Healthy Cooking for Kids

Healthy Cooking for Kids

BUILDING BLOCKS FOR A
LIFETIME OF GOOD NUTRITION

Shelly Null

St. Martin's Griffin ⚞ New York

Book design by Gretchen Achilles

Library of Congress Cataloging-in-Publication Data

Null, Shelly.
    Healthy cooking for kids : building blocks for a lifetime of good
nutrition / Shelly Null.
        p.   cm.
    ISBN 0-312-20639-9
    1. Cookery (Natural foods)   2. Children—Nutrition.   I. Title.
TX741.N85   1999
641.5'63—dc21   99-36858
                                                        CIP

First Edition: October 1999

10   9   8   7   6   5   4   3   2   1

I am blessed with parents who generously gave me the unconditional love from which I believe true happiness springs. This book is dedicated to them.

Through her kindness, compassion, and wisdom, my mother, Judy Smith Sullivan, has set an example and inspired me in every area of my life. Her constant support has helped to make this book a reality, and my life a better one.

My father, Gary Null, has provided a positive learning and working environment for me throughout my life. By virtue of his unparalleled knowledge and tireless ability to question and challenge, he has served as a role model in my efforts to make a contribution to the health and well-being of families.

I also want to express my appreciation and special thanks to my grandfather, Russel C. Smith. I can never forget my days as a little girl on his West Virginia farm, digging potatoes and getting covered in dirt and bugs. Nor can I forget his patient endurance of my first baking disaster, riding in his pickup truck, climbing in the mountains to harvest ginseng, and watching him cook on that big black stove at the cabin. His meals always included sweet corn, tomatoes, and his famous green beans, all of which he would pick fresh from the earth. Pap continues to be a loving, anchoring force in the life of our family; one could not wish for a stronger, kinder patriarch.

Contents

Acknowledgments

No book is the work of just one person, and so with gratitude I would like to acknowledge those who believed in this project's purpose and gave selflessly:

Charlie Spicer, for giving me the opportunity to share this book. He was there in the beginning, remained faithful to its completion, and guided it all the way.

Dorsey Mills, for her gentle guidance through the publishing process.

Joseph DelGiodice, for the culinary lessons.

Judy Smith Sullivan, for giving her all, from conception to completion.

Vicki Riba Koestler, for the energy and effort put toward the editing process, and for years of faith, encouragement, and patience.

YongSoo Ha, for his computer genius and loyal friendship.

Jodi Blanchard, who, by her creative, supportive spirit, helped me bring this labor of love toward completion.

Dr. Martin Feldman, for his sharing an understanding of food allergies, and especially for years of committed friendship and unshaking faith.

Maria Tarantino, for tasting foods with an uncanny judgment, and for brainstorming, editing, and being a creative guide and inspiration—her omnipresence has been a gift.

Libby Gandy, for developing the party section and sharing her bright light.

Recipe testers Hope and Vincent DeRosa, Rachine Jefferson, Dorothy Swiesz, and Susan Lacina, for the hours spent in that steamy Texas kitchen; and especially Rachel Reid, for her dessert contributions.

Mario Mastrandrea, for a fun culinary partnership and for sharing his wonderful mother, Carmela.

George Broglia, who, in his characteristic humorous way, helped me remember what is truly important and joyful in life.

Laura Gevanter, for her work on the food co-op section and the directory of physicians.

Pam Prager, for her sprouting expertise and friendship.

Doris J. Rapp, M.D., for her input to the section on pediatric allergies.

Ronald Cunnings, for his help in gathering information on food safety.

Paul A. LaChance, Ph.D., professor and chair, Rutgers University Department of Food Science, for his assistance in the area of nutrition.

Those in the field of organic agriculture, including—

Mark Van Horn from the University of California at Davis student farm and research facility.

Judith Redmond, Drew Rivers, and Paul Muller from Full Belly Farm.

Jeff and Ann Main from Good Humus Farm.

Julie and Jim Eldon and Sue and Steve Temple from Fiddler's Green Farm.

Paul Rabadan from Earthbound Farms.

Katherine DiMatteo from the Organic Food Production Association of North America.

Griffith McLellan from Quality Assurance International.

Jered Lawson, for his assistance in the area of community supported agriculture and his commitment to sustainable farming.

Gene Yeager from the BioDynamic Farming and Gardening Association, Inc., for his assistance with the topic of community-supported agriculture.

Leonard Diggs and Chris Bowland from the Farmery, Inc., for supporting the efforts of organic farmers and encouraging the education of private citizens in the area of sustainable agriculture.

Todd Koons from TKO Farms, for bringing organic produce to America's pantry and for the fine example he has set in management-worker relations.

Michael Miller from the National Sanitation Foundation and Daniel Di Resta, Ph.D., for their scientific expertise and help in the area of water purity and contaminants. Also, thanks to the numerous scientists and technicians who shared information for the section on water.

Estella Hall, life master and natural foods pioneer, for her friendship, faith, and unshakable optimism.

Meri Wayne and Mayumi Honda, for their work on the author photo.

Arden Kartalyan, for years of faith, devotion, and wisdom.

And Gerald Sullivan, who has been Grandpa Supreme to our children, and much more than a good friend to me. His strong but laid-back and unassuming way of loving is an example to all about the true meaning of family.

Foreword

If every child had parents who used the information in this book, we could prevent a major portion of the next generation's illnesses. That's because this is more than just a cookbook—it's a nutritional resource book, written by someone uniquely qualified to give the health interests of your family the priority they deserve. Rarely does a highly qualified chef also have a background in nutrition and health sciences. My daughter, Shelly Null, however, has both, and she has used these combined talents to write a most informative, original, and useful book for parents. The result can only be a great benefit for children.

Shelly Null has set very high standards for herself and her work. She has made sure that every recipe is nutritionally sound, delicious, easy to follow, and affordable. I am very proud of her achievements. This book is sure to have a positive impact and will be a mainstay in home libraries for a very long time.

—GARY NULL, PH.D.

Introduction

We all know there are countless negative influences and pressures to live by the dictates of our mass-market food culture. But overcoming them is not as difficult as one might think, and the rewards are well worth the effort. This book provides affordable, easy, delicious alternatives to the hot dogs, ice cream, soda, and pizza so many children are raised on. It's never too late to begin offering healthy alternatives. We will help you prepare for and cater parties featuring wholesome meals and desserts free of processed sugar that the whole family will love.

We often hear concerns and questions arising when it comes to the purity and nutrient content of our food. I've written this book to provide answers to these questions, and to offer a cookbook and comprehensive resource guide that will be an asset to every kitchen.

What's wrong with the typical American diet anyway? Generally, there are high amounts of saturated fat, refined sugars, salt, and caffeine, in a diet in which meat and dairy products are usually emphasized as main courses. By and large, Americans are overfed and undernourished, a situation that inevitably takes its toll on long-term health.

An ever-growing body of research is revealing that the major diseases Americans suffer and die from—cancer, heart disease, and stroke—are lifestyle related and thus to an extent preventable, and that their root causes often begin in childhood. What's more, many cases of childhood and adult imbalances, such as obesity, dental caries, hyperactivity, learning disabilities, and a vast array of other symptoms, have proven to be initiated or aggravated by poor eating habits.

We hear a lot about individuals with allergies these days, and the question arises, why are so many of us allergic to foods that used to be considered the staples of a healthy diet? The answer is, in large part, that farming and animal-raising techniques have changed drastically in the second half of the twentieth century, so that the nature of our food has changed. For one thing, animals are now routinely fed or injected with an assortment of antibiotics and hormones selected from the plethora of drugs serving the industry. Many of these drugs may be transferred to the human population via the meat, poultry, eggs, and dairy products consumed.

Also, fruits, vegetables, grains, and legumes produced with the use of chemical fertilizers and pesticides have residues of these chemicals, to which children may develop sensitivities. What's more, food additives such as colors, flavors, sweeteners, stabilizers, thickeners, maturing agents, and bleaches can also cause allergic reactions or impair the immune systems of young people. Over 3,000 such additives are currently used in the manufacture of America's food. Some individuals may consume up to 5 pounds of them per year. Many of these additives have not been tested as to their long-term effects, and others are allowed to stay on the market even though their harmful effects are known.

Infants and children show many signs of poor immune response as a result of dietary habits. Fluid accumulation in the ear and subsequent ear infection manifest most often in children with allergies, lowered immune function, and nutritional inadequacy. Tooth decay is associated with refined carbohydrates, especially sugar, and recent studies have shown it to be associated as well with insufficient levels of vitamins A, C, and E, and with low levels of the minerals calcium and zinc.

Many children and adults suffer ill effects from caffeine consumption, including insomnia, headaches, anxiety, irritability, indigestion, and irritation of the stomach and bowel. Recent surveys have indicated that some individuals drink as many as 5–10 colas a day—the caffeine equivalent of 2–5 cups of coffee. No one needs that!

What we do need are nutrient-rich foods in their natural state, a diet of fruits, vegetables, grains, legumes, nuts, and seeds. These foods will provide us with the necessary vitamins, minerals, protein, carbohydrates, and fats, while helping to avoid the problems associated with processed foods, meat, dairy, and other animal products.

As for meat and dairy products, we have been led to believe that these American mainstays are necessary in the diet if our children are to receive adequate protein and calcium. But who disseminated much of the literature on the subject? For decades the powerful meat and dairy industries have provided the "educational" information on health and nutrition to schools and other institutions. Only recently has their literature been superseded by scientific evidence not linked to industry interests.

What is now shown to improve the health is a diet based on foods low in cholesterol and saturated fat, and high in complex carbohydrates and fiber. Such a diet is one of the most beneficial, disease-preventive measures an individual or family can take. Vegetarians consume lower amounts of chemical residues, many of which are found concentrated in the fat stores of animals that consume large quantities of chemically grown and treated feed during their lifetimes. In fact, a vegetarian diet can reduce the risk of developing certain types of cancer, as well as hypertension, cardiovascular disease, diabetes, osteoporosis, arthritis, and obesity.

Studies show that legumes, grains, and seeds contain cancer-fighting components. Moreover, a diet rich in the nutrient beta-carotene, found in sweet potatoes and many other vegetables, is one of the best ways of battling heart disease and a variety of cancers. And prevention of these diseases begins in childhood, in fact, prenatally. Lucky is the baby who begins life with the breast milk of a healthy mother who has eaten wholesome foods throughout her own life and pregnancy.

Did you know that the baby-food industry is one of the most profitable in the American marketplace? The health of babies has been compromised in many cases for the sake of those who prosper from selling processed baby foods. Infant formulas contain ingredients such as corn syrup, sucrose, and cow's milk, which have been associated with food sensitivities and conditions such as colic, eczema, and irritability. Breast-feeding, on the other hand, has been shown to prevent the onset of food allergies. And breast-fed babies often suffer less from digestive ailments, and develop stronger immune systems.

As your baby moves on to solid foods, you can do her or him a great service by preparing fresh meals from organically grown ingredients. Many vitamins are destroyed by light as it shines on jars for extended periods on supermarket shelves. But when you make your own baby food, you control its freshness and purity, which means that your baby profits. You save money as well.

What it all boils down to is this: You can substantially reduce your family's susceptibility to a gamut of ailments with a healthy diet and pure water, by preparing fresh meals made from whole foods, and by continuing, as your children grow, to make health and good nutrition priorities in your household.

Healthy eating habits are best taught by example, and your greatest assurance of raising healthy children is to lead a healthy lifestyle yourself. If your kitchen is kept well stocked with a variety of nutritious foods, you make eating wisely easier for the whole family. And with a well-stocked pantry, when kids decide, as they often do, that they're bored with a particular food or recipe, it's easy to get creative and find an equally healthy alternative. Variety and innovation are essential to keeping your menus fun and responsive.

This book is filled with easy, economical, and delicious recipes to keep the whole family happy. Plus you will learn how to rotate foods in order to prevent allergies, how to make sure your water is pure, how to buy organic foods, and how to throw creative, healthy kids' parties. There's also information on vitamins and minerals, current food production controversies—in short, on all the topics that have been important to me in my own education as a natural foods chef, and as a parent. I should add that although this is a family-centered cookbook many of the recipes are delicious enough, sophisticated enough, and have enough eye-appeal to be hits with your adult guests. I don't believe in talking down to—or cooking down to—children, so be confident that there's no culinary condescension in this book.

Finally, this book is grounded in the belief that raising our children is our greatest vocation and a true reflection of who we are. Ultimately our success lies in theirs. If we set a conscious example, *they will follow*. As my children grew, so did this book. Our life together made it possible for this book to become what it has. They've been my biggest inspiration and most sobering critics. *Healthy Cooking for Kids* has the information and intent to empower and change lives. It is my heartfelt wish that you will use this book to better the health of your family and positively influence all those in your life.

—SHELLY NULL

PART ONE

A HEALTHY APPROACH TO FEEDING OUR FAMILIES

CHAPTER 1

KITCHEN STRATEGIES AND FUNDAMENTALS

Imagine letting your kids eat anything in your kitchen that they wanted. That's essentially what I do. I believe that one of the most important steps a parent can take toward having a healthy child is to have a healthy kitchen. So I keep only health-giving foods in my kitchen. And not only is my kitchen healthy—it's kid-friendly too. Snacks and goodies are left where they're easily grabbable by little hands. I can afford to do this because all the goodies are the good-for-you kind.

Kids who come over to my house can't believe it! Their eyes pop at the sight of so much food that's just there for the taking, much of it on racks that are at their eye level. Of course, it's all good stuff. I have large, wide-mouthed jars full of healthily prepared popcorn, nutritious cookies, granola bars, dried organic fruits, nuts, and seeds. On countertops I always have bowls of appealing fresh fruit. Also readily available are refrigerated fresh fruits and vegetables in easy-to-get-at bowls, healthy fruit spreads, and nut butters.

It's liberating to have a healthy, kid-friendly kitchen. There's no junk food to hide. On the contrary, you're showing everything off. You can feel good about your kitchen, and about what you're doing for your kids and their guests. Once you do this, you'll know exactly what I mean.

SOME KITCHEN PRECAUTIONS

I always stress that one aspect of having a healthy, kid-friendly kitchen is maintaining a kid-*safe* kitchen. If you're at all interested in the art of cooking, your child is at some point going to catch your enthusiasm and want to participate in the process. This is all for the good because when your junior chef helps you prepare a meal, it can be an enjoyable and educational experience for both of you. Plus kids really can contribute, lightening your work load. (Well, perhaps that depends upon their age!) But the point is, you always have to give safety your top priority. Although I'm quite adventurous when it comes to experimenting with a recipe or creating a new dish, I am a real conservative on the issue of safety. As a result of experience and observation, and after talking with a lot of people, there are three recommendations I can share in this area.

First, have your young chef or chefs help you only at those times when you're not rushed or distracted, so that you can supervise them fully.

Second, cutting vegetables and fruits is a job best done with properly sharpened knives. But kids and knives don't mix. I've seen bad accidents happen even with blunt knives, so please reserve kitchen cutting jobs for adults. There are so many other cooking chores children can do—getting ingredients, measuring, pouring, mixing, rolling, molding, etc.—that you can reserve cutting for yourself and still keep them busy and helpful.

Third, respect the danger potential of your stove. I believe working directly at the stove is something to be done by people aged 12 and over *only*. And your preteen or teenager should be carefully supervised when he or she is doing so. Also, kids who are going to be anywhere near a stove should have their long hair securely fastened. Kids are short; their loose hair is closer to the stove's flame than an adult's is; and therefore it can catch fire. Tragically, it's happened.

I offer you these ideas because I want your kitchen to be a happy, accident-free place.

GETTING A GOOD START

Providing a good nutritional foundation for young children consists of more than monitoring the types of foods they eat. Sure, we want our children to avoid eating anything unhealthy; that way they'll have the strongest immune systems possible and be able to combat the germs that always seem to be attacking kids. But we also want our children to *enjoy* eating healthfully. We want them to feel good about mealtime, so they can develop good eating habits that will stay with them throughout their lives. How best can we encourage good eating habits in children? It's easy—if you think like a child!

A primary thing to remember is that a child doesn't want to be scolded, prodded, or nagged at mealtimes. Neither does anyone else, for that matter, so a relaxing, peaceful atmosphere is the best idea for the entire family. So, as much as possible, try to avoid mixing negativity with food consumption.

Something else you should keep in mind is that children are small—so please offer them *small* portions. Young children can deal best with ½- to 1-cup portions of food; they can always ask for seconds if they want more. When given a very large portion, often a child is overwhelmed and, as a result, becomes uninterested. Then, she'll just pick, or not eat at all. Also, if you're introducing a new item to your child, it's often best to let him have a mini introductory portion to get acquainted with the new food and see if it's to his liking.

Many parents are faced with small children who will not eat much at all. This problem may stem from a lack of variety in meals or from a limited number of choices presented, leading the child to become bored. Put yourself in the place of a child receiving peanut butter and jelly or pasta day after day. Don't you think you might get bored? But you wouldn't necessarily know how to say so, or that other culinary possibilities existed. So you might just lose your enthusiasm for eating.

My experience has convinced me to present a varied diet with numerous choices, for both meals and snacks. Lunches can be a little tricky since many children are not home at this hour, and you may have to pack a cold lunch. Still, you should be able to come up with a different lunch for each weekday. Breakfasts and dinners should present no problem at all since the children are home and hot meals can be prepared, offering so many different options.

Anyone cooking for children should keep plenty of cookbooks handy for inspiration so that neither you nor the children become bored. Remember—recipes do not have to be followed exactly. Some people seem to think that recipes are carved in stone, but really they're nothing more than suggestions, and as such they can be jumping-off points for endless variations. Develop a recipe repertoire, of both recipes you follow exactly and adaptations you've come up with. Soon you'll be able to place a list of recipes your child likes on the front of the refrigerator and only serve any one item on that list once every 2–3 weeks. This way your child will experience a varied diet and not get bored with any one meal. Once you think in terms of variety, you'll probably find yourself adding new options to the list all the time. Fresh ideas are the key to continued success when feeding kids.

So are fresh fruits and vegetables. I stock many in-season fruits and vegetables, since they make for more varied eating as the seasons progress. Fruits should be washed after you take them home and put out in a bowl, while some fruits, such as grapes, need to refrigerated. When the children open the refrigerator, healthful items will be right at their fingertips. In the summer months I will prepare fresh fruit like blueberries, strawberries, or cherries for snacks, always keeping them readily available to the children. Remember that any pure fresh fruit contains water, enzymes, vitamins, and minerals, and is better for your children than sweetened snacks. And remember too that many fresh fruits and vegetables are naturally sweet or flavorful and will appeal to most children whose tastes have not yet been spoiled. Many times people will overly sweeten or salt foods, which leads children to acquire unnatural and unhealthy tastes. If you guard, early-on, against this kind of taste subversion, it's much easier than trying to correct it later.

Seasonal eating of different foods will result in a naturally varied diet, since certain items will be eaten only in certain months, preventing children from becoming too bored with the same foods. Enjoy the flow of the year by including your children in the seasonal activities of gathering foods. Children love to be involved in the picking of berries, tomatoes, pumpkins, apples, and other foods from their actual origins. Spring, summer, and fall are the best for this, while in winter we get a little boost by opening our canned treasures from other seasons.

THE SAVVY PLANNER

This last idea—canning or freezing produce—is something you can do to make life in the kitchen easier for yourself. A variety of foods, such as tomatoes, beans, apples, peaches, and berries, can be canned when they're in season to provide great eating during the off-season. Another thing you can do to save time and energy is, when you're cooking a special dish, to prepare a larger quantity than you need and freeze some of the portions.

Have you tried this freezing strategy before, only to fall prey to the UFO syndrome? I'm talking about the unidentified frozen object syndrome, when you clean out your freezer and find all sorts of mysterious parcels of undertermined origin that have been buried in there for who knows how long. So much for saving time and energy, you've thought, as you've thrown these UFO's out.

Life doesn't have to be like this, however. You can identify and date everything you freeze. But, more important, you can, as you freeze each item, enter it on a list that you keep *outside the freezer;* on the refrigerator door is a good place. You'll be surprised how such a list will help you when you're running short on cooking time or supplies. You'll know instantly what's available without having to explore through the Arctic realms, and you'll be able to use the oldest items first. As you defrost any item, remember to cross it off your list, and you'll have an ever-updated menu-planning aid. It's amazing what modern technology (in this case, pencil and paper!) can do.

Something parents might like to make large quantities of is cookie dough. You can freeze several portions of a healthy cookie dough, and then, if you're having kids over, you can pull out a batch of dough that morning and—presto—you have an activity to occupy the children, as well as a treat.

One other kitchen efficiency idea: Do you find yourself with good intentions buying a lot of fresh produce, only to throw it out as it goes bad in your refrigerator? Maybe you're storing it in plastic bags. Don't.

Just because in many stores you use plastic bags to gather your produce and get it weighed, doesn't mean you have to keep it in these when you get home. The problem is that moisture accumulates in the plastic and hastens the degradation of the produce. So transfer what you've bought to crisper bins or store it open in the refrigerator. Why waste food, not to mention money and time?

DIGESTION MADE EASY

What if you've stocked your kitchen with only nutritious foods, you're feeding your child 3 healthful meals a day, and you're still hearing the most frequent of childhood complaints—he's getting stomachaches. What can you do?

There are several things you can try. First, don't give him those 3 healthful meals a day! Instead, try giving him many small, healthful meals during the day. Eating the standard 3 meals can cause indigestion since the body is presented with large amounts of food at once, causing the digestive system to overwork. So if your child is stomachache-prone, try the small-meal approach; it's a better one for proper weight maintenance too, so it could be a good lifetime habit to get into.

Also, pay attention to the mood of your child's meals, and especially to the pace. Hectic pacing adds to stress, which can cause stomach upset in the susceptible child. Plus speed-eating means inadequate chewing, which results in foods passing through the digestive tract with their nutrients being less than fully assimilated. That's why I recommend investing time when your kids are young in teaching them to eat slowly and chew their food thoroughly. The payoff will be fewer stomachaches, better nutrition, and probably a lifetime of being better able to relax and enjoy the eating experience.

Something else you should be aware of is that drinking beverages during meals interferes with digestion because it dilutes the saliva's digestive enzymes, as well as digestive acids in the stomach. Thus you might want to help your kids break the habit of washing food down with excess liquid. Liquids should be consumed 15 minutes before the meal to hydrate the system, with only an occasional sip during the meal to moisten the palate.

Other ideas for avoiding stomachache:

- Watch portion size—large could mean tummy trouble.

- Children's after-dinner eating should be limited to easily digestible snacks.

- Some foods are hard to digest raw unless they're in small bits; these include carrots, broccoli, daikon, and radishes. To ease digestion, think in terms of carrot strings and similar tiny pieces.

- Is allergy a problem? Mucus from allergic reactions to foods can cause digestive upset. Be careful of the frequency and proportions of suspected allergenic foods ingested. For instance, a small amount of wheat once in a while may be fine, but a few meals of it over a couple of days may cause problems with your child's digestive system.

For more information on easing digestion, see the section on optimal food combinations in the Appendix.

KID MEETS WORLD

A problem that all health-conscious parents eventually face is that most of the rest of the world isn't health-conscious. So you could be going along very nicely, setting up your kitchen with only healthy choices and laying the foundation for good nutrition, when—boom!—your child becomes more independent and ventures into school and other households and a monkey wrench is thrown into the machinery. Your child now wants the same commercially packaged devil's food snack cakes and fruit rolls that everyone else has! What do you do?

I had this problem myself recently, and I started out being quite disheartened about it. Here I was, writing a book about good food for kids, and my own children were coming home from school crying for these sugar- and preservative-laden goodies.

I spoke to a friend about this, telling him I felt I was losing the nutrition battle with my own children. His response was that I was not losing but, on the contrary, winning with flying colors. My children had been instilled with basic facts on nutrition that went beyond the knowledge of most adults. They knew which foods were richest in nutrients and what happens to our bodies if we don't eat well and nourish them. I was then inspired and ready for one more round of Mom versus junk food at school. That day we came up with recipes for more healthful fruit rolls and for blueberry muffins. And the next day at school, the other children wanted some of what my kids were having. Victory!

I'm not saying it's easy when your child meets the world. It can be quite difficult. My victory was for 1 day only, and each day presents me, and parents everywhere, with new challenges. Here are some ideas for meeting them.

Education, as my friend pointed out, is vital, both for the present and for the long run. So talk with your child about the food choices you make and the reasons you make them. Part of this health education is giving your child positive reinforcement when he makes good choices on his own. This positive reinforcement is so important in that it will carry your children through some of their most difficult times with a sense of self-worth, respect for their bodies, and high self-esteem. Their later lives will be so enriched for it.

TEENS AT THE TABLE

These thoughts about adolescents are intended mainly *for those who don't yet have one.* Why? Because that's when you've got to lay the groundwork—before your children reach their teens. If there's one phrase that's associated with the teenage years in American culture, it's peer pressure, and if you have any hope of countering peer pressure's strong effects on your children, it will be that you've taught them—early on and by example—your values and your ways of doing things. In the area of nutrition this will mean that you've lived by your belief that nourishing the body in a healthful way is important, and that you've demonstrated, perhaps with aids like this book, that it's easy and fun to do so. If you have, then, hopefully, your healthy approach to eating will now be theirs as well.

The teenage years accelerate the trend of your child's pulling away from home. So when your teen is at the table, a good deal of the time it's not going to be *your* table that she's at, but another—in a friend's house, a school cafeteria, a fast food restaurant. Can anything good be said about fast food places? Well, yes. Due to consumer pressure, some fast food establishments are trying to serve healthier menu items. So if you've educated your child about nutrition, when he's in a fast food place, he might be moved to choose one of the healthier items on the menu, for example, veggie pizzas, bean burritos, or a salad. An even more encouraging thought—maybe he will persuade his friends to go someplace where the really good food is. They might just like it, too!

Are these scenarios unrealistic? Maybe. It depends, of course, upon the particular child, and upon the particular circumstances as well. It's not always easy, or even possible, to find something wholesome to eat at a restaurant, or at a social event away from home. And sometimes a person just doesn't want to. A teen is, after all, a person who makes his or her own choices most of the time.

In any event, if you do at present have a teenager, here are a few ideas to consider for those times when he or she *is* at your table:

Teens and parents may eventually have differences; it's part of the growing-up process. But there's nothing that says it has to happen at mealtime. Keep mealtime fight-free.

Cooking with your young child is educational for him. Cooking with your teenager is educational for *you.* Creating a meal together provides a natural opportunity for chatting, and for finding out what's on your child's mind and agenda at the moment.

If you've had enough kitchen adventures together, by the time your child is into his mid-teens he should be able to plan and cook an entire family meal by himself. Encourage him to do so. Enjoy!

Finally, let's say your high school or college student, despite years of a health-conscious upbringing and all your best current efforts, slides down into the typical less-than-healthful teen dietary ways. Fat, salt, and sugar are in. Vegetables and fruits are out. Whole grains are not a priority in her life, nor are any of the nutritional precepts you've taught her over the years. You feel like a failure.

Don't. Because here's my bet: Your child's going to grow up and eventually start her own family. Then some of the good habits you've inculcated in her are going to surface as she nurtures and feeds her own child. Watch for this. You'll see it. It will be the beautiful legacy of healthful living that you've created in your own kitchen.

CHAPTER 2

IS OUR FOOD SAFE?

The many technological advances of the twentieth century have generated greater change than has occurred in all previous centuries combined. The world is smaller as a result of some of these advances, and life is more convenient for many, but there are prices to be paid for these benefits. In the area of health and nutrition, industrial pollution has seeped into our air, water, and soil, and during the past several decades our food has increasingly been produced using factory methods. High-tech, high-input chemical practices are routinely employed to produce food in greater quantities and with longer shelf life—and with compromised nutritional value. This food often comes in highly processed, prepackaged form.

We must seriously consider the nature of what we feed ourselves if we are to encourage optimal health. We can't automatically assume that every product available in supermarkets, restaurants, or school cafeterias is wholesome and nourishing. Let's look at current practices in agriculture, food processing, and preparation, and discuss some healthful alternatives.

Please note that the aim here is not to shock or frighten anyone. My thought is simply that we should empower ourselves with knowledge, as this is the first step in taking appropriate responsibility for our families' health and well-being.

FRUITS AND VEGETABLES

When examining the safety of our food, we have to look at the methods used to produce it. For much of the past century, the American farming system has been dominated by the use of chemical fertilizers, pesticides, and monocrop (or 1-crop-per-area) production. While this system has certainly produced an abundance of food, some questions arise. We have to ask, how safe and nutritious is this food? Also, what is the environmental price paid for our agricultural bounty?

Chemical Fertilizers

Chemical fertilizers are a combination of nitrogen, phosphorus, and potash. These products do force a higher yield from the soil; however, they also cause the destruction of many essential living soil organisms and elements responsible for transporting important nutrients to the plant. In addition, the nitrogen in these fertilizers clings to plants' root systems, further blocking nutrient absorption.

Chemical Pesticides

These petrochemical insecticides, herbicides, fungicides, fumigants, and rodenticides don't just kill the bugs that nibble at our crops, they also kill beneficial organisms that naturally control pests, and that digest organic matter to create richer, nutrient-dense soil. What's more, chemical pesticides can encourage the mutation of pests into superspecies that resist previous levels of application. This means that greater amounts of even more toxic chemicals become necessary. And this in turn leaves greater amounts of poisonous residue in soil, water, and crops—and eventually in our children's developing bodies.

Monocrop Production

Monocrop production refers to the production of only one crop year after year on a particular piece of land. This is a highly productive method of cultivation. The problem is, though, that since crop rotation is minimal, as is the practice of periodically leaving the ground fallow (or uncultivated), the soil becomes worn out. As a result, in monocrop farming the soil needs to be treated with more and more chemical fertilizers and pesticides, which quickly perpetuates the vicious cycle of factory farming.

The Costs of Modern Agriculture

The overall environmental effect of these high-tech, high-input practices is a chain reaction of monstrous proportions that damages several ecosystems. Agricultural chemicals build up in the soil, leaving a lowered level of vital organic matter, fewer nutrients, and greater levels of soil erosion. The crops grown in this devitalized dirt are more susceptible to pest infestation, more laden with chemical residues, and far less nourishing than they could be. As for flavor—well, comparisons with cardboard have been made.

The direct connection of disease to agricultural chemicals must be considered as well. Children are the most vulnerable since they consume proportionately higher quantities of foods that receive heavy chemical treatment, such as apples, pears, bananas, fruit juice, and peanut butter.

One problem is nitrogen, which is far and away the main component in chemical fertilizers. Nitrogen builds up in foods, and when eaten, especially by children, it gets transformed, to some extent, into toxic nitrosamines. Nitrosamines can cause less oxygen to be delivered to bodily systems, and it's been linked to stomach cancer. Excess nitrogen also disrupts the amino acid profile of food, creating a product with less absorbable protein.

Chemical pesticides are another health threat in that the residues they leave in soil and on food are often at dangerous levels. For several reasons, children are the ones who are most vulnerable to the ill effects of these often neurotoxic chemicals. First, when it comes to foods most heavily treated with pesticides, children far outconsume adults in proportion to body weight. Second, children usually consume greater quantities of a lesser number of foods than adults do, which means that there is more chance of a child's being overexposed to the several pesticides used on a specific food. Third, children have immature digestive systems that absorb these toxic substances more readily. Plus, once absorption takes place, their less developed immune systems have a harder time protecting other developing systems from detrimental effects. This is especially true for the nervous system, which can suffer irreversible damage from excess exposure to neurotoxic organophosphate pesticides. Carcinogenic pesticides are also at issue here; it's been estimated that by age six, about 30 percent of a child's lifetime risk of cancer from pesticides has already been incurred. While about 100 pesticides have been labeled as possible carcinogens by the EPA, this does not take into account the many so-called inactive ingredients with which the pesticides are mixed, which can also pose health threats.

Our children must also contend with chemicals used to preserve produce during shipping to increase cosmetic appeal, and to extend shelf life. Phenols, used on food during the train and truck journey from farm to store, are so extraordinarily toxic that just a gram and a half (about 1.5 paper-clips-worth in weight) can cause vomiting, internal damage, and convulsions. Dyes, mineral oil (a petroleum-based oil), and various waxes similar to those used on floors are applied to produce such as cucumbers, peppers, tomatoes, apples, pears, and citrus fruits, to add a bright shiny appearance and to lengthen their storage and selling life.

What Can We Do?

Being alarmed at what's happening to America's food supply makes no sense unless we're prepared to do something about it. And there are a variety of things we can do. For one thing, we can start at the top, demanding of the EPA and other government agencies, such as the Food and Drug Administration and the Department of Agriculture, that they be more vigilant in protecting us from the dangers of agricultural chemicals. They've got to revise what they call tolerable levels of exposure to these toxins by taking into account current dietary trends and the fact that we are often zapped with the synergistic effects of anywhere from 2–8 pesticides per food. They must update their testing methods, since only a very small percentage of our food supply is tested for excess chemical residues. Also, their current methods are unable to detect many of the pesticides they themselves have deemed carcinogenic. Many feel pesticides recognized as carcinogenic and neurotoxic should be banned from production entirely. At the very least, in setting tolerance limits and in testing foods, federal authorities must take into account the special sensitivities of our children.

Another demand we can make: Federal authorities should act swiftly to close legal loopholes that permit toxic chemicals to enter our food supply via the international route. This can occur when stockpiles of now-banned pesticides are sold outside the United States, usually to impoverished Third World nations whose produce is then imported back into this country and right onto our kitchen tables.

The Resurgence of Organic Farming

Another thing we can do to help build a safer food supply is to encourage the resurgence of what has come to be known as organic farming. Actually, organic farming is nothing newfangled or radical; prior to the twentieth century it was the only way of producing food. Today, as the dangers of factory farming are becoming increasingly apparent, it's making a comeback. What's happening is that an increasing number of people are realizing that it's time for our nation to move toward a more balanced and sustainable system of agriculture. They're understanding that if we're going to produce food that is nutrient rich and life supporting on an ongoing basis, the earth's living, web-like network of ecosystems must be respected and nourished in a gentle, natural way that doesn't take out more than it leaves in. They're acknowledging that to further disrupt this delicate balance is to endanger our soil, food, water, air, and wildlife—and our own lives.

And it is all these understandings that form the scientific and philosophical underpinnings of today's organic farm movement. While organic farming varies in its application, certain things are constants— there is no use of synthetic fertilizers, pesticides, dyes, waxes, or preservatives. The benefits of this approach to food production are several: Organic farming nourishes the soil, encourages nutrient-rich, delicious crops, and leaves behind no toxic chemicals to threaten the environment, wildlife, or humans.

This thousands-of-years-old system is based on proven ecological and agricultural principles and has advanced in recent years to produce enough food not just for small villages or communities, but entire nations. One main principle of organic farming is that if you feed the soil, you nourish the plant, and this is done using several methods. Compost—decomposed vegetable and plant matter, and manure—is applied to the soil to act as a natural fertilizer. This encourages healthy plant growth without the harmful effects of excess nitrogen. Crop coverings such as soybeans and other leguminous plants add important nutrients back into the soil. Mulch—shredded leaves, bark, and other matter—when spread around plant beds, helps control erosion of soil and retain moisture, and acts as a mild fertilizer as well. Planting a variety of crops on a rotational basis and leaving sections of land to rest unplanted are important in preventing the loss of the nutrients and microorganisms that are vital to a healthy growing environment.

Another principle of organic farming is natural pest control. Natural pest control requires no petrochemicals, causes no water, air, soil, or food contamination, and frees us of concerns about carcinogenic or neurotoxic chemicals. One technique of natural pest control is interplanting, the process of cultivating companion crops near each other to ward off insects and parasitic infestation. Such companion crops include garlic, onions, marigolds, and nasturtiums. Beneficial insects such as ladybugs can also be introduced into the growing medium to effectively control crop-consuming insects. Crops can be covered or surrounded with plastic sheeting, which serves as a barrier against insects, birds, or rodents. Natural substances such as pheromones or plant-derived sprays are used to treat disease and insect problems in crops, and to prevent such problems.

These natural cultivating techniques provide all that is needed for the perpetuation of a healthy soil ecosystem. Plants, beneficial insects, and microorganisms flourish together in a balanced way, each adding to the well-being of the others, as well as the soil. And even though use of organic growing techniques cannot protect food from chemical residues that come from exhaust fumes, factory emissions, and acid rain, it can assure us that our environment—and ultimately our families—are not under the assault of tons and tons of toxic chemicals every year.

Shopping Organic

In an ideal world we'd all have the time, energy, and land to produce our own organic vegetables if we wanted to, and perhaps some of us are fortunate enough to be able to be self-sufficient in this way, if only to a limited extent with a small backyard garden or even a few terrace flowerpots. But in general, if we want to eat organic produce, we have to buy it. In a nation of high-tech products, this isn't always easy, so here are a few thoughts on shopping for organically produced food.

First, when shopping for organic products, always look for third-party certification verifying that the food has in fact been organically produced. Independent certifying bodies, such as QAI (Quality Assurance International), inspect and test crops, soil, water, farms, processing and packaging facilities, and distribution sites. This ensures that no chemical treatments are applied and that the highest levels of purity and hygiene are maintained. Many involved in organic farming believe that there should be a federal regulation about what constitutes organic farming. Some attempts have, in fact, been made to achieve this. (For information about what has been done in this area, you can contact: U.S. Department of Agriculture; Agricultural Marketing Services; Director, Public Affairs; Room 3510 South; Washington, D.C. 20250. Phone: [202]720-8998.)

You might wonder why organic produce often costs more than conventionally grown produce. The answer usually lies in the shipping and distribution. Since conventional produce is often unripe when picked and then ripened overnight by ethylene gas fumigation, and since it is often treated with preservatives for shipping, there is much less crop loss. Organic produce, by contrast, is often more ripe when picked, and then allowed to ripen further during shipping, which means that more loss occurs during transport. Also, distributor markup can be high, and these prices get passed on to stores, and ultimately to consumers.

A promising solution to the price problem is one that brings together the farmer and the consumer and provides freshly picked organic produce at a fraction of the cost of store-bought organic produce. It's called community-supported agriculture (CSA). The concept is simple: Community members team up with growers of organic fruits, vegetables, herbs, and in some cases, grains, dairy products, and meat or poultry. The community directly supports growers financially and in turn receives food with no distributor costs and no store markup. Some exciting things about CSA's are that members have direct contact with the growers of their food, they have access to farms, and they can sometimes help with cultivation or harvest. Children especially enjoy this, and for many urban youngsters the CSA is their first glimpse of nature at work.

CSA's also reacquaint us with the idea of eating foods in season. This helps our bodies and minds adapt to the climate changes that occur as the year progresses. Of course we can still enjoy our favorite organic food year-round by freezing or fresh-canning (with Mason jars). For more information on this innovative, affordable way of acquiring food, and to learn about CSA's in your area, contact: The Biodynamic Association; P.O. Box 550; Kimberton, PA 19442. Phone: (800)516-7797.

Another way of purchasing organic products is through organic farmers' markets, which are popular in many areas and will often provide an opportunity for a ride in the country or even a visit to the city. These open-air markets sometimes offer baked goods and crafts as well as produce.

Food co-ops provide yet another way of buying organic. Co-ops are usually owned and operated by their members and take the form of either a buying club or a storefront.

Your local natural foods store will often carry organic produce, sometimes locally grown. If not, or if prices are too high, speak to the manager about special ordering at a discounted price. One more source—your local supermarket—may carry organic produce. As organic products become increasingly popular, more supermarkets do seem to be picking up on the trend. If this isn't the case where you live, keep in mind that supermarket managers will usually find a way to acquire products if the shopper is insistent enough. When shopping for supermarket produce, speak with the produce manager; insist on information and quality and you'll receive it.

If you do buy conventionally grown products, remember to scrub (no soap) and rinse vegetables and fruits very thoroughly. Remove outer leaves from green vegetables and peel any fruit or vegetable that has a skin so as to lessen the chance of consuming wax. Also, when necessary, frozen vegetables are all right to use since they are usually frozen shortly after picking (many organic varieties are available). Frozen vegetables should be unseasoned and sugar- and additive-free. But do avoid canned vegetables; not only are they significantly depleted of nutrients but they often contain excess salt, sugar, or preservatives.

If at all possible, do not buy produce or related products, such as juice or jams, that have been grown or processed outside the United States, since other countries may use some of the nastiest agricultural chemicals, many of which are banned from use here. This will not only protect you and your children, you'll also be providing incentive for change in countries where farm workers are exploited and exposed on a daily basis to these dangerous substances.

ANIMAL PRODUCTS

Dairy Products

Milk has been touted as the most natural food for children to consume. This assertion is both true and untrue. It is true that, for infants, the best sustenance by far is milk from their mother's breast. Infants who are breast-fed tend to develop stronger immune systems and closer emotional bonds with their mothers than bottle-fed children do. That is why babies should be breast-fed for 6 months to a year or longer, if possible. During this time, as through the entire pregnancy and before, the mother should be nourished on a varied, whole-foods diet. For the many mothers who work outside the home, breast pumps can make their milk accessible on a regular basis.

After weaning, children should be fed soft or pureed foods, cooked fruits, and juices. While cow's milk is ideal for calves, it is problematic for humans. Milk and dairy products in general are very mucus-forming, and dairy is in fact one of the most common food allergens in the Western diet; it can play a major role in year-round hay fever and asthma. Also, many people have difficulty digesting lactose (milk sugar) and casein (milk protein). Symptoms can include phlegm in the throat, a stuffy nose, clogged ears, and persistent ear infections. Gastrointestinal symptoms can include abdominal cramping and gas, bloating, diarrhea, constipation, and bad breath. Sensitivities or allergies to dairy can also cause leg aches, hyperactivity, bed-wetting, and fatigue.

From a nutritional standpoint, milk is said to be the perfect builder of strong bones, bright smiles, and big muscles. However, the source of much of this information is the dairy industry itself. The fact is that many important nutrients in milk, such as protein, vitamin A, and especially calcium, are more abundant in—and more easily absorbed from—plant-based foods such as leafy greens, cruciferous and root vegetables, beans, and nuts and seeds. (See the nutritional tables in the Appendix.)

Many healthy shoppers know that dairy products are now available free of bovine growth hormone (rBGH—see section on genetically engineered foods) and are third-party-certified organic. Also available are organic yogurt and goat's milk products. While these are positive developments, there is a healthier choice for those who cannot resist the milk and cheese family. There are now many varieties of delicious, nutritious alternatives to dairy foods made from soy, rice, oats, nuts, and seeds. These come in beverage, cheese, yogurt, and frozen dessert (ice cream) form. This option eliminates the mucus-forming, allergenic, high-cholesterol, inhumane, and environmentally unsound factors that are part and parcel of the dairy industry. Healthy nondairy options are available as third-party-certified organic products and are included in this book in every recipe that would otherwise include cow's milk, cheese, yogurt, ice cream, sour cream, and butter. When shopping, be sure to check labels and go for variety; this will ensure that your family reaps the nutritional benefits of the many products on the "healthy shelves."

An added note about soy: While soy products are only a segment of the nondairy spectrum, it is almost impossible to ignore the mounds of well-publicized research documenting the health-promoting and protective properties of this remarkable legume. I'm sure that more information is on the way to further encourage the use of the many products made from soy.

Eggs

Due to its protein content and, specifically, its amino acid balance, the egg has sometimes been called a perfect food. Eggs are also rich in nutrients such as B vitamins. We should, however, realize that eggs are mucus-forming and are allergenic for many individuals. Raw or uncooked eggs can also pose a significant threat of infection with salmonella and other microbes. While organic eggs come from healthier hens that live happier lives, and have shells that are thicker and more resistant to microbial infection, there is a healthier option. On a nutritional and culinary level, we don't have to look far to replace eggs with healthier, protein- and fiber-rich, cholesterol-free foods that present no microbial hazards or nutritional drawbacks. For baking, entrees, and other recipes that provide alternatives to eggs, simply browse through the recipe section of this book.

If you do use eggs, they should be third-party-certified organically produced. If they are, the hens that produced them will have been more thoroughly nourished and humanely raised than factory-farm hens. They'll have lived with more space and access to fresh air and sunshine, and as a result, the eggs they produce will be healthier than most sold today and have thicker shells, which protect against parasitic infections that might be passed on to humans. Always check the freshness date on eggs, and buy just the amount you need. Remember, never eat raw eggs—in milk shakes, salad dressings, appetizers, dough, or in any other form.

Fish

Seafood has become increasingly popular among those concerned with the high fat content of red meat. It is true that fish is rich in protein, vitamins, and minerals, and generally low in saturated fat. It is often rich in omega-3 fatty acids, which are believed to be beneficial for cardiovascular health. Before you jump into the tank, however, there are some environmental safety and nutritional issues you should be aware of.

Environmentally, there are two main areas of concern, one having to do with wild-harvested seafood and one with farm raised.

Regarding seafood harvested from the wild, we are depleting the oceans, and as more people choose fish over other meats, overfishing will occur to an even greater extent. With the ocean's natural biodiversity being further upset, the complex food web with its natural checks and balances is altered, which could result in further extinctions if predator fish lose their prey. Another problem with ocean-harvested fish are nets used by fishing vessels. These nets catch tens of millions of tons of fish and marine mammals each year that are not intended to be caught but that accidentally get trapped in nets intended for other fish. The result is that the extra marine animals, or "by catch," get thrown back dead or dying because the fishing boats are not licensed to harvest those particular marine animals. So here we have not only a threat to the population of fish but a needless, wasteful one at that.

Regarding farm-raised fish, we should be aware that they also carry their share of problems. This practice generally crowds fish into very tight surroundings to maximize the harvest. This stressor leads to increased disease among fish, and increased use of antibiotics to combat infections. Also, farmed fish are fed in a similar fashion to other factory-farmed livestock. For example, farm-raised catfish and rainbow trout are often fed a popular brand of cat food. If you've ever read the label on a bag of dried cat food, you would have cause for concern about eating a fish that was raised on such fare. Remember, the old saying that we are what we eat carries a great deal of truth.

Another issue with fish farms is the pollution they produce. Due to the cramped living conditions, drugs, and commercial feed, the runoff from such farms can pose a threat to surrounding bodies of water. The pollutants that enter the surrounding ecosystems can harm the local plant life and can further spread through the food chain.

From the standpoint of safety, you should definately understand something about contaminants in fish. Briefly, they are divided into three types: natural, chemical, and microbial.

Natural contaminants, or toxins, often occur in fish feeding on coral reefs in the Caribbean, the Pacific Islands, and extreme Southeast Florida. Some fish poisoning also comes from gross mishandling after harvest. Natural toxins can become more of a threat if fish is not kept cold upon harvest and if the fish comes from the above high-risk areas, especially if they have been caught by recreational fishermen.

Chemical contaminants are found in many fish as a result of industrial pollution in both oceans and freshwater around the world. Pesticides like DDT, heavy metals (such as lead and mercury), and radioactive compounds are among the many chemical contaminants found in fish. By inquiring where fish are caught and avoiding larger predator fish that often have higher concentrations of chemicals, we can provide ourselves with some protection from chemical contaminants. Remember that children are particularly vulnerable to the effects of chemical contaminants, as are pregnant women, nursing mothers, and those in ill health.

Parasitic or microbial infection in fish is generally a result of improper handling. Fish processed under unsanitary conditions can be contaminated with fecal and other parasites. Also, eating undercooked or raw fish is an all too effective way to acquire dangerous microorganisms such as the hepatitis A virus, staphylococcus bacteria, and the bacteria that cause botulism. To help avoid microbial infection, one must obtain fish from a clean, reputable market; wash hands thoroughly; and sterilize all utensils. Also, no matter how fashionable it may seem, never eat raw fish. If you like sushi, try vegetable nori rolls instead.

On a nutritional level, it is true that fish is rich in protein, vitamins, and minerals. As mentioned before, some fish, like salmon and cod, are rich in omega-3 fatty acids. What you should keep in mind is that fish has cholesterol and zero fiber. Also, nutrients found in fish can just as easily be found in plant-based foods, which provide valuable dietary fiber and are void of cholesterol. In fact, flaxseed oil is twice as rich in omega-3 fatty acids as fish oil.

If you must consume fish, consider it part of a transition to a healthier plant-based diet, and limit your intake to once every week or two. At present, the safest fish to choose is third-party-certified organic tilapia, also called St. Peter's fish. Tilapia is naturally a vegetarian, which means it is lower in concentrated contaminants when compared to predator fish. Also, feed such as soy, alfalfa, and cultivated algae can be obtained in certified organic form. In preparation, remember to use a separate cutting board and plate, sterilize your utensils, and wash your hands thoroughly after handling.

I would encourage you to refer to the recipe section of this book for nutrient-packed recipes that are easier and quicker to prepare than fish, and are super-pleasurable to the palate.

Poultry

Chicken, an American staple for generations, has become even more popular in the past 20 years. As with fish, those seeking to reduce cholesterol and saturated fat turn to poultry as an alternative to red meat. But poultry does cause a rise in cholesterol in the human body. Also, poultry brings to your table all the drawbacks of today's factory-farm practices. These include unsanitary conditions due to overcrowding, the use of antibiotics to control infections, and pesticide and agricultural chemical residue. For these reasons, along with the fact that poultry endure painful lives and inhumane slaughter, many have chosen the more ethical, healthy alternative of eating a varied plant-based diet. Even when considering organically raised poultry, we cannot escape the nutritional facts that it is a cholesterol-rich, protein-dense flesh food with no fiber or enzymes of its own to aid its processing in the human digestive tract, which was designed to break down plant foods. As with other animal products, there is no nutrient present in poultry that cannot be obtained from a plant-based diet.

If you do choose to eat chicken, choose only third-party-certified organically raised, free-range varieties. This will ensure that the chickens you buy have eaten only organically grown feed and have been raised under humane conditions, meaning they've been less crowded and have had access to fresh air, sunshine, and space to run freely. In other words, these chickens have generally lived happier lives than most.

When preparing chicken, be sure to remove all skin, which accounts for most of the fat. Also, to protect against salmonella, a microbe present in many chickens, cook chicken thoroughly and be sure that no pink meat or juices remain. To prevent cross-contamination with these and other microbes, wash hands thoroughly and wash all cutting boards, knives, and other utensils.

Try to limit chicken consumption to every other week, and serve it with salad and vegetables. These high-fiber, high-water-content, enzyme-rich foods will aid in digestion of the chicken.

Pork

Pork is a meat that soon goes by the wayside when people switch to a healthier diet, and for good reason. Pigs undergo the same type of treatment that other animals experience in factory farms. Pigs, more than other livestock, are highly intelligent and emotionally complex creatures capable of a wide array of feelings, so their mistreatment is even more disturbing to many who are ethically opposed to the consumption of animal products. Nutritionally, pork is a disaster for humans. This is especially true in the case of processed pork products like cold cuts, bacon, and sausages. In this case we have—combined with high cholesterol, saturated fat, and sodium—carcinogenic nitrate and nitrite compounds to contend with.

So do your family a big favor: Switch from pork to the plant-based, nutrient- and fiber-rich, cholesterol-free, low-fat foods that you will encounter throughout this book.

Beef

In the standard Western diet, beef has been a mainstay, especially since the prosperity boom that followed World War II. For years it was believed that beef was necessary for strength, vigor, and overall good health. After all, protein and iron are so abundant in beef that it should be a must for growing children, athletes, expectant mothers, and virile men. Of course, we now know that along with these nutrients and our positive cultural images come high cholesterol and saturated fat levels, total lack of fiber and living enzymes, and all the horrors of the inhumane treatment cattle endure at today's factory farms.

Beef cattle, dairy cows, and veal calves suffer in terribly crowded conditions, receive antibiotics to combat ever-present infections, and are injected with growth hormones to increase size, weight, and therefore profitability. The process of slaughter is usually quite gruesome, as often fully conscious cows and calves experience extreme terror and excruciating pain before and during the killing process.

Another issue with cows is the recently banned practice of adding cow meat to cattle feed. This process of cannibalizing cows is believed to be responsible for a form of bovine spongiform encephalopathy (mad cow disease). There is a strong possibility that BSE is connected to new variant Creutzfeldt-Jacob Disease (nvCJD). This is a disease that has struck a number of young people (from teens to forties) in Great Britain in the past 10 years. It has as yet not been officially diagnosed in the United States. This disease is physically and mentally debilitating, and in the end always fatal.

Nutritionally, many people have decided that the risks of eating beef outweigh any possible benefits. Foods like beef, which are high in cholesterol, saturated fat, sodium, with higher relative concentrations of environmental and agricultural toxins, have been linked to many degenerative health conditions. Some examples: cardiovascular disease, cancer (including colon, breast, and prostate), arthritis, gout, and gastrointestinal conditions. For these health reasons, and for ethical reasons, beef is usually one of the first foods eliminated when people change to a more health-supporting diet. Remember, you can get your protein, iron, and other nutrients, along with fiber, phytonutrients, vitamins, and minerals, without the many drawbacks of beef consumption.

THE VEGETARIAN ALTERNATIVE

Vegetarianism is the practice of avoiding animal-based food products and choosing plant-based foods instead. Those who adopt these habits do so for a variety of reasons, including health, ethical, environmental, and religious ones.

In the area of health, vegetarianism can bring many rewards. Both adult and child vegetarians can benefit from increased dietary fiber and antioxidant nutrients, such as beta-carotene and vitamins C and E, which are so plentiful in fruits, leafy greens, and cruciferous vegetables. Another benefit is the abundant chlorophyll and other phytochemicals found in leafy greens, sea vegetables, and sprouts. Chlorophyll can be an effective detoxifier to help the body get rid of environmental and dietary contaminants. Also present in fruits, sprouts, vegetables, grains, beans, nuts, and seeds are living enzymes that aid in the efficient digestion and metabolism of foods, thus contributing to improved body functioning and increased energy.

Yet another benefit of living the vegetarian lifestyle has to do with what is avoided, specifically cholesterol, excess saturated fat, and pathogenic microbes present in animal products. Moreover, we can help protect our growing children from the many hormones, antibiotic and pesticide residues, and heavy metals that build up in beef, poultry, fish, and dairy products. These residual toxins are far more concentrated in animal products than in vegetarian foods.

Vegetarianism also encourages far greater efficiency in food production. In the case of beef, every pound of meat produced requires more than 10 pounds of grain used as cattle feed. It's been calculated that almost twice the world's current population could be fed by the quantity of food that goes toward cattle production yearly. Since this inefficient type of food production is one of the reasons why the world's rain forests are being destroyed at an alarming rate, it seems wise to ask if there's not a better way.

Vegetarianism is also a more compassionate way of living, considering the fact that animals raised for food production often endure overcrowded, painful lives and meet with miserable and inhumane deaths. This is, in fact, a prime reason why many vegetarians have chosen their dietary path.

One question a vegetarian may be asked is, "How do you get your protein?" The answer can actually be as simple as, "by chewing and swallowing." The fact is that by eating a varied diet of grains, beans, vegetables, fruits, nuts and seeds, and other high-quality products such as soy foods and sprouts, we can easily get all the protein we need in a form that is easy for the body to break down. By using the wide variety of foods in the recipe section and menu planner in this book, parents can be assured that all necessary amino acids are present in their family's diet, thus maximizing the benefits of ingested protein.

Another high-profile issue for vegetarians has been that of vitamin B_{12}. Previously it was thought that only animal products contained this important vitamin. Now it is understood that B_{12} is created by bacterial activity in the presence of the mineral cobalt. So while the vitamin is present in animal foods, it can also be synthesized in the human gut by a substance called "intrinsic factor," using mineral-rich plant foods as the raw material. Also, by using foods like blue-green algae, brewer's yeast, and, to a lesser extent, fermented products, including tempeh and miso, we can have abundant amounts of vitamin B_{12}. It should be noted that the human body is capable of stockpiling supplies of this vital nutrient. Therefore, anyone who eats any B_{12}-rich food (from either an animal or plant source) can draw from this reserve for several years in order to meet the body's requirement of about 2.5 micrograms daily. Nevertheless, many vegetarians, and nonvegetarians as well, choose to take a high-quality multivitamin/mineral supplement to ensure that they receive all necessary nutrients, including B_{12}, on a daily basis.

The last of the big concerns about vegetarianism has to do with calcium. Some vegetarians who avoid dairy products may wonder if they take in enough of this mineral, and parents, especially, wonder if children can get enough calcium without a high dairy-product intake. In actuality, leafy green vegetables, sea vegetables, and many beans, seeds, and nuts contain more abundant supplies of calcium than dairy foods do. Thus the good news for the many children who have difficulty digesting highly allergenic and mucus-forming dairy foods is that there are a variety of calcium-containing alternatives. What's more, when animal proteins are removed from the diet, more calcium is absorbed and retained by the body. So the bottom line here is actually more calcium for children's growing bones, teeth, and connective tissue. (Refer to the nutrient charts in the Appendix for more information.)

What it all adds up to is that if your family wants to become vegetarian, with a little bit of intelligent menu planning you'll be losing nothing nutritionally, and gaining a lot. Of course if you're eating the full range of animal products now and want to stop, a question may arise as to how to go about it. What's the right way to change your eating habits?

Actually, there is more than one way. People take different approaches. In embarking upon the vegetarian journey, some people jump right in, completely changing their eating habits overnight, while others choose a methodical step-by-step transition diet, eliminating one or two animal products at a time. Generally, beef and pork are the first to go. After a short while they are almost never missed, especially by children, whose habits are less firmly established and who are more flexible. Poultry generally sticks around a little longer before moving to the wayside, with fish being the next to go. Some will hang on to eggs and dairy foods, while others will keep going until they consume no animal products whatsoever. This is sometimes called veganism. This option enables us to bypass any possible negative health or environmental effects of animal product consumption while simultaneously bringing us to a more responsible, compassionate standard of ethics and planetary stewardship. Also, as we enter the new millennium, we have advanced so much on a culinary level that no animal products, even eggs and dairy foods, are indispensable in creating delicious, wholesome food.

FOOD IRRADIATION

In irradiation food products are exposed to a field of radiation of between 10,000 and 300,000 rads (a rad is a unit of measure in the process of irradiation) as a way of preventing spoilage and killing pests without the use of chemical preservatives and pesticides. It's been used to sterilize Army rations, food for astronauts, and laboratory and hospital equipment. Unfortunately, the process has some less than healthy consequences. Upon being exposed to radiation, foods undergo a significant loss of nutrients, including vitamins A, B complex, C, E, and K. Moreover, the amino acid balance of food can be altered, rendering protein less usable by the body.

But nutritionally deficient food is the least of the problems irradiation presents. When food is exposed to radiation, highly reactive free-radical compounds are formed, which cause a chain reaction of cellular damage. These free radicals in food get eaten and introduced into our bodies. In humans, free-radical activity causes cellular damage, along with a vulnerability to various forms of cancer. In fact, degenerative disease in general, and the whole aging process, are thought to be connected with free-radical activity.

The free radicals formed by irradiation also give rise to various other chemicals, such as benzene and formaldehyde, both of which cause mutations and are highly suspected of being carcinogenic. Some other dangerous compounds formed in the irradiation process are glyoxal, a mutagen; orthoquinones, which are carcinogens; and carbonyl compounds, which are cellular toxins. Irradiation can also be related to an increase in aflatoxins in foods infected with fungal spores. The concentration of this naturally occurring yet highly carcinogenic mold can jump by up to a hundredfold.

In addition to the health effects caused by eating irradiated foods, there are other concerns about irradiation. For one, the process itself can be an occupational hazard for those involved in it. Even though safeguards exist, there is always the potential for worker exposure to dangerous gamma radiation. Also, irradiation can be an environmental hazard because of the possibility of contaminated cooling-water leakage.

Fortunately, and thanks in part to public outcry and state-level legislation, irradiation in the United States is usually carried out only on herbs and spices. However, the FDA has already opened the door to irradiation of other foods, such as fruit, vegetables, grains, and poultry. What steps can you as a consumer and parent take to stop this? There are several.

First, purchase only those herbs and spices that are organically grown and labeled as nonirradiated. Second, to avoid the small amount of other foods that may be irradiated, such as fruits, vegetables, poultry, or teas, insist that your store manager provide written assurance, visible to all, that no irradiated foods are knowingly sold in that store. Third, call or write to companies making prepared and processed food to be sure all ingredients have not been irradiated. Let them know that you will not purchase products made with irradiated ingredients. Remember—when profits are involved, companies listen. Fourth, familiarize yourself with the "radura," the symbol used to signify that a food has been irradiated. No written labeling is required at this time.

Finally, contact your government representatives and demand anti-irradiation legislation and appropriate restrictions; they too will listen if they feel that votes are on the line. For more information on irradiation and companies that do and don't use it, contact:

Food and Water
389 Vermont Route 215
Walden, VT 05873
Phone: (800) EAT-SAFE

Americans for Safe Food, Center for Science in the Public Interest
1875 Connecticut Avenue NW, Suite 300
Washington, D.C. 20009
Phone: (202) 332-9110

Public Citizen Health Research Group
1600 Twentieth Street NW
Washington, D.C. 20009
Phone: (202) 588-1000

GENETICALLY ENGINEERED FOODS

Genetic engineering of food products, one of the latest high-tech food production "advances," occurs as follows: The genetic code of a food is deciphered, one or more specific genes are removed, and these are then restructured or replaced by synthetic genes or genes from other organisms. The new gene is then recombined with the genetic structure in order to gain a desired result. This is different from the traditional practice of hybridizing plants since, in genetic engineering, genes from completely different organisms can be combined. Thus, we already have the development of tomatoes with flounder genes and bacterial genes, corn with firefly genes, catfish with trout genes, potatoes with chicken genes, and pigs with human genes. The goal here is to lengthen sale life and maximize profit.

The above-mentioned tomatoes containing the genetic material of bacteria are already on sale in the West and Midwest, marketed as the MacGregor Flavr Savr. These tomatoes are said to be able to remain on the vine to ripen longer without rotting. However, they are still usually picked unripe, but remain on the produce shelf longer, thus extending their sale life.

Since these "transgenic" plants, and others, are being newly introduced into the complex array of nature's ecosystems, the long-term effects of their introduction are unknown. That is why many in the scientific community feel there is cause for reexamination of policies allowing gene transferring practices. Their concerns include the creation of new bacteria resistant to antibiotics, the creation of new viruses from plants engineered with viral genes, harm coming to animals that eat plants engineered to have "genetic pesticides," and a threat to the natural genetic diversity of wild plants by the passage of pollen from their genetically engineered counterparts. Another concern is that since the federal government does not require these products to be labeled as genetically engineered, those who oppose this practice for religious, philosophical, or ethical reasons may unknowingly consume them.

Perhaps the most well-known case of genetic engineering is that of cows treated with recombinant bovine somatotropin (rBST), also known as recombinant bovine growth hormone (rBGH). This synthetic hormone, developed by the Monsanto pharmaceutical company, has been used by dairy farmers since 1994. Farmers, consumers, and many in the scientific community have serious concerns about the use of rBGH. While rBGH does increase a cow's production of milk by up to 25 percent, it carries with it a price. Treated cows become more susceptible to a painful udder infection called mastitis. In mild, or subclinical, cases of mastitis, cows produce milk with higher levels of bacteria and pus. More severe cases force the use of additional antibiotics, which often leave residues in our milk. Milk from rBGH-treated cows can also have higher levels of hormones called insulin-like growth factors (IGF-1). In humans, IGF-1 can be absorbed through the intestinal wall and may be related to various cancers, including breast and prostate cancers, as well as a condition called acromegaly, characterized by overgrowth of bones in the face and limbs. RBGH-treated cows often suffer from leg and foot ailments, chronic body sores and lacerations, and digestive and reproductive disorders.

Milk from rBGH-injected cows is used in the full array of dairy products, including cheese, ice cream, yogurt, and even infant formula. This is of particular importance since the developing bodies of children are more vulnerable to contaminants. In fact, this is just one more of the many reasons that children should be nursed for at least six months to one year, or until they can digest soft foods and juices.

As consumers we should be aware that there is already a milk surplus in this country and therefore no logical reason to unnaturally and painfully increase cows' production of milk. And we should note that treating cows with bovine growth hormone has been banned in Europe, Australia, and New Zealand.

Even though there is no law requiring the labeling of this tainted milk and other genetically engineered foods, there are several steps we can take to avoid their consumption. The first is to avoid dairy products and purchase only third-party-certified organically grown produce. Any dairy products that we do use should be organic, or, at the very least, labeled free of rBGH.

As consumers we must insist that our store managers provide us with the purest products available, ones not subject to genetic engineering. We must also contact food producers and let them know that we will choose other products if theirs do not meet our standards. If we care about the quality of our children's food, we're going to have to constantly monitor it, and to speak up about what we want.

For more information on rBGH and genetically engineered foods in general, contact:

Consumers Union (publisher of *Consumer Reports* Magazine)
101 Truman Avenue
Yonkers, NY 10703
Phone: (914) 378-2000
Fax: (914) 378-2901

MICROWAVES

When food and liquid are exposed to microwave radiation, their molecules vibrate together, causing them to heat quickly. This is the principle behind the microwave oven, which in recent years has become a very popular fixture in many kitchens. People who keep a busy schedule use microwaves for defrosting and reheating, as well as cooking, and thoroughly enjoy their speed and convenience. Yet despite their popularity, microwaves pose problems that should be discussed.

First, an operating microwave can generate a magnetic field of about 3 milligauss (mG) through a radius of 8 to 12 feet, extending the distance of most kitchens. Fields as low as 2 milligauss have, in some studies, been linked to negative health effects, including some forms of cancer. Note also that children may well be among the chief recipients of these magnetic fields because they often use the flameless microwave as an easy way of preparing snacks and frozen meals.

Second, microwaves can produce free radicals in food, which can be related to a myriad of degenerative conditions.

Third, a microwave oven with a faulty seal (seals can wear out with age and use) can cause microwave leakage, which can cause severe burns and neurological problems if direct contact with human flesh is made.

A final consideration, but a no less important one, is the fact that microwaves can cook unevenly, and often leave cold spots in food. In the cases of unevenly cooked beef, pork, chicken, fish, and eggs, this can be dangerous, since microbes like *E. coli,* salmonella, and trichinosis can survive the cooking process and cause serious illness. Similarly, microwaves can produce very hot spots in food, so your child may unknowingly take a bite and get a serious mouth burn.

Given these health concerns, and considering the fact that it takes only a little more time and forethought to prepare food conventionally, it would be best to avoid the use of microwave ovens altogether.

CHAPTER 3

OUR WATER, AND WHAT TO DO ABOUT IT

This is a cookbook, so it's supposed to be about things you cook. Why, then, does it have such a large section on water? Well, for one thing, you cook *with* water. You may take it for granted, but water is actually the number-one staple in your kitchen. Not only that, but we ingest more water than any other single food; in fact our bodies are made up largely of water—about 70 percent. When you look at things this way, you can see why pure, safe water is vital to the healthy growth of children, and to the maintenance of health in adulthood. And you can understand why, whether you live in a city or a suburb, on a ranch or in a cabin, you and your family need to investigate and consider the quality of the water you are cooking with and drinking.

Most Americans drink and cook with tap water, piped into their homes by a major water utility. But how much do you know about your tap water?

First, you should understand that there are two sources for tap water—surface water and groundwater—and that these are intimately related, since the stream, lake, and river waters that make up surface water can seep down into groundwater aquifers. The second thing to understand is the reality that both surface and groundwater may contain a slew of pollutants. These include microorganisms, toxic metals and minerals, organic chemicals, and radioactive substances. Because of this pollution, in nonrural areas water utilities treat water with the aim of reducing contaminants to "acceptable" levels. However, our water is often drawn from such polluted sources that it requires purification beyond the capabilities of most water treatment facilities.

In rural areas, most homes get their water from wells that tap into porous underground formations, or aquifers. But there are problems here too. The groundwater in these aquifers is susceptible to pollution from naturally occurring toxic and radioactive metals and minerals. In addition, groundwater in agricultural areas is susceptible to pollution from surface water irrigation and pesticide runoff. Plus, pollutants can enter private water systems through unsanitary springs, unsealed holding tanks, and wellheads. Such pollutants can include algae, animal waste products, insects, and decaying plant matter.

Another common cause of water pollution can be the breakdown of the pipelines that transport water to our homes. Corrosion of the pipes can lead to the release of various contaminants, such as lead and cadmium, into the water. There are also various toxic substances that can be released into the water when impurities react with components of plastic water pipe and with chlorine.

Given all this, there has been growing concern since the early 1970s about the increasing number of harmful substances found in our water. Today, the Environmental Protection Agency monitors our public water supplies, together with federal, state, and local governmental agencies. However, of the thousands of possible contaminants found in drinking water, the EPA regulates about 80–90. And for many of these contaminants, the limits are too high, several times higher than those allowed by European countries.

Another problem is this: In the United States, while we have been concerned with treating water to eliminate the short-term health risks—which are primarily bacterial infections or acute poisoning—the long-term health effects of water contaminants have been overlooked, both in terms of single pollutants and possible synergistic effects of combined pollutants. This is unfortunate, particularly for children, because extended exposure to water pollutants can pose a danger of chronic low-level nervous-system poisoning, a wide range of illnesses, and weakened immunity. While scientists may say that one part per billion of a pollutant in a substance will have no ill effects, we do not know if this is really so, especially when considering the smallest among us. The accepted maximum contaminant level (MCL) allowed for a substance may in fact be many times the amount that is dangerous to small children. With this in mind, then, it's easy to see why we cannot be too careful about monitoring our water.

WHAT'S IN OUR WATER?

Contaminants in our water may include microorganisms; toxic minerals and metals; organic chemicals; radioactive substances; and additives. This section will examine each of these five categories of contaminants.

Microorganisms

Microorganisms that live in water can cause a variety of diseases, such as hepatitis, giardiasis, typhoid, and flu. This class of contaminants includes bacteria, viruses, and protozoan cysts. Both municipal and private water systems can harbor any of these.

A common type of bacteria found in water is fecal coliform bacteria, which come from human and animal waste. While these can be killed by the application of chlorine, the presence of local coliform bacteria often indicates that there are also hard-to-detect and potentially more dangerous organisms, such as viruses.

As for these, viruses are the smallest type of pollutant—much tinier than bacteria—and thus they're difficult as well as expensive to detect. Most viruses are harmless to humans and are killed during the chlorination process; however, not all viruses can be killed during water processing, even in a properly functioning treatment plant. Viruses can cause a wide range of illnesses, from colds to the flu to hepatitis. Since many cases of viral illness last less than 24 hours, they're often not attributed to contaminated water supplies, although water may in fact have been the cause.

The final type of trouble-causing microorganism commonly found in water is protozoan parasites, the two of particular concern being giardia and cryptosporidium. These critters have a hard-shelled exterior that protects them from the chlorination process in water treatment facilities. When ingested, they can attach to the intestinal lining and suck up nutrients meant for their host. What's problematic is that, while water companies are required to test for the presence of bacteria, they're not necessarily required to check for protozoan parasites. Since symptoms in cases of parasitic illness do not disappear immediately, and since these types of illnesses can easily be identified by physicians, protozoan-caused diseases are commonly traced back to water supplies.

Minerals and Metals

Minerals are substances that are not derived from plant or animal sources and that occur naturally in sand, clay, and rock formations, from which they can enter our water systems. Minerals and metals can of course also enter our water supply from man-made sources. While many members of this group aren't harmful, many can be toxic; those that pose a threat to health include aluminum, arsenic, asbestos, barium, cadmium, chromium, copper, fluoride, lead, mercury, and silver. Especially toxic to children are mercury, cadmium, and lead.

Because it's been so widely used in the past, and despite its great potential to cause harm, lead is still prevalent in the plumbing systems of homes, schools, and office buildings. Plumbing systems are often comprised of copper piping joined by lead solder. The copper stays in place but the lead can leach into the water. Another common offender is our faucets, which are typically made of brass alloy that contains some lead. When water remains in the faucet and pipes for several hours, lead can leach into it. All of this is unfortunate because lead is accumulated in the body until it reaches harmful levels, at which time health problems ensue, particularly in children. Lead can interfere with a wide variety of body functions and cause problems such as learning disabilities, impaired growth and hearing, inhibition of red blood cell formation, and impaired neurological functioning. Severe cases of lead poisoning can even cause brain damage.

Developing fetuses are also susceptible to lead's detrimental effects, which can include reduced gestation time and low birth weight.

Organic Chemicals

Organic chemicals are substances that come directly from plant or animal matter, or are manufactured from it. Examples are synthetic fertilizers, pesticides, and various fuels. Many organic chemicals are toxic, and thousands have been found in public water supplies.

One class of this kind of pollutant is volatile organic chemicals, or VOC's. These are nonparticulate substances that can vaporize, and they're especially dangerous because they can be absorbed through the skin when a person is bathing or washing dishes. A VOC that commonly shows up in our water supplies is benzene, which is found in paint removers and plastics. VOC's can be harmful to the liver, kidneys, muscular system, nervous system, and lungs. They have also been linked to cancers and birth defects in children.

Health-threatening pesticides constitute another class of organic chemicals that turns up in our water supply. An example is alachlor, a known carcinogen that is nevertheless very widely used in this country as an agricultural pesticide and herbicide. It's been found in drinking water supplies in virtually all states. Two other agricultural organic chemicals are nitrates and nitrites. These by-products of agricultural fertilizers are proven carcinogens and they're potentially harmful to infants.

Lastly, polychlorinated biphenols, or PCB's, are a family of more than 200 chemicals used primarily in electrical equipment and by large companies. These potent carcinogens are found in many of our water systems and have often been illegally discharged by industrial processes as waste into surface water supplies.

Radioactive Substances

Radioactive water contaminants can be in mineral form, or they can be gases. Some naturally occurring ones that are present in water systems include radon, radium, uranium, and potassium 40. Man-made radioactive water pollution can come from uranium mining, coal-burning electrical generators, and smelting plants, as well as from water discharged by nuclear power plants, nuclear weapons facilities, radioactive material disposal sites, nuclear-powered ships, and hospitals.

Radon is a naturally occurring gas. It is the breakdown product of the radioactive mineral uranium, and is particularly concentrated in water passing through rock strata of granite, shale, phosphate, or uranium. Radon evaporates when exposed to air and is thus not a concern with surface water sources such as reservoirs, rivers, or lakes. Also, if your water has been aerated or processed through an open-air tank, radon is not a problem. It can, however, be a threat if your water source is groundwater that comes directly into your home from an underground source, with no air exposure.

Radium, uranium, and potassium 40 may be of concern to those living in small communities with municipal water supplies or with private wells. Since water companies are required to test for these radioactives, it may not be a bad idea to obtain a copy of your municipality's annual water report. Also, since radioactive water pollution has been linked to childhood leukemias, it would be advisable to have your water tested if it comes from a private well.

Additives

Additives are chemicals used in the treatment of public water systems; they include chlorine and fluoride. The danger here is that chemical interactions at water treatment facilities can transform certain compounds into more dangerous contaminants.

Chlorine, the most noticeable additive, is used to reduce the risk of water-borne bacteria, including those that cause cholera and typhoid. But chlorine is not without its own risk. Chlorine used in municipal water supplies often binds to organic materials such as leaves, creating potent carcinogens called trihalomethanes (THM's), which are found in all public water systems in varying concentrations. Also, longterm exposure to chlorinated tap water raises the risk associated with bladder, colon, and rectal cancers.

Fluoride, an additive put into the drinking water of more than 100 million people in this country for the purpose of preventing tooth decay, is a poison whose level of ingestion must be carefully regulated. Since it's difficult to accurately measure the amounts of this additive, the levels in drinking water can vary greatly from day to day, and when one considers the fluoride ingested from other sources, such as toothpaste and supplemental tablets, a safe standardized intake is almost impossible to ensure.

Approximately half of the U.S. population lives in areas with fluoridated water, and their water systems are supposed to be fluoridated at the level of about 1 part per million. Overfluoridation of water supplies in the 1–4-ppm range can cause fluorosis, a discoloring of the teeth. Other symptoms that can occur are skin rashes, headaches, gastric distress, weakening of the immune system, kidney damage, heart problems, and cancer, particularly bone cancer.

As an alternative to fluoride, I recommend a holistic approach to preventing tooth decay. Eliminate all refined carbohydrates from your child's diet. Replace these with fresh whole foods, including fruits, vegetables, whole grains, nuts, seeds, and legumes. Proper care in pregnancy, and maintenance of the child's overall health in infancy and childhood, combined with good nutrition, regular checkups, brushing, flossing, and keeping the mouth generally clean, are all part of this approach. Also, ample intake of zinc, phosphorus, calcium, magnesium, and vitamin C will help make the teeth strong.

HOW TO HAVE YOUR WATER TESTED

To address our concerns responsibly, we must inform ourselves and use our common sense. We must ask: Is there any safe level of a cancer-causing substance? Then, we must identify which contaminants are present in our drinking water. We can seek out water-testing companies or purchase inexpensive home test kits to help us make educated decisions regarding the use of the water that flows so freely from our kitchen tap.

The first step is to obtain an annual water-quality report from your water supplier. You are entitled to this report free of charge under federal and state laws. You can get one by sending a brief letter to your water supplier. In it, ask for all reports that have come out over the past year measuring organic chemicals, VOC's, total dissolved solids, pesticides, radioactive chemicals, metals, minerals, and alkalinity in the water supplied to your address.

Keep in mind that the water in the report that you receive has not yet been exposed to the contaminants in the transportation system of piping from the water treatment facility to your home. That means that certain contaminants—e.g., vinyl chloride, organic chemicals, and asbestos—may not be included in the report, even if they're in your water.

That's why your second step in information gathering is to have your tap water tested. Most water-testing companies will test for coliform bacteria, toxic metals, nitrates and other organic chemicals, particulates, and fluoride. You should understand that no test facility can detect every contaminant possible. Also, testing for radioactive contamination, asbestos, and protozoan parasites may require laboratories other than the standard water-testing labs.

Should you check for radioactive pollution? People who might consider this are those whose water supply is downstream from a nuclear facility or a uranium mining facility, or those whose water comes from a private underground well. As far as radon testing goes, you should check your air first. Only if radon is present in your air is water contamination a possibility.

Asbestos testing is a good idea for those whose water transportation is made up of old cement water pipes. Those who might need bacteria or protozoan cyst testing would be people who have confirmed giardiasis or cryptosporiasis, or those who believe their well may not be fully sealed. Since testing can be expensive for both asbestos and protozoans, it is often less costly to assume you have these problems to some degree and purchase a purification system that will remove protozoan cysts and asbestos.

Different labs have different methods of testing and reporting results, and you'll need to check with your test facilities for instructions on properly reading your water-test reports. However, the reports supplied to you by these testing labs, and by your water supplier, will provide enough information for you to make a more informed choice regarding water-purification systems and bottled water.

Listed below is an independent water-testing laboratory that you can contact to have your water tested for contaminants at very reasonable rates. You may already have an idea as to which class of contaminants has presented problems in your community in the past. If not, it is best to get a comprehensive report. After you call the lab and tell them which tests you would like, they will send you the sample containers and instructions. Then, you will draw a sample of your water and sent it to them. You should receive your report within a few weeks.

National Testing Laboratories, Inc.
6555 Wilson Mills Road
Cleveland, OH 44143
Phone: (800) 458-3330

"Watercheck Test Series": 14 metals, inorganics and physical factors, VOC's, microbiological (coliform bacteria).

Organic chemicals—pesticides, herbicides, and PCB's.

Radionuclide contamination testing for gross alpha and gross beta, and testing for radon available upon request.

HOME PURIFICATION SOLUTIONS

There are several types of water purification systems suited for home use, the most common ones being filtration, reverse osmosis, and distillation. No one system can remove all contaminants, so, depending on which kinds of contaminants are present in your water, you may need one system or a combination of systems. Some are countertop units with easy hookup capability, while others offer the option of installation underneath your sink, to provide maximum countertop surface area.

Filters

The simplest type of purification system is the filter. A filter can be any of various media used to trap and remove undesirable contaminants from tap water.

Sediment filters are used for removing large particles of dirt, sand, and total suspended solids, called TSS. Filtration of sediments is usually the first step in a multifilter purification system since these large particles will often damage more sophisticated systems. The filter material is generally a pleated film, which is durable and effectively resists bacterial growth. Sediment filters come in sizes ranging from coarse to very fine, and the size you need will depend on the size and number of TSS in your water. Sometimes the sediment content is so great that more than one step of sediment filtration is required.

Carbon filters are used to remove tastes and smells coming from certain minerals and from hydrogen sulfide gas. In addition, carbon will remove organic chemicals (including VOC's), additives, and radon. Some carbon filters will greatly reduce soluble lead and other toxic minerals, as well as some microorganisms. Look for ones that have been certified by the National Sanitation Foundation, a reputable testing organization for water purifiers. One possible drawback to carbon filtration is the tendency for bacteria to get trapped within the filter. This problem can easily be remedied by changing the filter at least every three months.

Carbon filters usually come in two forms: granular and block. The block carbon is often preferred over the granular since the water remains in contact with a greater surface area of the filter for a longer period, thus removing a greater amount of contaminants. Also, due to the structure of the solid carbon block, there is less bacterial proliferation. Some carbon filters are labeled bacteriostatic due to the addition of silver; however, this is ineffective in removing bacteria or blocking their buildup.

When using a carbon filter, remember to change it at regular intervals, and allow your water to run for at least 30 seconds before use. If you follow these precautions, a block carbon filter can be a sensible home purification solution, although if you have a really severe problem you might want to incorporate it as one facet of a reverse osmosis system.

Reverse Osmosis Systems

Another type of purification system is called an RO, or reverse osmosis, system. An RO system eliminates organic compounds (including VOC's), toxic metals/minerals, and radioactive minerals. In addition, it will partially remove microorganisms. RO treatment works as follows: Water comes in contact with a membrane and contaminants are trapped on one side while most of the water flows through to produce a pure water supply. The contaminants, dissolved in a small amount of water, are expelled through a drain.

Membranes used in an RO unit can be of two types—cellulose triacetate (CTA) or thin film composite (TFC). If you receive your water from a municipal supply you will probably need a CTA membrane, since it can better tolerate chlorine. TFC membranes are appropriate for those using well water.

Even though RO systems do an excellent job of ridding water of a wide range of pollutants, they are not without their drawbacks. They can be expensive to purchase and maintain. Adequate water pressure must be available to make the system efficient. And while some RO units can produce purified water quickly, others take several hours to make a gallon of water. Also, water is often wasted in the RO process, so be sure to look for a recirculating unit that refilters water, or an inline unit, which uses the water flow through household pipes. All good RO units have an automatic shutoff valve (flush), which prevents water wastage when the holding tank is full.

Many different RO systems are available, depending on your needs, and these systems will generally be combined with a sediment prefilter and carbon posttreatment filter. Before you purchase an RO system, your supplier should test your water to let you know which type of unit is best for you. Some companies will provide installation, while others will require you to hire a plumber for this task.

Distillation

A third type of purification system, distillation, is an effective way to remove toxic minerals and metals, radioactive substances, and additives from your water. It will partially remove organic chemicals (except VOC's) and some microorganisms, but not all bacteria. Distillation involves water being heated to its boiling point and then being transported as vapor to the other side of the unit, where it recondenses into liquid after having left its contaminants behind. The disadvantages of this method are that it does not eliminate VOC's, it is a process that generates heat and moisture, it can be time-, space-, and electricity-consuming, and it can be very costly.

HOW TO MOST EFFECTIVELY PURIFY YOUR WATER

PROBLEMS	SOLUTIONS
Microorganisms	
bacteria	block carbon, distillation
cyst protozoa	block carbon, distillation
viruses	RO, distillation
Organic chemicals,	
including VOC's	block carbon, RO
Toxic metals/	RO, distillation, block carbon
minerals	RO, distillation

PROBLEMS	SOLUTIONS
Radioactives	
radon	block carbon
uranium and radium	RO, distillation
Additives	
chlorine	block carbon
fluoride + flocculents	RO, distillation
Suspended solids	pleated film sediment filter
Tastes and smells	block carbon, distillation

Other Measures

For those times when drinking tap water is unavoidable, there are ways to make it safer. Boiling water will kill most bacteria and evaporate chlorine and other VOC's. Also, letting the tap run for 1 minute will flush toxic metals that have leached into the water from plumbing fixtures and pipes overnight.

BOTTLED WATER

Are all bottled waters the same? The answer is no. There are 5 types of bottled water, including distilled, drinking, natural source, mineral, and specialty water.

First, purified, or distilled water, is tap water that has been disinfected, demineralized, aerated, and filtered. Since distilled water has been demineralized, it has a tendency to leach plastic from its container in order to make up for its lost minerals.

The second type of bottled water is called drinking water; it, like purified water, is tap water that has been filtered, removing sediment and some harmful chemicals; aerated; and disinfected. Both drinking water and distilled water are treated with ozonation and ultraviolet light to kill bacteria. The difference with drinking water is that after it's purified, beneficial minerals are reintroduced.

Natural-source water, often called spring water, comes from a spring, aquifer, or artesian well that is mineral rich. Despite its association with purity, spring water can contain toxic metals, minerals, organic chemicals, and radioactives. However, this kind of bottled water does have the advantage of being bottled at the source, thus avoiding contaminants often associated with the transportation system. If you do buy natural-source water, look for brands that reveal the location of the spring, to ensure their authenticity. Good spring water can be a very effective alternative to problematic tap water.

Mineral water can be either natural spring water rich in minerals, or tap water with minerals added or removed. The FDA has exempted these waters from regulation, so when shopping, choose a brand that carries the NSF (National Sanitation Foundation) seal of approval.

Finally, specialty water is tap or spring water to which flavor and/or carbonation have been added. Because it's considered a beverage, specialty water is not subject to FDA regulation. I would therefore recommend using specialty water on an occasional basis, as opposed to every day.

When purchasing bottled water, look for glass bottles if possible, and purchase your water from a store with a high turnover rate. When water is exposed to temperature fluctuations, the release of plastic components into the water is hastened, giving it a plastic taste. Also, do not store your water in sunlight, since this will encourage the growth of microbes.

Quality Bottled Waters

The following bottled waters are recommended for their purity and lack of contaminants. They are certified by the NSF and/or the Food and Drug Administration.

Alhambra Natural Water	*Georgia Mountain*
AquaPenn Spring Water	*Hawaiian Sparkling Water*
Artesia Texas Mineral Water	*Ice Mountain Main Spring Water*
Aspen	*Leisure Time Spring Water*
Big Spring Water	*Mendocino Mineral Water*
Calistoga Mineral Water	*Mountain Valley Spring Water*
Carolina Mountain Spring Water	*Mount Olympus Spring Water*
Chippewa Spring Water	*Naya Spring Water*
Cloister Spring Water	*Ozarka Spring Water*
Crystal Geyser	*Poland Spring Natural Spring Water*
Crystal Rock Spring Water	*Puro Spring Water*
Culligan	*Roaring Spring Water*
Diamond Water	*Triple Springs*
Ephrata Diamond Spring	*Triton*
Eureka	

CHAPTER 4

BE PREPARED

Some people take cooking in stride, while for others it is a terrible burden. The difference usually lies not in the area of cooking skill but in having an organized, well-stocked kitchen, as opposed to a poorly stocked, disorganized one. With a wide variety of staple items stored in the pantry, you won't have to run to the store every time you want to turn on the stove. Instead, if your child wants his or her favorite dinner, or if a recipe catches your eye, you can immediately roll up your sleeves and enjoy the oldest creative process in the world—cooking. Even the most skeptical individuals will enjoy cooking once they've lived in the "be-prepared" mode for a while. It's the stress-free way of operating in the kitchen.

In this chapter you will find some basic products that you may want to keep on hand, along with suggestions for their use.

GRAINS

Throughout history, grains have been the staple food product for the vast majority of the world. The largest percentage of one's diet should come from complex carbohydrates, of which grains are an excellent source. Grains are also a fiber-rich source of vitamins, minerals, and proteins.

Grains can be used for breakfast cereals, tossed into salads, or thrown into soups, or they can constitute the main component of meals. A convenient and versatile way to use them is in the form of flakes, which are made by a process of quick exposure to dry heat and rolling in a steel press. Grain flakes are nutrient rich and quick cooking, and they make a great hot cereal or addition to baked goods. Then of course there's ground grain, or flour, that most versatile of kitchen staples that can be used in breads and muffins, main dishes, snack items, puddings, and baked desserts.

The grain kernel is composed of four parts. The inedible outer covering is called the husk. Under the husk is the first edible layer, called the bran; it contains soluble and insoluble fiber. The second edible layer is called the germ, and it's rich in protein, vitamin E, and several members of the B complex family. Innermost in the kernel is a starchy portion called the endosperm. The endosperm is responsible for nourishing the seedling while the plant is in its beginning stages of growth.

When a grain is kept in a state where all three edible portions of the kernel are intact, it's referred to as a "whole grain." When it goes through a process of refinement, the bran and the germ are removed, leaving the endosperm. The more a grain is refined, the more nutrient and fiber content it loses. Most commercially available grains are both hulled and degerminated, removing fiber and over 20 nutrients. Then a few chemically synthesized vitamins and minerals representing just a fraction of the total nutrient spectrum are added to the starchy endosperm in an attempt to replace what's been lost. The lost fiber, however, is not replaced, nor is the delicate balance of the full range of nutrients that are present when all three edible parts of the kernel are left in their natural state. Because fiber and nutrients are lost, refined grains are more difficult to digest and metabolize than whole grains are.

So when buying grains, whole grains are best. And when purchasing a whole grain, it's most economical and environmentally friendly to purchase organic grains, in bulk. They should be stored in airtight containers in a cool place. Plastic containers, tightly sealed jars, or bags that zip closed are all good for this purpose. Before using whole grains, check them for stones and then rinse with pure water in a colander.

Flour

Grain will keep for several months, but flour won't. That's why flour should be purchased in small portions and stored in the refrigerator or in a cool place. As with grain, store flour in tightly sealed containers, jars, or plastic bags that zip closed. This will help prevent infestation by grain moths and will also help prevent rancidity, which, unfortunately, is more likely to occur in a whole-grain product than in a refined one since the nutrient-rich and oil-rich germ is left intact. (When a grain is stripped, bleached, and literally devitalized, it will have a much longer shelf life. But some trade-offs aren't worth making, especially when it comes to your family's nutrition.)

When flour is made, grain immediately begins to oxidize and lose its nutritional potency. Grinding your own will give you the freshest possible product, and save you money too. The grinding process takes only a few minutes and is the best way to get fresh whole-grain flour. You can use either a manually operated or electric flour mill. The hand mills are usually made of wood and can be purchased through health food stores or mail order, while electric mills can be purchased in appliance stores. My own preference is a manually operated mill. It's easy to clean. Plus electric machines are noisy and will often raise the temperature of the flour to undesirable levels, thus hastening its degradation. Electric mills can also be messy; the last time I used an electric machine to make flour for fresh pasta I ended up covered from head to foot in flour dust! But of course the choice is yours; the important thing is that, if you have the time, freshly ground flour is a superior product.

Most flour that Americans purchase and consume is bleached, but bleached flour should be avoided as much as possible, and whole-grain flours used instead. As for wheat flour, the most commonly used type, it's available in 5 main varieties (I'm not even considering bleached). First, there is regular whole-wheat flour, which is made from hard red winter wheat and has the germ and bran intact. The second alternative—not as good nutritionally—is unbleached white flour, made from hard red winter wheat with the bran and germ removed. Sometimes the germ is added back in; try to find this kind in natural foods stores if you want to work with unbleached white; it makes for a rich but delicate taste in baked goods. Third, there is whole-wheat pastry flour, which is soft red winter wheat with the germ and bran intact. Fourth, there is whole durum flour, which comes from durum wheat with the germ and bran intact. Fifth, there is simply durum flour with the germ and bran removed.

Pasta

Any section on grain wouldn't be complete without discussing pasta. Traditionally, pasta is made from durum wheat, also called semolina; however, the days of a cook's being limited to old-fashioned macaroni are long gone. Today, pasta is available in a wide variety of shapes, sizes, textures, and colors, and it's made from many different grains. Some of these are brown rice, corn, buckwheat, rye, and whole wheat. Sometimes, vegetables such as spinach, tomatoes, beets, carrots, and pumpkin are dried into powders and added to pasta dough, imparting unique flavors and vivid colors. When purchasing pasta, look for a whole-grain product. It generally has a higher nutrient content and less chemical processing in its past.

When cooking pasta be sure to follow the directions on the package, and be prepared to strain and rinse (if appropriate) quickly to prevent overcooking. Al dente is best!

Seitan

Seitan, sometimes called "wheat meat," is a chewy, protein-rich, cutlet-like product made from wheat flour and water. When these are mixed, the glutinous portion of the flour concentrates, forming the seitan patty. This versatile food comes in a variety of textures and is a great substitute for meat-based dishes. You can use it in such main-dish items as stews, chili, stir-fries, and burgers.

Most seitan is made from organically grown wheat flour, but check the label to play it safe. It's best to choose unseasoned seitan to avoid excess sodium and to maximize your options with the product. But if you choose preseasoned seitan, be sure it has no MSG, hydrolyzed vegetable protein (HVP), sugar, or artificial ingredients.

Mochi

Mochi is a unique food product originating in the Far East, but now very popular in American natural foods stores. It's made from steamed, pounded, sweet brown rice. This flat, compact cake can be toasted, steamed, baked, and added to soups. It has a chewy texture and expands to many times its original size, so a small piece goes a long way. It can also be cut and placed in a waffle iron for a chewy, sweet waffle.

Mochi comes in a variety of flavors and can be stored frozen for months. Look for mochi that is made from organically grown rice and in a desirable flavor (e.g., cinnamon raisin). Some mochi comes with perforations that make breaking and slicing easier. This product has a place in every healthy kitchen, especially where family members are allergic to wheat products.

Types of Whole Grains

The following is a list of grains that you may want to keep on hand in your kitchen. When you cook them, grains should be simmered covered for the allowed cooking time, or until all of the water has been absorbed. Then turn off the heat, cover, and let stand for 5 minutes. Fluff with a fork and serve.

Amaranth: a small, sweet round kernel highest in protein among grains, which, along with quinoa, is native to South America, although China leads the way in growing it today.

Barley: a cereal grass kernel hulled into scotch or pot barley, it was the first grain to be cultivated in ancient times.

Corn: the kernel of a starchy vegetable native to the Americas and first cultivated by the Incas. Corn is found in many varieties—white, yellow, blue, popcorn, masa, and grits.

Kamut: pronounced "ka-moot"—a highly nutritious ancient wheat with a nutritional value superior to that of modern hybridized wheats. It's a relative of durum wheat with a more easily digestible form of gluten.

Kasha: (buckwheat, roasted)—a hearty grain staple in many Eastern European countries and China. Kasha can be purchased in coarse, medium, and fine groats.

Millet: a mild-flavored highly digestible alkalizing grain (not acidic to the body). Rich in protein, millet was a staple food of many ancient cultures, including those of Egypt, India, and China.

Oats: a cereal grass kernel native to America and Europe that can be purchased as whole groats, steel cut, and rolled.

Quinoa: pronounced "keen-wa"—a round grain, which, along with amaranth, has the highest protein content among the grains and is rich in all eight essential amino acids and many vitamins and minerals. This ancient grain originated in the Andes mountains of South America. Since the seeds mature at different times they must be harvested by hand, making quinoa a bit more expensive than most grains.

Rice: a water grass native to India, Southeast Asia, and China. Rice comes in various varieties, including: long-, medium-, and short-grain, sweet, wild, white basmati, brown basmati, white texmati, and brown texmati. You can also buy separate components, i.e., cream of rice, rice bran, and rice germ.

Rye: a cereal grass low in gluten with a rich hearty flavor. Its low gluten content makes rye well tolerated by those with wheat allergies.

Spelt: an ancient grain that's recently been rediscovered. This close relative of wheat may be an option for those with a sensitivity to wheat.

Teff: the smallest grain in the world, native to Ethiopia. Teff is a rich source of minerals, fiber, and protein. It's sweet and molasses-like in flavor and gelatinous in texture when cooked. It is difficult to chew and most nutritious when the seed is opened, so it's best sautéed or soaked first.

Triticale: a new cereal grass with good protein content made by a hybrid cross of rye and wheat. Those with a wheat allergy might find triticale useful.

Wheat: the world's most cultivated grain crop. Wheat was first cultivated in China and Egypt and can be found in many varieties and forms, including durum (semolina), soft red winter, and hard red winter. Products made from wheat include whole-wheat berries, bulgur (steamed and cracked), wheat germ (raw or toasted; toasted is more flavorful, with a negligible difference in nutrient value), farina (cream of; it's the coarsely ground endosperm of wheat), wheat bran, wheat flakes, and couscous (cracked and pelletized endosperm of durum wheat).

HOW TO COOK WHOLE GRAINS

1 CUP DRY GRAIN	WATER	COOKING TIME
Amaranth	3 cups	25–35 minutes
Barley (pearled)	3½ cups	60–75 minutes
Buckwheat (kasha)	2 cups	20 minutes
Kamut	3 cups	90–120 minutes
Millet	3 cups	20–25 minutes
Oats		
rolled	3 cups	10–15 minutes
steel cut	4 cups	30–40 minutes
Quinoa	2 cups	20 minutes
Rice		
brown basmati	1½ cups	45 minutes
brown texmati	2 cups	45 minutes
short-grain brown	2½ cups	45 minutes
sweet brown	2 cups	45 minutes
long-grain brown	2 cups	45 minutes
wild	3½ cups	60 minutes
white basmati	1¾ cups	15–20 minutes
white texmati	1¾ cups	15–20 minutes
Rye (berries)	3 cups	90–120 minutes
rolled or flakes	3 cups	15–20 minutes
Spelt	2 cups	50–60 minutes
Teff	4 cups	25–30 minutes
Triticale	4 cups	105–120 minutes
Whole-wheat (berries)	3 cups	90 minutes
bulgur	2⅔ cups	25 minutes
couscous	1½ cups	10 minutes
flakes	3 cups	20–25 minutes

LEGUMES

Legumes, which include beans, lentils, and split peas, are a highly nutritious, low-fat family, and can be a favorite food if they're prepared with imagination and a small amount of care. Legumes are an excellent source of protein, complex carbohydrates, B vitamins, iron, and other important minerals, and they're fiber rich as well. They are an excellent accompaniment to any meal, although they can constitute a main course by themselves.

Legumes can generally be purchased organically in three ways—fresh; dried; or precooked, in cans and jars. Here we will talk about both dried and precooked legumes, since fresh beans are rarely seen except at farmers' markets. (If you do purchase them fresh, they can often be treated as fresh vegetables and cooked for short periods until tender.)

When choosing dried beans, look for those that are whole and without cracks or pinholes, which can indicate insect damage. Also, beware of beans that are cloudy or fuzzy-looking, since this can be a sign of mold or fungus. To ensure even cooking, beans should be uniform in size, because larger ones take longer to cook. Last, look for a nice bright color, which is a sign of freshness. Even though long-stored legumes retain their nutrient content, they do take longer to cook and can be a little tough to chew.

Dried beans can be stored in the plastic bags in which they're purchased, or if you've bought them in bulk, use plastic bags that zip closed, airtight plastic containers, or tightly sealed glass jars.

The first step in preparing dried legumes is to sort through them on a clean flat surface to "weed out" any stones or debris. They should then be rinsed in clean pure water to wash off any dirt. As for the cook-

HOW TO COOK LEGUMES

2 CUPS PRESOAKED BEAN	WATER	COOKING TIME	PRESSURE-COOKING TIME
Adzuki beans	8 cups	120 minutes	15–20 minutes
Black beans (turtle)	8 cups	90 minutes	10–12 minutes
Black-eyed peas (cow)	8 cups	50–75 minutes	8–10 minutes
Chickpeas (garbanzo)	8 cups	180 minutes	10–12 minutes
Fava beans (broad)	8 cups	180 minutes	12–14 minutes
Lentils (green, all types)*	7 cups	40–45 minutes	10–14 minutes
brown*	7 cups	35–40 minutes	8–10 minutes
french*	7 cups	35–40 minutes	8–10 minutes
red*	7 cups	20–25 minutes	6–8 minutes
Lima beans (large)*	8 cups	60 minutes	3–4 minutes
Mung beans	8 cups	60–75 minutes	5–7 minutes
Pigeon peas*	8 cups	30–45 minutes	10–12 minutes
Pink beans	8 cups	60–120 minutes	7–8 minutes
Pinto beans	8 cups	150 minutes	10–12 minutes
Red beans	8 cups	60–75 minutes	4–5 minutes
Red kidney beans	8 cups	90 minutes	10–12 minutes
Small white beans (navy)	8 cups	150 minutes	6–7 minutes
great northern beans	8 cups	120 minutes	6–7 minutes
Soybeans	8 cups	180 minutes	10–15 minutes
Split peas (all types)*	8 cups	60–75 minutes	10–12 minutes
White kidney (cannellini)	8 cups	90 minutes	6–8 minutes

*No soaking required.

HEALTHY COOKING FOR KIDS

ing, the indigestibility of beans is often talked about and sometimes laughed about. The gassiness from beans is caused by complex starchy sugars that often go undigested until they mix with bacteria in the large intestine. This digestive and social dilemma can be easily remedied with the following prescription. Dried beans should be soaked overnight in 3 times the quantity of water per measure of beans. (Note: Legumes that do not require soaking are split peas and lentils.) They should then be drained, rinsed, and covered with pure water for cooking. To prevent foaming during the cooking process, you can add a strip of the sea vegetable kombu or a tablespoon of expeller-pressed vegetable oil (see page 42). Kombu adds flavor and nutrients, shortens cooking time, and increases legumes' digestibility. To keep beans from becoming tough, add salt and any acidic ingredients such as tomatoes, lemon juice, vinegar, honey, or molasses last.

Cooking times for legumes range from 25 minutes for red lentils to 3 hours for some of the harder beans. It may take a little longer to cook them, but the advantage of using dried beans is that when they are stewed for a while with vegetable stocks or fresh herbs, they will take on flavors that precooked beans added to dishes won't.

I would suggest investing in a pressure cooker if you can. A new and improved species of pressure cooker has come on the market in the past few years that will decrease the cooking times for many legumes by as much as three quarters. Look for a manual spring valve release system in your pressure cooker. Since steam does not escape, the internal temperature is increased, less water is needed, more nutrients are retained, and noise is virtually nonexistent. Another important feature to look for is an automatically locking lid, which ensures that the lid cannot be removed until all of the pressure is released. This feature can prevent serious injuries.

When using your pressure cooker, place your soaked legumes inside and cover with 3 cups of water for every cup of legume. (Note that dried beans soaked overnight will often increase in volume 2½ times, so that 1 cup of dried beans expands into 2½ cups soaked.) With lentils and split peas no soaking is necessary; simply cover them with 2 inches of water. Pressure-cooking times will vary for different pressure cookers.

Canned or jarred precooked beans shouldn't be ruled out. They're good when time is lacking, and their convenience makes them an invaluable addition to the cupboard. When purchasing canned beans, choose a variety that has not been preseasoned, since MSG and other chemicals are often added. Also, preservatives like EDTA, BHA/BHT, and any other additives, should always be avoided. Beans should be packed in an enamel-lined or lead-free can (avoid dented cans) or in a clear glass vacuum-sealed jar. Drain and rinse the beans in pure water before you use them.

To increase protein and other nutrients, try sprouted beans, or prepare with a whole grain such as brown rice or kasha. There are many kinds of beans readily available for purchase; for variety and adventure in shopping try an ethnic market or natural foods store.

The Joy of Soy

A widely used member of the legume family is the highly nutritious and versatile soybean, the derivatives of which are so spectacular that they merit a section all of their own. Soybeans have been used around the world throughout history. They can be used as whole beans or grits, they can be ground into flour, or they can be processed into tofu, tofu hot dogs, tempeh, or miso. Soybeans are rich in protein, low in saturated fat, and packed with many nutrients, such as B complex vitamins, vitamin A, calcium, iron, potassium, phosphorus, and polyunsaturated fatty acids. Sprouting soybeans will markedly increase their vitamin C content.

It's not often that soybeans are prepared whole as other beans are, but they can be. After you rinse and soak them, they can be pressure-cooked for 20 minutes, then added to soups or stews. Precooked soybeans can also be added to stir-fries, pot pies, soups, burritos, tacos, dips, and casseroles. Or season the precooked beans and present them along with a colorful array of steamed and raw vegetables. Sprouted soybeans are tasty and highly nutritious, plentiful in fiber, and wonderfully crunchy. They're a great addition to salads and crudités. Soy sprouts must be steamed or otherwise heated for 5 to 10 minutes since they contain a natural enzyme inhibitor that makes digestion difficult.

Soy flour is made by hulling, heating, and cooling soy beans and then grinding them into a rich flour that can be used in baking. The flour comes in low-fat, defatted, and full-fat form. I don't recommend defatted soy flour because it's often treated with chemical solvents in processing. But low-fat soy flour is a reasonable alternative since the beans are treated with a mechanical press to remove oil, a process that leaves no chemical residue. Full-fat soy flour is also free of chemical residues, and can be used very effectively in many recipes.

Tofu, or soybean curd, is made from strained soy milk coagulated with nigari (a sea water mineral) or various mineral salts like magnesium chloride or calcium chloride. Vinegar or lemon juice is sometimes used, though less frequently. Tofu is rich in protein and can be compared to ground beef in this regard. It's low in saturated fat and mild in flavor. In fact, it absorbs the taste of the foods it's prepared with, which makes it an excellent addition to almost any dish.

Tofu comes in a variety of textures, each of which is great for different purposes. Extra-firm or firm tofu can be grilled, stir-fried, scrambled in place of eggs, or chopped as a meat substitute. Soft or silken-style tofu can be used for its binding properties in place of eggs, or used in place of sour cream and cream cheese for custards, pies, and creamy soups. It can also be pureed for blender shakes, frozen desserts, and dairy-free whipped cream. Baked or pressed dried tofu is appropriate for specialty dishes or appetizers requiring a meat-like texture. A similar consistency can be attained at home by draining, freezing, and then defrosting tofu before using it.

When you shop for tofu, you'll find that it's usually available in one of three ways—in sealed plastic containers filled with water, in aseptically sealed cartons, or in bulk buckets filled with water. I prefer not to use bulk tofu, for sanitary reasons. The water is often not changed regularly and sometimes proper utensils are not used to remove the tofu from the container. Aseptically packaged Japanese-style silken tofu has a delicately smooth consistency and a shelf life of several months. Despite these advantages, I don't recommend this style of tofu either because it is often very highly processed and the packaging can be treated with unlisted chemical preservatives.

The tofu that's most readily available is packaged in plastic containers with purified or spring water; this is my choice for regular use. It's the least processed form, and is free of preservatives (always check the label, though) and is often made from organically grown soybeans. It is sometimes called Chinese-style tofu. Look for the most recent freshness date and store it in a tightly sealed plastic container with fresh pure water. The water should be changed daily until the tofu is used completely. If tofu develops an oily, slimy surface or a foul odor, it should be discarded. However, this will happen only rarely if the tofu is saved properly and used within a week of opening.

HEALTHY COOKING FOR KIDS

Tempeh is another highly nutritious soy product that has been used for generations in the Far East, especially in Indonesia. It is a cake made from pressed, cooked soybeans and a rhizpous or bacterial culture. This added culture causes a white mycelium mold to form, which partially breaks down the beans, increasing digestibility for the consumer. Tempeh normally comes in flat square or rectangular blocks wrapped in tightly sealed plastic. Often, grains, seeds, or seaweeds are added to the mixture to increase nutritional content and subtly enhance the already pleasant flavor.

Tempeh is easily digestible and is a highly absorbable source of protein, iron, calcium, zinc, and B vitamins—most notably vitamin B_{12}, which is usually most abundant in animal-source food. Tempeh can be stir-fried, barbecued, skewered with vegetables like shish kabob, or chopped as a meat substitute for sauces, sandwiches, or pizzas.

When purchasing tempeh, always look for a recent freshness date. It will store well for a few weeks in the refrigerator and for several months in the freezer. You can tell if tempeh is spoiled if it has a fuzzy multicolored surface or spots and an ammonia-like odor. I've tried many varieties of tempeh and my favorite by far has quinoa and sesame seeds added to it. This type is one of the highest in protein and lowest in sodium and fat, and in my opinion it's definitely the very best tasting.

Soy cheese is a popular lactose-free alternative to cow's milk cheeses. Soy cheese usually contains tofu, lecithin, sea salt, soy milk, and casein, which is a milk protein added for coagulation. Various flavors are available, such as Cheddar and Mozzarella. In addition, spices are sometimes added, such as garlic or jalapeño peppers. For those who desire completely dairy-free soy cheese (caseinless), it is available; however, it requires a bit more heat and moisture to melt.

Miso is a centuries-old product from Japan that is used to flavor soups, sauces, main courses, and spreads. It's a protein-rich paste made with cooked soybeans, salt, water, a fermenting culture, and sometimes various grains, such as rice or barley. Traditionally, this mixture is left to ferment from about 6 to 24 months and develops a unique flavor and aroma, just as all fine fermented foods do. Some miso is made using a nontraditional fast method that relies on chemicals and various additives to speed the process. Needless to say, my preference and only choice is traditionally fermented, organically produced miso that is unpasteurized. This is readily available at any natural foods store. Natural foods stores will also sell pasteurized miso that's been traditionally fermented and often organically produced, but the beneficial live cultures and delicate nutrient balance are negatively affected by the pasteurization. So this form of miso should be a second-string choice.

Along with a high protein content, beneficial cultures, and enzymes, miso contains several vitamins and minerals, such as potassium, iron, calcium, phosphorus, and B complex vitamins. Miso is also naturally abundant in sodium, so it should be used judiciously. When choosing miso, purchase containers from the refrigeration section of your natural foods store. Generally, longer-aged, darker-colored misos are heavier in taste and aroma, while the shorter-aged, lighter-colored misos are milder. Lighter miso can be used as the base for spreads, dips, creamy light sauces in main meals, dressings, and even desserts. The darker miso can be used as the base for soups, stews, and meatless entrees that require a rich hearty flavor.

Miso makes a wonderful broth when you mix it with a small amount of water and stir well to form a smooth paste. Add this to a pot of warm water with vegetables such as carrots, scallions, and seaweed. Be sure not to boil your miso, as this will kill the active cultures; just bring it to the simmering state. When storing miso, seal and place it in the refrigerator. Years ago I asked a friend who runs a natural foods market about how long I could keep miso, and he remarked that it will outlive both of us. This may be an exaggeration, but I have yet to see a spoiled container of miso.

Tamari soy sauce is a dark, rich-tasting, salty liquid seasoning originating in Japan. Traditionally it comes either from the liquid runoff from the miso-making process or from brewing soybeans with water, salt, and sometimes wheat. It is then naturally aged in wooden casks for about a year and a half. In a natural foods store, wheat-free soy sauce is generally referred to as tamari, while soy sauce with wheat is called natural shoyu or natural shoyu tamari. When you're shopping, look for a brand that does not contain grain alcohol. In addition to naturally brewed soy sauces, there are commercially made, artificially fermented supermarket soy sauces, with plenty of preservatives, caramel coloring, etc. These should be avoided at all costs; if your grocer doesn't carry a natural brand, request that he or she order some.

Soy sauce is most appropriate when used in small quantities for its saltiness and as a flavor enhancer in stir-fries, salads and dressings, grain and legume dishes, and entrees.

SEA VEGETABLES

Sea vegetables, sometimes called seaweed, are a nutrient-packed group of foods that grow wild in the ocean. In the Far East seaweed has been consumed for generations, with Japan leading the way in the use of this versatile food for over 200 years. Sea vegetables are rich in many nutrients, especially minerals like calcium, phosphorus, potassium, iron, and iodine, which are absorbed from seawater. Many varieties are plentiful in beta carotene, B vitamins, and protein, and throughout history many cultures have credited sea vegetables with the ability to detoxify the body from harmful contaminants. In fact, sea vegetables do have the ability to leach heavy metals from the system due to their alginic acid, a substance that binds metallic ions onto itself and keeps them from being absorbed in the intestine. The bound metals are then passed out of the body via the eliminatory organs.

Sea vegetables can be delicious, nourishing, and versatile additions to any kitchen. They can be cooked into beans and vegetable soups, soaked and chilled as a salad, used as condiments, shredded and sprinkled over grain dishes, and mixed into stir-fries. One type, called agar, can even be used as a healthy substitute for gelatin in puddings and other desserts.

Sea vegetables can be purchased in natural foods stores or in some oriental markets. Be sure that the seaweed products you buy contain no MSG, preservatives, or other additives. They usually come in plastic or cellophane bags and are sometimes carried in bulk. When seaweed is chosen from bulk containers, the leaves should be whole or as large as possible. Seaweed products can be stored in their original bags or in airtight containers. When using sea vegetables, rinse them first to remove sand and debris. Some types should be soaked briefly and sometimes simmered or otherwise cooked before eating; follow the directions on the package.

When cooked into bean dishes, sea vegetables like kombu will help increase nutrient content, flavor, and digestibility. Any cooked sea vegetable leftovers should be refrigerated and used within 5–7 days.

If you and your family have never tried sea vegetables, start off slowly in order to get used to the unique tastes and textures. Following are the most commonly found sea vegetables and their uses.

Agar: used as a natural gelatin for desserts; should be purchased in flake form.

Arame: soaked for salads and main dishes.

Dulse: rinsed and eaten raw or in salads.

Hijiki: sautéed, stewed, or added to main dishes.

Nori: rolled with rice and vegetables, added to soups, or ground and sprinkled into snack foods, salads, or main meals.

Kelp: used in vegetable soups, or ground and sprinkled into salads, main courses, and snack foods.

Kombu: used in soups and to cook beans.

Wakame: used in stir-fries, salads, and soups.

SPROUTS

Sprouts of various sorts, especially when freshly grown at home, are a nutritional gold mine easy to incorporate into the diet. And they're inexpensive, to boot! Sprouts are delicious in salads, on sandwiches, and thrown into cooked soups.

A sprout is simply a previously dormant seed that has had its enzymes awakened by the addition of water and time (usually a few days to become ready for eating). The most interesting and valuable aspect of this process is that a whole array of nutrients are created or dramatically increased as the germinating embryo awakens. Enzymes become active and vitamin content soars—as much as three to twelve times. Proteins are converted to their more usable components—amino acids. Starches also become more digestible. Minerals become more assimilable and if, after a certain point, the young sprout is exposed to light, chlorophyll is produced.

Sunflower sprouts are my own all-time favorite, but alfalfa is probably the most familiar sprout and the easiest to begin with if you're making your own sprouts. It's easy; here's all you do: Get a large-mouth quart-size or larger jar. Soak a heaping teaspoon of alfalfa seeds in a full jar of water overnight (6–8 hours). Then use a fine strainer to rinse the seeds well with fresh water and drain them. Return the seeds to the jar and top it with an air-permeable covering such as nylon net screening, polyethylene window screen, or cheesecloth; fasten the material around the mouth of the jar with a rubber band or rubber jar rim (the kind found on canning jars). Invert the jar and leave it in a dish rack with a small towel draped loosely over it to keep out the light (but not the air). Rinse and drain the seeds 2 or 3 times a day.

In about 5 days, you'll be ready to harvest. Transfer the sprouts into a bowl of water and gently swish them around, by hand or with a fork, to separate the sprouts and remove the husks, which can impede freshness. If you like, at this point you can put them back in the jar for 1 more day (remember to rinse at least twice a day) and expose them to indirect sunlight. And, amazingly, you'll get chlorophyll! If you don't get to your sprouts right away, that's all right; you can refrigerate them. You'll find, however, that when you make fresh sprouts, it's rare that they don't get eaten.

When sprouting, be sure to use organic seeds, beans, and grains that are a bright, uniform color, as well as a uniform texture and size. Damaged seeds can ruin a whole batch of sprouts, so sort through them prior to rinsing. This will also allow you to remove any stones or other debris. Rinse thoroughly to get rid of soot and any other residue.

A word about freshness: There is nothing like it. That's why I recommend sprouting a small amount of seeds every day or so rather than having one huge mega-harvest. With smaller amounts maturing in a series, your sprouts are always fresh, and this method really isn't significantly more work. Sprouting is fun! Experiment! There are several good books available on the subject to help you along.

NUTS AND SEEDS

Nuts and seeds are rich sources of protein, B complex vitamins, minerals, unsaturated fatty acids, and fiber. They can be eaten as snacks, toasted, sprinkled on salads, tossed into stir-fries, or baked into grain or vegetable nuggets. They can be added to desserts and snack foods or ground into nut butter. When combined with beans, nuts and seeds have a near-perfect amino-acid profile (perfect means all 8 essential amino acids are present in the proper proportions), yielding highly absorbable protein. Sprouting nuts or seeds improves the protein and nutrient content and makes this highly concentrated food source easier to digest.

To help ensure freshness, buy nuts and seeds in small quantities. Also, I recommend purchasing them in the least refined state possible. If you choose the preshelled variety, the process should be done by hand or machine, since the chemical shelling procedure introduces chemical-based solvents to "melt away" the shell. For this same reason, blanched nuts should be avoided. The skins can easily be peeled by hand. Seeds and nuts that appear dried, prune-like, or wrinkled and with holes should be avoided. These are signs of age, possible spoilage, and insect damage. Avoid nuts and seeds that are seasoned and spiced, since sugar, MSG, excess salt, and oils are often used in the processing.

It's a good idea to buy nuts in their raw state and oven-roast at home in a baking pan or a heavy skillet. This is not only cost-effective, but it assures you that no unhealthy ingredients are used. Plus there's nothing quite like the rich smell of roasting nuts and seeds floating through your kitchen.

When purchasing nuts or seeds in bulk, check for a rancid odor and look for any signs of dark spotting, webs, or visible infestation by moths or other insects. A white fuzzy appearance is a sign of mold, and this is a clear warning not to consume. There is one mold in particular that is very hazardous, and it's not always easy to detect. This carcinogenic mold is called aflatoxin and often flourishes inside the shells of peanuts. Aflatoxin develops in humid climates, so when choosing peanuts the safest variety is Valencia, which is grown in a dry climate.

At home, nuts that are preshelled should be stored in a dry, airtight container and kept in a cool, dry place. Nuts that are still jacketed in their own protective shell can be stored in a large bowl or in an airtight container for longer periods of time without spoilage.

Since nuts and seeds are such concentrated foods, they should not be eaten in large quantities at any one sitting. Generally, a handful at a time is an appropriate portion. One facet of nuts and seeds that you often hear concern about is the quantity of fat present. While most nuts and seeds are rich in the more desirable unsaturated fats, some have higher levels of saturated fats; these include coconuts, Brazil nuts, pecans, pine nuts, and macadamias.

Better Butters

This section would not be complete without discussing nut and seed butters. These are made by grinding the nut or seed into a paste-like consistency. Choose nut and seed butters with no hydrogenated oils, mono or diglycerides, sugar, salt, or any other additives. The butters should go from the grinder to the jar. You can even make your own with the use of a Champion juicer.

Today, we have so many nut and seed butters to choose from that there's no need to fall into the peanut butter rut. On any visit to your natural foods market, you can discover other butters that your child may take a fancy to, such as those made from almonds, cashews, filberts, pistachios, sunflower seeds, and sesame seeds (this product, tahini, has been used for generations in the Middle East). Of course your store will have natural peanut butter too (do remember to choose only Valencia peanut butter if you're purchasing this; and, by the way, peanuts are really beans, not nuts).

Just as with whole nuts and seeds, the butters made from them should be purchased in small quantities at any one time and should be stored in the refrigerator. Also, remember that it is normal for natural nut and seed butters to separate. Simply stir the oil back in before using to achieve a uniform consistency.

Here are some of the many nuts and seeds that are available:

Nuts

Almonds	Macadamias
Brazil nuts	Peanuts
Cashews	Pecans
Chestnuts	Pignolia (pine)
Coconuts (unsweetened, unsulfured)	Pistachios
Filberts (hazel)	Walnuts

Seeds

Alfalfa	Poppy
Caraway	Pumpkin
Chia	Radish
Clover	Sesame
Cress	Squash
Fenugreek	Sunflower
Flax (linseed)	

Non-dairy Milks

There are many products available to take the place of traditional cow's milk. These non-dairy milks come from such healthy sources as brown rice, soybeans, and nuts.

In natural foods stores, the most common milks found are soy milk and rice milk. Soy milk is generally made from filtered water, soybeans, kombu, vanilla extract, and sometimes a sweetener such as barley malt. It comes in plain and assorted flavors, is rich in protein and calcium, and is now often fortified with vitamins A and D. It also comes in low-fat varieties. Another option is rice milk. This product is not as rich as soy milk and has the consistency of low-fat cow's milk. It's often made from brown rice, water, safflower oil, and a touch of sea salt. Rice milk also comes in assorted natural flavors, and in fortified varieties, but my favorite is the unsweetened original because of the simplicity of its ingredients and its versatility. I include it in many recipes, from pancakes to baked goods. Soy and rice milk come in aseptically sealed cartons and can be stored sealed for 6 months. Once opened, they should be used within 2 weeks.

At home, milks can be made from soy powder and also from nuts and seeds such as almonds, cashews, sesame seeds, sunflower seeds, and coconut. Simply toss any of the above, or a combination, into a powerful blender with some pure water and a bit of honey or fruit juice, and blend on high speed until smooth. These milks should be refrigerated and used within a few days.

For coconut milk, the only varieties that should be used are those that contain no preservatives, stabilizers, sugar, mono and diglycerides, or other additives. Whether homemade or store-bought, coconut milk should be used sparingly, since it contains a considerable amount of saturated fat.

FATS AND OILS

Fats and oils are members of the lipid family and have been used for thousands of years for cooking and skin care. Saturated fats, which are most abundant in animal foods, should be avoided as much as possible. Consumption of excess saturated fat over the long term has been linked with heart disease, cancer, and other degenerative conditions. Unsaturated fats, which are most abundant in plant-based foods, have several beneficial nutrients present in their chemical makeup; these include vitamin E, lecithin, and essential fatty acids.

Beans, grains, nuts, seeds, and vegetables that are rich in unsaturated fats can have their respective oils separated from their kernels, nuts, or leaves for use in food preparation. Vegetable oils are generally pressed in one of two ways—they're either mechanically (or expeller) pressed or they're solvent-extracted. Solvent extraction is done by adding a chemical—usually petroleum based—to the product, thus drawing out the oil. This method is convenient and inexpensive, but it's also unhealthy. The oil produced is often laden with petrochemical residues and has no place in the healthy kitchen. The traditional expeller pressing method is a mechanical process in which the base product is placed in a press and the oil is squeezed out. Sometimes chemicals are added to extract more oil, so look for oils that are 100 percent expeller-pressed.

Sometimes expeller-pressed oils are further filtered, bleached, or deodorized to create a clear, light consistency, and to increase shelf life. These refined oils with their uniform color and long shelf lives are also often treated with preservatives, antifoaming agents, and degumming chemicals. It is far healthier to choose oils that receive no further treatment after the initial pressing. These unrefined oils have no chemical residues, and maintain their natural flavor, aroma, and color. They also have their own natural antioxidant, vitamin E, nature's preservative and an important nutrient for good health.

When purchasing, choose glass bottles to avoid plastic compounds leaching into your oil. Oils should be kept in a dark, cool, dry place and purchased in small quantities, to help ensure freshness when no preservatives are used. Also, beware of hydrogenated oils; these are oils whose carbon molecules are saturated with hydrogen atoms to make the oil more solid at room temperature. The problem is that the hydrogenation process creates trans fatty acids and a highly saturated, unhealthy fat. Hydrogenated oils are often used in the making of desserts, convenience foods, snacks, fast foods, vegetable shortening, and margarines. Even margarines sold in natural foods stores contain hydrogenated or partially hydrogenated oils, along with some liquid safflower or soy oil.

Oils can be used on salads and in baking, and drizzled as a condiment on grain and bean dishes. They can be used for light sautéing, but do remember, when sautéing, to measure by the teaspoon or tablespoon (3 teaspoons equals 1 tablespoon) to prevent overuse. Also, allow the pan to get hot before adding the oil, thus preventing overheating of the oil, which creates saturated fats.

Today, there is a wide variety of natural, unrefined oils, each of which is advantageous for different purposes. There are also naturally produced vegetable oils that are highly saturated and thus poor choices for foods, but fine for body care products. These are palm oil, palm kernel oil, and coconut oil. Oil from the cottonseed, a nonfood crop, should also be avoided, since cotton is treated with pesticides not intended for foods. Cottonseed oil is often used in snack and fast foods.

As much as possible, the unrefined, mechanically pressed oils that you choose should be organically produced, to avoid any pesticide residues lingering in their fatty acid structure. The following is a list of oils that are available organically grown and in their unrefined state, along with appropriate uses.

OILS	USES
Almond oil	Salads
Avocado oil	Salads
Canola oil	All-purpose
Corn oil	Baking, sautéing
Flaxseed oil*	Blender drinks, salads
Hazelnut oil	Salads
Olive oil (extra virgin, first pressing)	Salads, condiments, spreads and dips, entrees
Olive oil (virgin, second pressing)	Sautéing, entrees
Safflower oil	All-purpose
Sesame oil	All-purpose
Sesame oil (toasted)	Condiment for specialty dishes and salads
Soy oil	Baking
Sunflower oil	All-purpose
Peanut oil	Stir-frying, popcorn
Walnut oil	Salads
Wheat germ oil	Salads, blender drinks, breakfast cereals

*Flaxseed oil is very rich in the essential fatty acids linoleic and linolenic acids, and is twice as rich as cod liver oil in omega-3 fatty acids, which appear to have some value in the prevention of cardiovascular disease.

Spectrum Spread

A high-quality product made from expeller-pressed canola oil, Spectrum Spread can be used to replace butter or margarine. It is dairy free, nonhydrogenated, free of tropical oils, and low in saturated fat and sodium.

Lecithin

Lecithin is a phospholipid present in soybeans that comes in granulate and liquid form. Lecithin is also produced by the liver and has several functions in the body, such as improving digestion and metabolism of fats and regulating blood pressure. In liquid form it can be used in sautéing vegetables and as a very effective binder in baking. The granular form can be sprinkled on salads and casseroles, pureed into soups, and blended into fruit shakes. Granular lecithin is also a great binder for baked products.

Lecithin lends a buttery taste to foods and helps prevent fats from oxidizing in the body. Look for pure lecithin from soybeans—not eggs—and store in a cool, dark place.

SWEETENERS

Refined Sugar—The Dangers

From the time children can eat solid food, they are bombarded with refined sugar. They sure like the taste, but unfortunately, along with this sweet white stuff comes a host of side effects. These include weakened immune systems, hyperactivity, dental caries, hyperacidic blood and saliva, and food allergies. In addition, the processing of sugar includes bleaching and filtering with bone ash (anyone concerned with the plight of our animal friends should be aware of this).

Nutritionally, sugar is completely void of anything beneficial, and it is strongly addictive. How many people have you seen who need something sweet after a meal or in the afternoon? How happy are they if their sweet fix is denied them? How much better do they feel when they get something sweet? But how long does this good feeling last? By now we should all be aware of what refined sugar does to our insulin levels and glucose balance as a whole—it creates a seesaw effect. Over time the pancreas can no longer keep tabs on these strong fluctuations. The result: hypoglycemia or perhaps diabetes.

So what do we do? We eliminate refined sweeteners all together, and in their place we use judicious amounts of natural unrefined sweeteners, fresh fruit, and whole foods in general. This will satisfy our natural desire for sweet foods without the harsh effects of sugar, and will make our bodies more resistant to strong cravings. In addition, the reduction of sodium that comes with a whole foods diet will automatically reduce sugar cravings.

Let's look at all the highest-quality natural sweeteners, any of which can be used to replace highly refined commercial sugars.

Fresh Fruit

Fresh fruit, my first choice for a natural sweetener, is actually one of the best in a variety of recipes. Fresh fruit is the least refined of all sweeteners, and it provides the benefits of fiber and other nutrients inherent in the fruit. Also, since a wide variety of fruits can be used, the array of flavors is seemingly endless. Fruits can be used raw in some recipes, either grated or cut into small pieces. They can also be cooked lightly and pureed before being added to a recipe. Applesauce is a prime example. Cooked, blended fruits make an ideal topping for pancakes, waffles, or toasted whole-grain bread.

Another way to use fruits as sweeteners is in the form of juice. Juices, preferably freshly pressed or squeezed, can be added to cooked sauces, or baked products. As a substitute for freshly made juice you can use unfiltered organically produced bottled juice; however, the flavor will not be as lively nor will the nutrient content be as high. Concentrated fruit juices can also be used, but do so sparingly, since they are more intensely sweet and more refined than fresh or bottled juices.

Dried Fruit

Another way to use fruits as sweeteners is in the dried form, which imparts the benefits of fiber and minerals. Always use unsweetened, unsulfured, unpreserved dried fruits, organically grown if possible. Dried fruits can be rinsed and dipped into boiling water for a couple of minutes to kill any bacteria and soften. They can then be chopped, processed, or soaked in fresh water to be reconstituted. The soaking water can also be used to add sweetness to cooked foods. The following dried fruits make good sweeteners:

Apples	Papaya
Apricots	Peaches
Bananas	Pears
Cherries	Pineapple
Currants	Prunes
Dates	Raisins
Mangoes	

Natural Fruit Spreads and Jams

Natural fruit spreads or jams are great for sandwiches, snacks, and dessert recipes. Choose only brands that are sweetened with whole fruit or fruit juice. Stay away from anything with sugar, fructose, or corn syrup, as well as artificial sweeteners, flavors, colors, or preservatives. Whenever possible, purchase organically produced varieties.

Date Sugar

Date sugar is simply ground-up dried dates. It has a rich, delicious taste and is considered a whole food, since no part of the fruit is removed. Date sugar can be used in place of granular sugar—only less is needed since the flavor is strong. This natural sweetener is rich in fiber and minerals.

Honey

Honey has been used as a food, a sweetener, and even a medicinal product for thousands of years. It has natural antibacterial qualities and, when uncooked, it has beneficial living enzymes. It will also provide small amounts of B complex vitamins and minerals. When choosing honey, look for one that is unheated and unfiltered. This will ensure more complex sugars and minimal processing beyond what the bees take care of. Also, when honey is unfiltered, other beneficial elements, such as propolis and pollen, are allowed to remain.

The most common types of honey are clover and wildflower. Orange blossom honey is also available at natural foods stores, as is buckwheat honey, which has a robust flavor and aroma. Honeys with spices and flavorings are available too, but I don't recommend these since the quality of the spice or flavoring is difficult to determine; they also tend to be expensive. Honey can be used in baked goods or as a topping, just as table sugar is used. As a general rule, less is needed.

Honey should be packaged in glass and stored in a cool, dry place. Refrigeration is not necessary. If honey crystallizes or becomes solid, it can be made liquid by placing the jar in a pan or bowl of warm water (boiling isn't necessary).

One important note of caution about honey: Raw honey may contain spores of the clostridium botulinum bacteria, which is harmless to adults and children over 1 year of age, but can cause botulism in infants. This is a severe illness, so it is best not to give honey to a baby under the age of 12 months, even though some physicians will allow it at 6–8 months of age. This is not a cause of panic, just a call for caution and good common sense. Besides, children under 1 should not be inundated with anything sweeter than mother's milk anyway.

Maple Syrup

Maple syrup is a high-quality natural product with a remarkable flavor and aroma. It's the boiled sap of the maple tree, which grows in the Northeast, New England, and Canada. Generally, it takes about 3 trees or 50 gallons of maple sap to make a gallon of syrup. Maple syrup is not a nutritional powerhouse, but it does supply small amounts of minerals such as calcium, phosphorus, and iron.

When choosing maple syrup, be sure to look for a product that's 100 percent pure maple syrup. Beware of pancake syrups, maple-flavor toppings, or other such artificially produced, chemical-laden substances. It's best to buy the organically produced variety, since commercial maple growers often use formaldehyde pellets in processing to keep the taps flowing freely. Also, ask your store manager to find out if all-stainless-steel buckets are used to gather the sap, since some buckets have lead in their seams. Or better yet, inquire with the maple farm that supplies your store. Just get the name from the back of the bottle.

When using maple syrup, remember that even though it is not highly refined, it does have a concentrated sweetness. The strong taste and aroma go a long way in flavoring food, so don't use too much. For example, when you're topping pancakes, don't drench them; 2–3 tablespoonfuls are plenty. Getting into the syrup-sparing habit is economical, and a good way to teach children not to become dependent on heavy sweetness in foods, but rather to appreciate the subtleties of a delicious, wholesome food product.

When storing maple syrup, choose a cool, dark place without excess moisture. To decrease the chances of mold, store only enough to last for a couple of months, or a season at most. Keep the container snugly sealed, and remember to wipe the top to keep it from sticking and attracting insects.

Malted Grain Syrups

Malted grain syrups such as barley malt and brown rice syrup are high-quality, mildly sweet products that can be used when a less intense sweetening is required. They have a greater amount of complex carbohydrates and are more appropriate for those with problematic fluctuations in blood sugar. These grain syrups are made from grains that are sprouted, and then cooked down to a thick syrup.

Barley Malt and Brown Rice Syrups

Barley malt is a dark, rich liquid with a distinct taste and characteristic aroma. Since this product has a powerful flavor, it's an acquired taste for some children, and it may be too powerful for delicately flavored recipes. However, barley malt is fine for gingerbread, nut cookies, and other hearty-tasting recipes.

Brown rice syrup is a liquid sweetener that's lighter than barley malt and has a more delicate quality. Both products are composed mostly of maltose, a complex sugar created by the breaking down of the starch molecule in the cooking process. Both are excellent for baking and can be found in all natural foods stores. When purchasing, look for organic varieties of barley malt and brown rice syrup. Do not pick anything with preservatives, sugar, or malt flavorings. Store in a cool, dry place.

Powdered Barley Malt and Rice Syrups

These powdered high-quality sweeteners have the consistency of confectioners' sugar. They're made by drying their respective liquids to a smooth powder form. They can be used as sprinkled toppings for baked goods or in frostings and glazes.

Molasses

Blackstrap molasses is the dark, heavy, full-bodied syrup that remains after sucrose is removed from sugarcane. Blackstrap has significant levels of calcium, iron, magnesium, and potassium. It is best used in multigrain breads, ginger-flavored baked goods, baked beans, and certain other hearty recipes. When shopping be sure to pick the unsulfured variety.

Barbados molasses is lighter and sweeter than blackstrap and is slightly more versatile. By nature it is unsulfured; however, it has considerably less nutrient content than blackstrap molasses.

When storing any type of molasses, keep it in a dry place, since dampness will cause mold to grow on it. Also, be sure to wipe the bottle opening and lid to facilitate use.

Amasake

Amasake is a delicious, rich, exotic beverage made from brown rice and a natural fermenting culture called koji. Long popular in Japan, this thick, sweet liquid can be used as a sweetener for puddings, confections, baked items, hot cereals, or pancakes and waffles. Amasake can also be diluted and added to fruit shakes and served warm with nutmeg as a healthy replacement for eggnog. When purchasing amasake, be sure to check the expiration date, since it is perishable. Also, you can buy it frozen. Store amasake in the refrigerator and use within 1 week, or, if it's frozen, within 1 month.

Fruit Source

Fruit source is an excellent, high-quality sweetener that comes in both granular and liquid form. It is made from granulated natural brown rice syrup and granulated grape juice. When you measure it, it works much the same way as commercial sugar does, and it can be used in any recipe calling for sugar.

Maple Sugar

Maple sugar in its pure form is simply maple syrup dried to granules. Since it is expensive, it's best used as a topping for cookies and other baked goods. Be sure that what you have is made from 100 percent pure maple syrup, with no additives or other sweeteners.

Commercial white sugarcane sugar:	stripped, denatured, bleached
Brown sugar:	white sugar with added molasses
Turbinado/raw sugar:	only slightly less processed than white sugar
Sucanat:	dried unrefined sugarcane juice, somewhat processed
Corn syrup:	highly processed and refined
Fructose:	highly processed; derived from corn syrup, not fruit
Aspartame:	chemical-based artificial sweetener with possible health-threatening side effects
Saccharin:	chemical-based artificial sweetener with possible health-threatening side effects

EXTRAS

Green Products

Green foods, such as the juice from wheat, barley, alfalfa, or kamut grass, and micro-algaes such as spirulina, chlorella, and blue-green algae can be a valuable addition to the health-supporting lifestyle. Green products are a rich source of chlorophyll, a powerful detoxifier; beta-carotene and other carotenoids; enzymes; and many vitamins, minerals, and phytonutrients. The micro-algaes are also, ounce for ounce, rich in protein, with an amino acid profile virtually identical to that of human tissue; they're rich, as well, in vitamin B_{12}, a critical nutrient lacking in many of today's foods. By virtue of their low position on the food chain, green foods are lower in environmental toxins and richer in life energy from the sun than other foods.

When shopping for the cereal grass juices be sure you are getting the juice, not powdered grass. (Heat drying destroys the vital nutrients, so look for freeze-dried.) Make sure that whatever you purchase is organically grown and certified as such. Wheat grass juice is often available freshly pressed at juice bars; just double-check the quality.

When shopping for micro-algae be sure the brand is certified organic and freeze-dried. Chlorella should have a cracked cell wall. When buying both micro-algae and cereal grass juices, check the production and expiration dates for freshness.

Why Carob and Not Cocoa?

Cocoa is made from the beans of the cocoa tree. These beans are roasted, cracked, and ground into chocolate liqueur, which is then separated by a hydraulic press into cocoa powder and cocoa butter. Chocolate and cocoa contain the stimulants caffeine and theobromine. Caffeine can cause hyperactivity and irritability in children. Other unhealthy aspects of chocolate are tannic acid, which has been shown to retard growth in laboratory animals, and oxalic acid, which can block calcium absorption.

Luckily, there is an alternative to chocolate—carob. This is a wonderful product filled with beneficial nutrients, including calcium and magnesium. The carob pod, which comes from a Mediterranean evergreen tree, contains pulp and seeds. The pulp is ground into carob powder, and its rich sweet taste and aroma are great for recipes that call for a chocolate-like flavor and color. Wholesome carob bars and chips may take a bit of patience to find, but they are available. When purchasing, look for bars or chips that have no dairy solids, hydrogenated oils, sugar, or palm kernel oil. If you cannot locate carob chips without these unhealthy ingredients, carob bars—which are easier to find—can be chopped into pieces.

If using chocolate is an absolute necessity (even though it usually isn't), choose cocoa powder that is unsweetened and free of additives such as alkali and mono and diglyceries. Steer clear of those ready-to-mix chocolate drinks. Chocolate chips are available in natural foods stores sweetened with barley malt and without dairy products or preservatives. Remember to read those labels.

Sea Salt

Salt and seasoned salt can be useful if purchased carefully and used judiciously. When buying salt, choose only unrefined sea salt with no additives, such as dextrose and sodium aluminosilicate, which are present in regular table salt. These ingredients prevent caking and keep salt flowing freely. They are also very unhealthy. Caking is a minor issue, especially if you use only a small amount of salt, which should be the case anyway. Sea salt contains more trace minerals from the ocean.

When purchasing seasoned salts, choose those with no sugar, chemicals, or other additives, such as MSG or HVP (hydrolized vegetable protein), both of which can cause allergic reactions in many individuals. The best products consist of unrefined sea salt mixed with natural herbs and spices, or with ground seeds.

Vinegars

Vinegars, which have been used for preserving and as condiments for over a thousand years, are made from the diluted acid of fermented grains or fruits. Apple cider vinegar is generally recognized as the healthiest type to use. It has mostly malic acid, which is cleansing and detoxifying, as opposed to acetic acid, which in excess can cause digestive irritation. Apple cider vinegar is great on salads. When purchasing, look for a vinegar that is unfiltered and organically produced.

Brown rice vinegar is a milder product often used in specialty recipes and salad dressings. It has a low acid content and a delicate flavor. It is expensive, so you may want to use it sparingly. Choose a brand from a natural foods store made solely from brown rice, organically grown if possible.

Balsamic vinegar is a mild wine vinegar from the Modena region of Italy. Its sweet exotic flavor makes it a popular ingredient in salad dressings, but since it's expensive and has naturally occurring sulfites, it should be used moderately. Fortunately, its full-bodied quality makes this possible; a little goes a long way. Choose a brand from organically grown grapes with no added sulfur compounds.

White distilled vinegar should not be used as a food product, ever. It is usually made from chemically treated grains and is highly acidic. However, it's an excellent ingredient for nontoxic homemade cleaning fluids for windows, floors, and countertops.

Natural Flavorings

Natural flavorings can be used in a variety of recipes, especially those for baked goods and desserts. While extracts contain alcohol, flavorings are alcohol free, using pure vegetable glycerin, or soybean or canola oil as the extracting medium. They may also contain alpha tocopherol (vitamin E). The benefits of using alcohol-free extracts are, first, that there is no bitterness, and, second, that even if they're left uncooked you don't have to worry about your children consuming alcohol.

Alcohol-free extracts or flavors are available in natural foods stores; look for those that have no corn syrup, sugar, preservatives, or artificial flavoring or colors. Pure alcohol-free extracts may cost a little more, but the advantages make the few extra pennies a worthwhile investment. I always have almond, lemon, orange, vanilla, and maple on hand.

Herbs and Spices

Used properly, herbs and spices can make low-sodium, low-fat whole foods flavorful, aromatic, and appealing to the eye. Do remember that when you use dried herbs and spices rather than fresh, you should use less, since the dried form is stronger.

Herbs, which are the leaves, flowers, and stems of aromatic plants, should be fresh when possible. They should be organically grown and never irradiated or treated with fumigants. These rules apply to dried herbs too, which should also be free of salt, MSG, and any other additives. Choose dried herbs that are as close to whole as possible, instead of finely ground powders. Crushing by hand before using will allow the aromatic oils to be released from the leaf.

Spices come generally from the buds, root, and bark of plants. When choosing spices, try to get the whole bud or root and grind it yourself for a stronger, fresher flavor and livelier aroma. Spices should also be organically grown if possible, with no fumigants, additives, irradiation, or MSG. As with herbs, it pays to read the fine print on the label.

Both herbs and spices should be purchased in small quantities and stored in dry, airtight, well-sealed jars or plastic containers, to help safeguard them from insect damage.

Herbs

Basil	Oregano
Bay leaf	Parsley
Celery salt	Peppermint
Chervil	Rosemary
Cilantro	Sage
Dill weed	Savory
Fennel leaf	Tarragon
Marjoram	Thyme

Spices

Allspice	Cumin (ground or seeds)
Anise seeds	Curry
Caraway seeds	Dulse flakes
Cardamon	Fennel seeds
Cayenne	Five-spice powder
Chili powder	Garlic powder
Cinnamon	Ginger
Cloves	Kelp flakes
Coriander	Mace

Mustard (dry)	Peppercorns (white, pink, black)
Nutmeg (whole and ground)	Red pepper flakes
Onion powder	Saffron
Paprika (sweet Hungarian)	Turmeric

Vegetable Bouillon

Vegetable bouillon cubes and broth powders should be chosen with great care because they often contain high levels of sodium, as well as MSG, HVP, preservatives, sugar, and artificial flavors. Look for a brand that has natural herbs and spices, soy powder, dried vegetable powders, and some sea salt. Broth powders come in a variety of flavors and can be added to stocks, soups, stews, and sauces. Use them carefully, though, since even the wholesome brands are moderately rich in sodium.

Baking Powder

Baking powder is a valuable leavening ingredient in muffin-making and for other baked goods. Baking powders are mixtures of dry acid or acid salts and baking soda, with starch or flour added to standardize and stabilize the mixtures. "Double-acting" with respect to baking powder means that the product will liberate carbon dioxide twice—first during the mixing stage, when it reacts with moisture, and then again when it's heated during the baking stage. Your baking powder should always be aluminum free and low sodium, if possible. Choose a brand in a glass jar instead of an aluminum can, and store it in a cool, dry place.

Pure Starch Thickeners

Natural starch thickeners such as cornstarch, arrowroot, and kuzu can be used to add viscosity to sauces, puddings, stews, and other foods.

Cornstarch, extracted from the inner portion of the corn kernel, is the most readily available and inexpensive of these products. Look for pure cornstarch with no additives. Arrowroot powder is derived from the tropical starchy root of the same name. It is my favorite starch thickener since it is convenient to use and not allergenic, as cornstarch can be. Like cornstarch, it must first be dissolved in cold water or another clear liquid to work properly. As with other thickeners, choose pure arrowroot with no chemical additives, sugar, or preservatives. Kuzu powder, the starchy portion of the kuzu plant root (the plant is called kudzu in North America), is imported from Japan. It's an effective thickener that is claimed to have alkalizing and other therapeutic effects on digestion. Kuzu also contains calcium, phosphorus, and other nutrients. It is the most expensive and the favorite of many natural foods chefs. When purchasing kuzu, choose a brand from a natural foods store and be sure to look for a rock-like texture, a sign of pure kuzu. Powdery textured kuzu, by contrast, is probably not really kuzu but cornstarch or potato starch with a more expensive price tag.

Condiments

When picking out condiments like mustard, ketchup, barbecue sauce, and relish, be sure they contain no sugar, artificial flavors, colors, preservatives, MSG, or other chemical additives. Look for organic, natural varieties with natural herbs, spices, sea salt, and apple cider vinegar. Unsalted varieties of almost every condiment are available.

COOKWARE AND BAKEWARE

Just as important as the foods we feed our children are what we prepare and serve them in. For pots and pans, it's best to use stainless-steel, cast-iron coated with enamel, and glass ceramic cookware.

Why Not Stainless Steel for Everything?

Stainless steel, which usually comes with a copper- or aluminum-clad bottom to help disperse heat and eliminate scorching, is fine for steaming; boiling grains, beans, and pasta; and cooking nonacidic foods. However, it's best not to cook acidic fruits, vegetables, and sauces in stainless steel, since some studies have shown that nickel can leach into the food during the cooking process. If acidic foods must be cooked in stainless steel, it's best to transfer them to another container for refrigerator storage.

Cast iron has been used for generations and is almost indestructible. It's an excellent conductor and retainer of heat that allows food to cook evenly without burning. Also, cast iron tends to increase iron levels in foods prepared in it, especially acidic foods. This iron is readily usable in the body and does not present a problem except for those with a disease called hemochromatosis, in which excess iron accumulates in the body. (In this case iron lined with enamel can be used.) Cast-iron cookware should be cleaned with a mild soap and sponge and dried thoroughly. Be sure not to soak, and remember to wipe a bit of oil on the inside to prevent rust. With enamel-lined iron, do not use metal utensils or scrubbing pads, since this will damage the inner cooking surface, and enamel ingestion is not desirable.

Using glass ceramic cookware is an excellent way to avoid the leaching of metal into your food. This kind of cookware is the most noncorrosive available, and it can go from the refrigerator to the stove to the sink without shattering. Glass ceramic cookware will withstand very high temperatures, so it can be used for oven baking or roasting as well. With glass ceramic pieces, avoid metal utensils or steel scrubbers, since they can scratch the surface.

Why Not Copper or Aluminum?

Copper is an excellent heat-conducting metal that often clads the bottom of stainless-steel pots and pans. This is the best place for copper, since when it contacts food it gets absorbed, and in excess it can cause diarrhea and vomiting. Keep copper-bottom pots clean, since stains are hard to remove once they're "heated on."

Aluminum is an effective heat conductor that is also best when it clads the bottom of stainless-steel cookware. If aluminum pots and pans must be used, do not cook acidic foods in them or use them for refrigerator storage. This will prevent the leaching of this toxic heavy metal into your family's foods. Another caveat: Scraping aluminum pots with metal utensils will release minute aluminum shavings into foods. Use wooden spoons instead.

Bakeware Basics

When choosing bakeware such as cookie sheets or muffin pans, the best choices are tinned steel (tin) or stainless steel, rather than aluminum. If aluminum is all that's available, it can be lined with parchment paper or paper muffin cups to keep batters and dough from contacting the surface.

KITCHEN EQUIPMENT

The following is a list of equipment useful for the avid cook. It's not a bad idea to consult with a consumer magazine before equipping your kitchen, in order to compare brands and familiarize yourself with various options.

Practical Investments

Pressure cooker
Juice extractor
Food processor
Citrus juicer—for fresh lemon, orange, and grapefruit juice
Blender—for fruit shakes
Mini coffee grinder or mini food processor—for spices, herbs, and garlic

Helpful Luxuries

Flour mill—for grinding flour
KitchenAid mixer—for kneading dough
Champion juicer—for nut butters, fruit ice creams, fresh juices
Waffle iron
Wok—for stir-fries—use carbon steel

CHAPTER 5

ALLERGIES

Allergies are abnormal reactions to substances tolerated by most people. Some allergists have estimated that from 20–30 million Americans are allergic to some element in their environment, and that about 15 percent of the population has reactions severe enough to warrant medical attention. Many people, roughly 50 million Americans, have food sensitivities, although often these are very mild.

Classically, food allergy has been defined as a lifelong reactivity to a particular food, usually beginning in childhood. An allergic reaction occurs when the immune system incorrectly perceives a substance as harmful and produces excessive antibodies to fight that substance. When one thinks of food allergies, a picture comes to mind of a child breaking out in a rash after eating strawberries or having an asthma attack after eating peanut butter. Blood and skin tests performed by allergists are designed to detect and measure these antibody responses. Traditionally, if no IgE antibody response is present, allergy to food as a possible cause of symptoms is dismissed.

However, the type of food allergy just described is known as a type I or fixed food allergy, and this type constitutes only about 5–10 percent of all food allergies. Most allergic individuals exhibit what are known as cyclic food allergies or food intolerances, in which IgE antibodies are *not* produced. These, known as type II, represent the other 90–95 percent of food allergies, and yet very few allergists are adequately trained to detect and treat them. One reason is that it can take several hours for symptoms to appear in cyclic allergy, whereas in fixed allergy, symptoms appear almost immediately, making diagnosis easier.

Type II reactions may be quite mild, or they may aggravate such conditions as arthritis, asthma, or colitis. In fact, a vast array of symptoms may arise from these food intolerances. Unfortunately, food intolerance is often overlooked as the cause while symptoms are treated superficially. Years, or a lifetime, may go by without relief.

I often see children with dark eye circles and allergic eczema. Their mothers speak of having consulted numerous allergy specialists, of having implemented the prescribed treatments, and of still finding their children suffering. A surprisingly high number of babies and children are coping with symptoms such as colic, allergic eczema, fluid in the ear, asthma, hyperactivity, and behavioral problems stemming from recurrent food allergies.

Complicating matters, in cyclic food allergy one can become "addicted to" the food or foods to which one is allergic. Food "addiction" occurs in many food-intolerant or cyclic allergic patients. As part of the cycle, one craves the offending food or foods, and some type of withdrawal symptom such as sleepiness or depression occurs if the food is not ingested. After eating the offending food, a person may experience an initial "high," yet the reactivity is actually contributing gradually to chronic disease. Addictive food allergies are the most difficult to diagnose and treat. As with fixed food allergies and cyclic food allergies, parents can help alleviate addictive food allergies by eliminating the allergenic food or reducing the frequency of its consumption. For more information about eliminating allergenic foods, see the section on rotational diets, page 60.

ENVIRONMENTAL MEDICINE

The bright side of the allergy picture is that an updated scientific understanding of the problem is emerging through the work of doctors of environmental medicine. Their approach offers new and vital information on the diagnosis and treatment of allergies, and the testing procedures and treatments employed are relatively uninvasive and inexpensive.

When investigating the possibility of food allergies in their patients, environmental physicians also consider the additives, preservatives, and pesticides often found on and in today's foods. Even foods that are considered low allergy, such as rice and apples, can cause reactions in some. When this occurs the doctor must discover whether the allergy is to the food or to a man-made chemical that's been sprayed on the food.

I recently spoke with a woman whose 3-month-old baby was suffering from eczema and colic. The third allergist she consulted advised her to remove milk-based formula from the baby's diet, recommending a soy-based one instead. After 3 weeks, the baby was still symptomatic. The traditional allergist had not addressed the fact that the baby was sensitive to the additives and preservatives both formulas contained. Unfortunately, this picture is a common one.

Doctors of environmental medicine have shown that there is a direct link between allergies and the severity of many disease states. Chemicals used in and on foods or in one's environment can aggravate the debilitating symptoms of these diseases. When many symptomatic children are placed on allergen-free diets, symptoms are alleviated, overall health improves, and the need for medication diminishes. When allergens are reintroduced, the symptoms can be reactivated or exacerbated.

Recent findings in environmental medicine strongly indicate that many postindustrial diseases can be traced to the foods we eat most frequently. Cyclic food allergies seem to develop with habitual eating patterns, that is, with the daily consumption of the same foods, especially in those people genetically predisposed to allergy. For instance, when a person consumes orange juice every day for a number of months, she may develop an allergy to orange juice. Such allergies may take weeks, months, or years to develop. Other factors such as psychophysical stress, environmental stresses, and the condition of one's immune system, can influence the frequency and severity of the reactions.

The development of food allergies can begin in utero. A pregnant woman consuming the same foods on a daily basis throughout a 9-month pregnancy can cause her unborn baby to be predisposed to allergies to those foods. Babies can develop the same allergies as their mothers, either through the placenta while still in the womb or sometimes through breast milk as nursing infants.

Also, children inherit a predisposition to food allergies. Dr. Jonathan Brostoff, director of the allergy clinic at Middlesex Hospital in London, reports that if one parent has allergies, the child will have a 20 to 35 percent chance of developing them; if both parents do, the risk increases to 40 to 60 percent.

Much research is still needed on the field of infant allergy. Because babies cannot communicate verbally, diagnosis and assessment are complicated. Colic, an inflammation of the intestine and one of the most prevalent symptoms of food allergy in babies, has been linked to food allergy in a high proportion of those studied. Most babies suffering from this condition are bottle-fed. Although allergies can be passed to babies through breast milk, recent studies have shown that babies born into families prone to food allergy are less likely to develop such allergies themselves if they are breast-fed for at least 6 months.

A common problem seen in children today is hyperactivity. This condition has been linked to many foods, including sugar, chicken, dairy products, and corn and corn derivatives, and especially those foods containing antibiotics, preservatives, and other additives. Recent studies have indicated that food additives used in a plethora of products are an important factor in a great many cases of hyperactivity, and it's not unusual to find a child for whom additives are the sole problem. In fact, the widespread use of additives may explain why the incidence of hyperkinetic syndrome seems to have increased dramatically in the past 20 years. Mass production of "junk foods," the prevalence of chemicals used in growing, packaging, processing, and preserving foods, and the abundance of convenience foods rife with colorings, flavorings, preservatives, and other additives are wreaking havoc on the immune systems of American children. And rather than addressing the environmental causes of this problem, orthodox medicine often attacks the symptoms using drugs. The sad reality is that, today, the overmedication of American children has reached epidemic proportions.

In the case of hyperactivity, in one survey of 750,000 children seen for this condition, almost 30 percent were put on medication. A majority of these were given methylphenidate hydrochloride, better known as Ritalin. This is an antidepressant drug belonging to the amphetamine family.

The incidence of hyperactive behavior and learning disabilities has risen in the past decade from 2 to 25 percent of children, and is now as high as 40 percent in localized areas. Consider that a typical school cafeteria meal will usually include white bread, meat, soft drinks, and sugary desserts; these are among the foods that can often trigger hyperactivity as an allergic reaction.

The hyperactive child tends to exhibit distractibility, inappropriate responses, and irritability, often accompanied by aggression, tantrums, poor schoolwork, insomnia, wiggly legs, inappropriate behavior, depression, fatigue, tension, or a combination of these symptoms. Dr. Brostoff reports that 1.6 million American children have been labeled hyperkinetic or hyperactive. Seventy-five percent of them are boys between the ages of 5 and 13. Girls, although similarly sensitive to factors causing hyperactivity, may exhibit more passive behaviors such as inattention, poor speech, and mood fluctuations.

Food additives need to be detoxified by the body's enzymes and by the liver. But the very enzymes needed to break down the additives may be inhibited in their action by the additives, in a sort of Catch-22 situation that can contribute to hyperactivity in sensitive children.

How can you head off such problems? Variety and purity in the diet are the keys to preventing cyclic allergy. But if allergies are suspected, an environmental physician might be the best person to contact. A list of these physicians is found in the Appendix.

FOOD ROTATION

Something that environmental physicians tell us is that patients can play a role in diagnosing their own allergies, and in treating them. A person doesn't have to wait for the skin tests of an allergist to tell him if he's allergic to a particular substance. What those in environmental medicine are now saying is that through elimination testing, or through a rotational diet, we can find out for ourselves what foods to stay away from. Of course in the case of children, parents are the ones to take the active role in dietary manipulation.

Elimination Testing

The concept of elimination testing is quite simple, although when you're dealing with children—and babies—you should discuss any major dietary changes with your pediatrician, environmental physician, or other health practitioner. That said, here's how you conduct an elimination test to see if your child is in fact allergic to something you suspect she's allergic to: You eliminate that food completely from her diet. Then, see if her symptoms clear up. The disappearance of symptoms can take up to 12 days or so, after which you can have her eat the food once again on an empty stomach to see if the symptoms return. This will give a clear picture of her condition.

The Rotary Diversified Diet

Another approach to testing is to use what's called a rotary diversified diet. Plan a diet in which no single food is eaten more than once every 4 days. Keep a record of what is eaten and when, and after the first 5 days, start recording any symptoms that appear. If you suspect a particular food is an allergen, the next time it rotates into your 4-day plan, serve it alone as a complete meal. Then see if the symptoms recur.

The Test as Treatment

A plus to this rotational regimen is that you can use it not just as a test, but as treatment for an allergy-prone family member. While an individual with a fixed allergy may have to give up a food entirely, one with a cyclic allergy can often continue to eat the offending food or foods if they're not presented more often than once every several days. Four days is the usually suggested number, although every 5, 7, or 12 days may be appropriate for a more sensitive child. The idea is that the more often a food is eaten, the more likely you are to develop an allergic reaction to it at some point, or even an addictive allergic reaction. Conversely, if you rotate foods into and out of the diet, there will be a lessened chance of sensitivity. Food rotation is a way of keeping sensitivities at bay without banishing foods completely.

The bottom line is that if your child is allergic, you'll want to cut down on his or her consumption of the problematic food or foods—if not entirely, at least for 3 days out of 4. And this is where the art of cooking without allergenic foods comes in.

ALLERGEN-FREE COOKING

Allergen-free cooking is not something to be afraid of. It can actually be an exciting and rewarding challenge. Some people gasp, "You take away wheat, you take away dairy, eggs, sugar, and fish, and there's nothing left to eat anymore except vegetables!" This is a very limited way of looking at things, and, what's more, it's absolutely not true. If your child, you, or another family member has an allergy problem, you can view it as an opportunity to discover a whole new range of foods that you never even knew existed. You'll be embarking on the adventure of a more varied diet full of new and interesting things.

As you read this section, keep in mind that the chapter on stocking your kitchen (see page 33) will give you more ideas for creative ingredient substitutions. If you remember that patience, experimentation, and openness to the new are all parts of successful allergen-free cooking, you'll be coming up with some great dishes in no time.

Dairy Free

Dairy, one of the most common food allergens in the American diet, is probably one of the easiest to eliminate from recipes. There are plenty of substitutions you can make. First, plain soy or rice milk can be used—part for part—to replace cow's milk. Other substitutes are fruit juices and pureed fruits, which can be used in place of milk in some of the sweeter recipes, or as cereal toppings. Pureed vegetables can replace milk in creamed soup recipes, such as cream of mushroom or potato soup. Nut or seed milks, made in the blender, provide yet another dairy-free replacement.

Cheese can be replaced by many types of soy cheese, and by nut cheese. These are ideal for those allergic to lactose, i.e., milk sugar. For those completely allergic to all dairy products, remember that most soy or nut cheeses contain casein, a milk protein used for coagulation. Casein-free cheeses are available in various flavors, but they usually require higher temperatures for melting.

Butter can be replaced in recipes with pure vegetable oil; canola or safflower oils are good since they are mild in flavor. Olive oil can be used on bread or when a distinctive flavor is desired.

Egg Free

Eggs can be mucus- and gas-forming, and if you are having a problem with these you may want to cut down on their use. If you banish eggs from your kitchen altogether, their holding-together and rising qualities in recipes—such as those for cakes—can be compensated for by using ¼ cup drained tofu (I use the softest texture available) for each egg. Generally, batters made with tofu are thicker, rise less, and have a smaller yield.

Almond butter and other nut butters are great for holding cookie dough together.

Custards, puddings, and pie fillings can be held together with tofu, arrowroot, kuzu, and vegetable-based gelatins such as agar, or a combination of any of these. Mashed banana or cooked and drained starchy vegetables, such as sweet potatoes, pumpkins, and squash, will also hold some foods together effectively.

Wheat Free

Wheat-free cooking is something I've had to master due to my sensitivity to wheat products. Once you get the hang of it, you're open to having fun with all sorts of new grains. If you are one of the many who is sensitive to wheat, you may also be sensitive to barley, spelt, oats, rye, kamut, and triticale, because these are all related to wheat. While sensitivity to these may be less than sensitivity to wheat, I would recommend eating these grains no more than once a week.

If you're not using wheat flour, alternative flours include buckwheat, quinoa, barley, millet, amaranth, corn, soy, and brown rice. Since some of these and other whole-grain flours tend to become rancid, purchase small quantities, keep them refrigerated, or grind your own. Also, it is generally a good idea to use a small surface area when working with these flours since there is very little gluten in them to hold them together.

If you are a pasta fan and allergic to wheat, don't despair. Experiment with rice, corn, buckwheat, and quinoa pastas. Be sure to read the ingredients on any pasta box, because some labeled corn, artichoke, or buckwheat pasta will often contain some wheat, which is listed on the box as durum or semolina.

I've found that many brown rice pastas are excellent. There are also bean pastas, such as mung bean threads, which are similar to rice noodles. They're a little bit thinner than other noodles and sometimes you may need to soak them for 10 minutes in cold water before sautéing.

Here's a little trick I learned in cooking with wheat-free pastas: Bring the water to a boil, add a little oil, add the pasta, and continue to stir. *Do not let the water boil again.* If it starts, add cold water and stir again. Repeat this cold water and stirring procedure as often as necessary to prevent the water from boiling again. If you're vigilant about this, and cook below boiling level for about 10 minutes, you'll prevent mushiness in your pasta.

Corn Free

Corn-free cooking is not much of a problem because most people really don't use a lot of corn in their recipes. To replace cornmeal or corn flour, flours such as quinoa, millet, or amaranth can be used. Arrowroot can replace cornstarch. Rumford and Featherweight baking powder are the two corn-free brands I use. In place of corn syrup, there are many different types of sweeteners available, such as maple syrup, rice syrup, or honey. Corn oil can easily be replaced by safflower, canola, or sunflower oils. Most of the regular salt brands use dextrose, which can be a corn derivative, to stabilize the iodine. Unrefined sea salt or kosher salt are good substitutes, since they do not contain these or other additives.

PART TWO

RECIPES

CHAPTER 6

JUICES, SHAKES, AND OTHER DRINKS

Carrot Apple Classic

Preparation time: 5 minutes to prepare, 5 minutes to juice
Yield: 3–4 servings

Here's a live food classic whose vitamins, minerals, and phytonutrients provide your children with the energy they need to grow. It also makes a great introductory juice for anyone trying to embrace a healthier lifestyle. Its cool, mildly sweet, refreshing taste is the good life in a tall glass. By the time you finish slurping through your straw, you won't even remember the name of your favorite soda pop.

1 medium head romaine lettuce, washed well and with leaves separated
1 pound carrots, tops removed and cut into halves lengthwise
2 large apples, cored and quartered

1. Place a 4-cup-capacity liquid measuring cup under the juicer spout. Bunch up the lettuce and push it through the juicer feed tube, alternating it with the carrots and apples.

2. Pour into glasses and serve.

NOTE
■ **The lettuce will need to be pulsed through a juicer, alternating it with the remaining fruits and vegetables, or it will become stuck in the juicer.**

Chocolaty-Rich Carob Milk Shakes

Preparation time: 5 minutes
Yield: 3–4 servings

Chocolate milk shakes are an old-time classic. So here's a way to enjoy a classic and be healthy. Bananas provide wholesome sweetness, fiber, and potassium. Carob packs a wallop of color, flavor, and richness, as well as calcium and magnesium for strong muscles and bones. For variety, try freezing these to make frozen fudge sticks. And as difficult as it may be, don't forget that this is good for you!

2½ cups soy milk or rice milk

3 medium frozen bananas

2 tablespoons carob powder

2 tablespoons flaxseeds, soaked overnight and drained (optional)

½ teaspoon pure vanilla flavor

Combine the milk, bananas, carob powder, flaxseeds, and vanilla in a blender. Blend on high speed for 1–2 minutes or until smooth and creamy. Pour into glasses and serve with straws.

NOTE

■ **This recipe should provide you with 12 frozen pops: Pour the shake liquid into twelve ½-cup ice cream pop molds and place the molds in the freezer to set for about 2 hours. Remove the pop molds from the freezer and insert wooden sticks three quarters of the way into the molds, then place them back into the freezer until the entire pop is fully set (at least 2–3 hours).**

Georgia Peach Wake-Up Shakes

Preparation time: 5 minutes
Yield: 3–4 servings

Down in rural Georgia, in just the right season, you can find roadside farm stands with the most luscious peaches on earth. One time we cut some up and popped them in the blender to make a shake. Having won immediate approval from the family, this smooth nutritious drink is now a breakfast mainstay in our home during the summertime.

2 cups almond milk, soy milk, or rice milk

5 large peaches, peeled, pitted, and sliced (about 4 cups)

1 tablespoon honey

1½ cups ice cubes

Combine the milk, peaches, honey, and ice in a blender. Blend on high speed until smooth and frothy, 1–2 minutes. Pour into glasses and serve with straws.

NOTES

■ **For variety, try an equal measure of prepared (peeled and/or pitted) mangoes, papayas, fresh figs, or bananas in place of the peaches.**

- **For Georgia Peach "Ice Cream" Pops: Pour the shake liquid into twelve ½-cup ice cream pop molds and place the molds in the freezer to set for about 2 hours. Remove the pop molds from the freezer and insert wooden sticks three quarters of the way into the molds, then place them back into the freezer until the entire pop is fully set (at least 2–3 hours).**

Green Goddess Smoothies

Preparation time: 5 minutes
Yield: 3–4 servings

Here's a delicious nutritional gold mine for all vegetarians. People often wonder about protein and vitamin B_{12}. Combining sunflower seeds (soaked to increase enzyme activity and protein absorption), flaxseed oil, and organic spirulina (a great vegan source of B_{12} that, by weight, contains close to 60 percent protein) is an answer. As a micro-algae, spirulina represents the highest level of trapped energy from the sun of any known food. It's like drinking energy straight from the sun.

1 quart apple juice
2 medium frozen bananas
¼ cup flaxseed oil
¼ cup sunflower seeds, soaked overnight and rinsed
1 tablespoon plus 1 teaspoon spirulina
¼ teaspoon ground cinnamon

Combine the apple juice, bananas, flaxseed oil, sunflower seeds, spirulina, and cinnamon in a blender. Blend on high speed for 1 minute or until smooth and creamy. Pour into glasses and serve.

NOTE
- **It's best to start your kids on algae at an early age to develop their taste for nutrient-rich dark green foods. Add powdered vitamin C, herbal extracts, and acidophilus for morning and afternoon pick-me-ups.**

Kona Coast Coladas

Preparation time: 5 minutes
Yield: 3–4 servings

This creamy cool colada comes straight from a juice bar on the Kona coast of Hawaii. It is the favored drink of Ironman triathletes who stop in for this energy booster featuring local organic white pineapples, bananas, and baby ginger—all grown in the fertile volcanic soil. Every time I make these, it brings me back to that beautiful place; it brings a boost of energy as well.

1 quart pineapple juice
3 medium frozen bananas
1 cup Thai Kitchen Pure Coconut Milk Lite or vanilla nondairy yogurt
1½ teaspoons grated ginger (optional)

Combine the pineapple juice, bananas, coconut milk, and ginger in a blender. Blend on high speed for 1 minute or until smooth and creamy. Pour into glasses and serve garnished with pineapple wedges.

NOTE

■ **This recipe can also provide you with 12 frozen pops: Pour the coladas into twelve ½-cup ice cream pop molds and place the molds in the freezer to set for about 2 hours. Remove the pop molds from the freezer and insert wooden sticks three quarters of the way into the molds, then place them back into the freezer until the entire pop is fully set (at least 2–3 hours).**

Lemony Carrot Pear Juice

Preparation time: 5 minutes to prepare, 5 minutes to juice
Yield: 3–4 servings

When my firstborn was 8 months old, I introduced him to this juice. I was looking for one that was nutrient rich, not too sweet, but tasty enough for a beginner to enjoy. The pears provide a flavorful alternative to apples, and this juice can open the door to your children's drinking other fresh juices.

1 large bunch flat-leaf parsley (about ¼ pound)

4 medium carrots, tops removed and cut into halves lengthwise

4 medium cucumbers, cored and quartered

4 large pears, cored and quartered

½ small lemon, peeled and quartered

Place a 4-cup-capacity liquid measuring cup under the juicer spout. Bunch up the parsley and push through the juicer feed tube, alternating it with the carrots, cucumbers, pears, and lemon. Pour into glasses and serve.

NOTE

■ The parsley will need to be pulsed through the juicer, alternating it with the remaining fruits and vegetables, or it will become stuck in the juicer.

Lily Pond Pink Lemonade

Preparation time: 5 minutes

Yield: 4–6 servings

There's nothing like a tall glass of lively lemonade, accompanied by fresh strawberries and slurped through a colorful straw. Sound good? This recipe can get you rollin'.

1 quart pineapple juice

3 medium blood oranges, squeezed, with pulp discarded (about ¾ cup juice)

3 large lemons, squeezed, with pulp discarded (about 1 cup juice)

1 pint strawberries, hulled and sliced

40 large ice cubes

1. In a large pitcher, stir together the pineapple juice, orange juice, lemon juice, and strawberries until well combined.

2. Pour into glasses filled with ice cubes and serve with straws.

NOTE

■ An equal measure of apple-raspberry or apple-strawberry juice can be used to replace the orange juice.

Liz's Hot "Chocolate"

Preparation time: 1–2 minutes to prepare, 1 minute to cook
Yield: 4 servings

One of my favorite places to be is Ithaca, New York. It has an abundance of well-stocked health food stores, a festive farmers' market, outstanding vegetarian restaurants, and Liz Randol's delicious hot "chocolate"! Liz, a fun-loving and energetic doctoral student, worked at a local vegan-friendly restaurant, and her hot "chocolate" caught my attention the first time I ate there—and every time thereafter! This recipe was inspired by hers, and my kids won't let me stop making it.

3 tablespoons sifted carob powder
⅓ cup brown rice syrup
2 teaspoons pure vanilla flavor
1 quart soy milk
Ground cinnamon or ground nutmeg to taste

1. In a medium saucepan, combine the carob powder, rice syrup, and vanilla. Whisk together until well mixed. Add the milk and bring to a simmer over moderate heat, continue to whisk, and simmer for 30 seconds. Remove from the heat and, using the whisk or a handheld electric mixer, beat the hot "chocolate" until foamy.

2. Pour into mugs and serve immediately, sprinkled with cinnamon or nutmeg.

NOTES
- **For a super creamy texture use a thick soy milk such as Vitasoy Creamy Original.**
- **For fun, try experimenting with a dash of orange-, mint-, banana-, or coconut-flavored extracts.**

Nature's Own Strawberry Punch

Preparation time: 5 minutes to prepare, 2–5 minutes to chill
Yield: 4 servings

Here's a great alternative to that sugared, chemical-laden, neon-colored stuff kids drink so often. With fresh fruit, and no refined sweeteners or artificial coloring, you know it's healthy, as well as delicious and refreshing.

1 quart grape-strawberry juice blend

Three 12-ounce cans Knudsen's Strawberry Spritzers

12 hulled strawberries

1 large orange, sliced into ¼-inch-thick half-moons

20–24 ice cubes

1. In a large pitcher, combine the juice, spritzers, strawberries, orange slices, and ice cubes. Stir until well combined and refrigerate until chilled, about 2–5 minutes.

2. Pour into glasses and serve with straws.

NOTE

■ **White grape juice can be used to replace the grape-strawberry juice blend.**

Orange Cream Smoothies

Preparation time: 5 minutes to prepare

Yield: 3–4 servings

Remember those Creamsicles the ice cream man used to bring? Well, here's my version in a nondairy form. This smooth, delicious drink is sure to please any child, big or small, first thing in the morning. Or try pouring this into pop-holders and freezing for a fun snack in the afternoon.

3 cups freshly squeezed orange juice (about 9 large oranges)

3 medium ripe bananas

12 ice cubes (optional)

Combine the orange juice, bananas, and ice cubes in a blender. Blend on high speed for 20 seconds or until smooth. Pour into glasses and serve.

NOTES

■ **The addition of 6 fresh or frozen strawberries will give this smoothie strawberry pizzazz.**

■ **This recipe should provide you with 12 frozen pops: Pour the smoothies into twelve ½-cup ice cream pop molds and place the molds in the freezer to set for about 2 hours. Remove the pop molds from the freezer and insert wooden sticks three quarters of the way into the molds, then place them back into the freezer until the entire pop is fully set (at least 2–3 hours).**

Peach Perfection Smoothies

Preparation time: 5 minutes to prepare, 5 minutes to juice
Yield: 4 servings

I was fortunate to spend a day with the Main family of northern California, harvesting their organically grown peaches and nectarines. Then came one of those moments I'll never forget. I picked a perfectly ripe white peach from the branch and took a large bite; it was juicy and delicate, with a melony-sweet perfume that caressed my taste buds. In one word—heavenly! That's the genesis of this recipe.

1 quart apple juice
6 large peaches, peeled, pitted, and quartered (about 3 cups)
2 small frozen bananas
½ cup vanilla nondairy yogurt (optional)

Combine the apple juice, peaches, bananas, and yogurt in a blender. Blend on high speed for 1 minute or until smooth. Pour into glasses and serve.

NOTE
- If you can find ripe white peaches, do indulge yourself. If not, fresh or frozen yellow peaches will be just fine.

Pillow Party Cherry Cola

Preparation time: 5 minutes
Yield: 4 servings

At an early age, many kids become hooked on the taste of cola. This version is a natural, fruit-juice-sweetened alternative to sugary colas, free of all artificial colors, flavors, and additives. Kids love the addition of colorful cherries and orange slices.

Four 12-ounce cans Knudsen's Cherry Cola Spritzers
40 ice cubes
⅔ cup sweet cherries
1 large orange, cut into ¼-inch-thick quarter-moon slices

Pour the spritzers into tall glasses filled with ice cubes, and serve garnished with cherries and orange slices

Power Juice

Preparation time: 5 minutes to prepare, 5 minutes to juice
Yield: 3–4 servings

This is my personal juice of choice. It's chlorophyll loaded, enzyme rich, blood purifying, and energy boosting. With a little bit of apple my kids also love it.

2 large bunches flat-leaf parsley (about ½ pound)
1 small piece ginger (1-inch square)
5 large celery stalks
3 medium cucumbers, quartered
3 large apples, cored and quartered

Place a 4-cup-capacity liquid measuring cup under the juicer spout. Bunch up the parsley and push through the juicer feed tube, alternating it with the ginger, celery, cucumbers, and apples. Pour into glasses and serve.

NOTE

■ **The parsley will need to be pulsed through the juicer, alternating it with the remaining fruits and vegetables, or it will become stuck.**

Rainbow Juice

Preparation time: 5 minutes to prepare, 5 minutes to juice
Yield: 3–4 servings

This amazing juice, with its rainbow colors of red, orange, and green, will have everyone wondering what's in it. Its bright eye-appeal will certainly attract children. Topped off with a garnish of fresh carrot sticks and celery, this juice is purely delicious and definitely a must-try!

1 large bunch flat-leaf parsley (about ¼ pound)
2 medium carrots, tops removed and cut into halves lengthwise
3 large cucumbers, quartered
3 large celery stalks
2 large red bell peppers, cored, seeded, and sliced
1 large apple, cored and quartered
1 small piece beet (about ½-inch square)

1. Place a 4-cup-capacity liquid measuring cup under the juicer spout. Bunch up the parsley and push through the juicer feed tube, alternating it with the carrots, cucumbers, celery, peppers, apple, and beet. Pour into glasses and serve.

2. Garnish with carrot and celery sticks.

NOTE

■ **The parsley will need to be pulsed through the juicer, alternating it with the remaining fruits and vegetables, or it will become stuck.**

Soaring Eagle Hot Cider

Preparation time: 3–5 minutes to prepare, 20 minutes to cook
Yield: 6–8 servings

Back in the mountains of upstate New York and all of New England, from September to February, apples are freshly picked and pressed into cider. There, you can watch eagles ride thermals, and with a light spicing and slow simmer enjoy this festive warm drink as its flavor "soars" to the peak of perfection.

2 quarts apple cider

2 cinnamon sticks (2¾-inch lengths)

6 whole cloves

One 2 x ¼-inch-strip orange peel

¼ teaspoon whole allspice

1 large orange, sliced into ¼-inch-thick half-moons

Cinnamon sticks for swizzling

1. In a large saucepan, combine the apple cider, cinnamon sticks, cloves, orange peel, and allspice. Cover and bring to a boil over high heat. Reduce the heat to moderate, and simmer covered for 20 minutes. Strain and discard the cloves, orange peel, and allspice.

2. Ladle into mugs and serve with the orange slices and cinnamon sticks.

NOTE

■ **This cider is great for fall and winter birthday parties.**

Summer's Essence Strawberry Shakes

Preparation time: 5 minutes to prepare

Yield: 3–4 servings

These shakes are a throwback to West Virginia summers with my cousins at the local ice cream parlor—complete with pinball machine. Now, you can create healthy memories for your own kids during those hot summer days. Don't forget the pinball!

2 cups soy milk or rice milk

4 medium ripe bananas

1 pint hulled strawberries

2 tablespoons honey

Combine the milk, bananas, strawberries, and honey in a blender. Blend on high speed for 1 minute or until smooth and creamy. Pour into glasses and serve with straws.

■ For variety, try making pops. This recipe should provide you with 16 frozen pops: Pour the shakes into 16 ½-cup ice cream pop molds and place the molds in the freezer to set for about 2 hours. Remove the pop molds from the freezer and insert wooden sticks three quarters of the way into the molds, then place them back in the freezer until the entire pop is fully set (at least 2–3 hours).

Sunny Sombrero Punch

Preparation time: 5 minutes
Yield: 4 servings

The idea for this punch came from a trip to Mexico. The children especially enjoyed choosing from the abundant, fresh tropical fruits in the dinner punch bowl. Here's how I duplicate that experience at home.

1 cup pineapple juice
1 cup apricot nectar
1 cup orange juice
½ cup lemonade
1 cup sweet cherries (pitted)
1 cup seedless green grapes
1 cup cut-up fresh pineapple (½-inch cubes)
30 ice cubes

1. In a large pitcher or punch bowl, combine the pineapple juice, apricot nectar, orange juice, lemonade, cherries, grapes, pineapple, and ice. Stir together until well combined.

2. Pour into glasses, and serve with straws and spoons.

NOTE
■ Canned pineapple (drained) can be used to replace the fresh.

Tropical Nectar

Preparation time: 5 minutes
Yield: 3–4 servings

This absolutely tantilizing drink is one that everyone will love—kids and grown-up kids alike. It's filled with vitamins, electrolytes, and enzymes, and will definitely energize your day.

2 cups freshly squeezed orange juice
1 medium mango, peeled, pitted, and coarsely chopped
½ cup coarsely chopped pineapple
¼ medium papaya, peeled, seeded, and coarsely chopped
2 large kiwifruit, peeled and halved
2 cups ice cubes

Combine the orange juice, mango, pineapple, papaya, kiwifruit, and ice in a blender. Blend on high speed for 1 minute or until smooth and creamy. Pour into glasses, garnish with kiwifruit or pineapple wedges, and serve.

Velvety Vanilla Almond Milk

Preparation time: 6–8 hours to soak the almonds, 5 minutes to prepare
Yield: 1 quart

Out in Eugene, Oregon, the athletes drink almond milk all the time. It's common to see them quaffing it at the health food store early in the morning before a run or before making the journey to Crater Lake for hiking and cliff diving into that chilly blue water. They know that the mix of protein and other nutrients almonds offer is difficult to surpass.

1 cup raw almonds, soaked in 4 cups pure water for 6–8 hours (then discard soaking water, rinse well, and drain)
1 tablespoon pure vanilla favor
2 tablespoons brown rice syrup

1. Combine the prepared almonds and vanilla in a blender. Blend on medium speed for 30 seconds, increase speed to high, and continue blending for 1 minute or until homogenous.

2. Transfer the almond mixture to a cheesecloth-lined fine sieve and strain into a medium bowl (squeeze or use a spoon to stir and push the milk through while you pour, since it will be too rich to strain it through without a bit of mashing). Save the pulp for hot cereal, grain dishes, baked goods, or smoothies.

3. Rinse and dry the blender, then pour in the strained milk and rice syrup. Blend on high speed until smooth and frothy, about 1 minute. Transfer to a container and refrigerate for 1–2 hours or until chilled.

4. Serve as a cow's milk, rice milk, or soy milk substitute.

NOTES

- **This recipe can be used to make Brazil milk, hazel milk, or cashew milk by using an equal measure of each nut to replace the almonds.**
- **Almond milk can be refrigerated in an airtight container for 3–4 days. If it separates, reblend or simply shake it up in the container.**

CHAPTER 7

BREAKFAST FOODS

Alpine Granola

Preparation time: 5 minutes to prepare, 20–25 minutes to bake
Yield: 4 servings

Granola is great for kids almost any time. I serve it for breakfast, pack it in lunches, and keep jars of it for snacking at home. This particular recipe was introduced to me during a trip to Switzerland. My dear friend Florence Barbara had set some aside for the kids. My son then asked if I could make it at home, and I've been making it ever since. He's happy—and your kids will be too!

4 cups rolled oats
¼ cup oat bran (optional)
¾ cup coarsely chopped almonds (see Notes)
⅓ cup sunflower seeds
1¼ teaspoons ground cinnamon
3 tablespoons canola oil
¼ cup honey
⅔ cup raisins

1. Preheat the oven to 375°F. Line two 11 x 15-inch cookie sheets with parchment paper and set aside.

2. In a large mixing bowl, toss together the oats, oat bran, almonds, sunflower seeds, and cinnamon until well mixed. Drizzle in the oil and honey; then, using your hands or a wooden spoon, incorporate until well combined.

3. Spread the mixture evenly on the two cookie sheets. Bake on the upper and middle racks of the preheated oven for 15 minutes. Remove the sheets from the oven and, with a wooden spoon, carefully stir the granola on the sheets, respreading evenly. Return the sheets to the oven to bake for an additional 5–10 minutes or until the granola is golden. For uniformity in baking, rotate the sheets from top to bottom and front to back. Remove the sheets from the oven, slide the granola into a large flat sheet or baking pan, and cool completely, about 20 minutes.

4. Toss in the raisins and serve with soy milk or rice milk. Store in an airtight container.

NOTES
■ Be sure to chop the almonds coarsely, or they will cook faster than the oats and burn. The granola will continue to cook on the hot sheets even after being removed from the oven, so do transfer it to another sheet or pan to prevent burning.
■ For those sensitive to gluten, an equal measure of quinoa flakes (found in the cereal section of the health food store) can be used to replace the oats.

Anytime Baked Apples

Preparation time: 10 minutes to prepare, 40–45 minutes to bake
Yield: 4 servings

Baked apples are easy to prepare and the finished product is always a special treat. These apples are filled with classic flavors children love. They are great as a breakfast item, for dessert, or as an anytime snack, and boy, do they make the kitchen smell great!

4 medium Golden Delicious apples
¾ cup apple juice
¼ cup pure water
2 tablespoons honey
1 tablespoon freshly squeezed lemon juice
1 teaspoon ground cinnamon
½ teaspoon ground nutmeg
¼ cup raisins or currants
¼ cup coarsely chopped walnuts or pecans

1. Preheat the oven to 375°F.

2. Peel about 1 inch of skin from the top of the apples; using the point of a peeler, a melon baller, or a coring knife, core the apples, creating a large enough space for the filling (do not go all the way through). Place the apples into an 8 x 8 x 2¼-inch baking pan. Set aside.

3. In a medium mixing bowl, whisk together the apple juice, water, honey, lemon juice, cinnamon, and nutmeg until well blended.

4. Spoon the raisins first and then the walnuts into the apple cavity, then pour the apple juice mixture over the tops of the apples (the excess liquid will spill over into the bottom of the pan).

5. Bake on the upper rack of the preheated oven, basting several times with the pan juices, until the apples are golden and tender, about 40–45 minutes (the skin may split). To ensure uniformity in baking, halfway through the baking period rotate the pan from front to back. Remove from the oven and let cool for at least 10 minutes. Spoon the juice mixture over the apples, slice, and serve.

NOTE
■ **Granny Smith, Rome Beauty, Northern Spy, and Macoun apples hold their shape during baking and can be used to replace Golden Delicious apples.**

Baby Bear Oatmeal

Preparation time: 5 minutes to prepare, 10–12 minutes to cook

Yield: 4 servings

We all know that oatmeal is good for you. But what if you have a non-oatmeal-eating child, one who finds the stuff boring? Well, this creamy cereal filled with sweet apples, crunchy walnuts, and fragrant cinnamon is so far from boring that—who knows?—your child just may become a convert!

4 cups pure water
1⅓ cups rolled oats
1 large apple, peeled, cored, and coarsely chopped
¼ cup raisins or currants
¼ teaspoon ground cinnamon
½ cup coarsely chopped walnuts or sunflower seeds

1. In a medium saucepan, bring the water to a boil. With a wooden spoon, stir in the oats, apple, raisins, and cinnamon. Reduce the heat to low and simmer covered, stirring occasionally, for 10 minutes. Stir in the walnuts and cook an additional 1–2 minutes, or until creamy.

2. Spoon into bowls and serve hot, topped with a little nondairy milk and honey, or apple juice.

NOTE
■ **A pear can be used to replace the apple, and coarsely chopped almonds or pecans can replace the walnuts.**

Banana Cream of Buckwheat Cereal

Preparation time: 5 minutes to prepare, 10 minutes to cook

Yield: 4 servings

Here's a creamy, maple-flavored cereal that may remind you of that store-bought cereal your mother used to prepare. But this homemade version is healthier, more flavorful, and just as easy!

1 cup pure water

2 cups rice milk, soy milk, or nut milk

1 tablespoon pure maple syrup or honey

⅛ teaspoon ground cinnamon

½ cup cream of buckwheat (fine-groat kasha)

1 teaspoon pure vanilla flavor

1 cup coarsely chopped banana

¼ cup sunflower seeds

1. In a medium saucepan, bring the water, milk, maple syrup, and cinnamon to a boil. With a wooden spoon, stir in the buckwheat. Reduce the heat to low and simmer uncovered, stirring occasionally, for about 8 minutes. When the cereal is loose and creamy, stir in the vanilla, banana, and sunflower seeds until well combined.

2. Spoon into bowls and serve hot.

NOTES

- Farina can be used in place of the cream of buckwheat; you will need to whisk it in rapidly to prevent clumping. Cook for 2–3 minutes only, then serve with a little added milk.

- For variety, try coarsely chopped almonds, walnuts, or pecans to replace the sunflower seeds.

Belgian Mochi Waffles

Preparation time: 1 minute to prepare, 6–8 minutes to cook 1 batch

Yield: 4 large waffles

These waffles have been a favorite of mine for over 25 years. Back then, when a 6-year-old girl was taken by her vegetarian parents to Souen (a macrobiotic restaurant, then located on Manhattan's Upper West Side), the sight of fish, tofu, and steamed seaweed was a bit formidable. Fortunately these delicious waffles, made from glutenous, sweet brown rice called mochi, were also available. My parents knew that mochi, served with fresh organic berries and sweet adzuki beans, was a nutritional powerhouse, and so all parties involved were satisfied. I still eat these waffles regularly and am convinced that once you try them you too will be hooked. By the way, the added bonus is that this elegant-looking dish is ridiculously simple to prepare—just cut and cook for a few minutes!

One 12-ounce package Kendall Food Company Organic Mochi Rice Cake (cut into 4 equal pieces)

1. Preheat a Belgian waffle iron on a moderate to low setting until hot (it should not be smoking). Using a brush, lightly oil the iron.

2. Lay 2 mochi rice cake cubes—1 piece per waffle—onto the preheated iron. Allow the lid to close by itself as the mochi melts down. Cook on a moderate to low setting until the steaming stops and the waffles are golden brown, about 6–8 minutes.

3. Serve topped with The Very Best Chunky Applesauce (page 100), Maple Glazed Bananas (page 93), sweet adzuki beans (see Note), stewed fruit, apple butter, honey, or a little pure maple syrup.

NOTE
- **For sweet adzuki beans, add a little brown rice syrup to cooked adzuki beans (page 38).**

Blueberry Buckwheat Silver-Dollar Pancakes

Preparation time: 10 minutes to prepare, 4–6 minutes to cook 1 batch
Yield: forty-two 2-inch pancakes

These multigrain hot cakes have it all. They're rich in protein and fiber (thanks to oat bran and buckwheat), fluffy (thanks to nondairy yogurt), and need not a drop of syrup since they're loaded with fruit. The silver-dollar size means easy eating for kids, and by the way, an entire batch of 42 contains only 2 tablespoons of oil.

¾ cup unbleached white flour
½ cup buckwheat flour
½ cup oat bran
1 teaspoon baking powder
1 teaspoon baking soda
¼ teaspoon sea salt
1 cup soy milk, rice milk, or nut milk
½ cup nondairy yogurt
2 tablespoons canola oil
1 cup ripe banana, coarsely mashed
½ cup blueberries
½ cup strawberries, hulled and sliced

1. In a large mixing bowl, combine the flours, oat bran, baking powder, baking soda, and salt. Whisk together until well mixed. Set aside.

2. In a medium mixing bowl, whisk together the milk, yogurt, oil, and banana until well blended.

3. With a rubber spatula, gradually add the wet ingredients to the dry, making sure they are well blended before each addition. Scrape off any excess batter from the side of the bowl. Stir in the berries until well combined.

4. Heat a griddle or large cast-iron frying pan over moderate to high heat, and brush lightly with oil.

5. Spoon the batter—about 1 tablespoon per pancake—into the prepared pan and cook over moderate to low heat until bubbles form and the edges start to dry, about 2–3 minutes. Using a metal pancake turner, flip the pancakes over, and cook on the other side an additional 2–3 minutes or until done. Continue until the remaining pancakes are made (you may need to re-oil the griddle between batches).

6. Serve topped with The Very Best Chunky Applesauce (page 100), pureed fresh fruit, or a little pure maple syrup.

NOTES

- **For those sensitive to wheat, an equal measure of either spelt or Lundberg brand brown rice flour can be used to replace the unbleached white flour.**
- **If frozen berries are used, they should be rinsed and drained to remove any excess moisture.**
- **To keep the pancakes warm, layer them in a baking dish (covered with a kitchen towel) and place in an oven set at the lowest temperature.**
- **These pancakes can be cooked ahead of time—then frozen between pieces of waxed paper in a sealed plastic container—for a quick morning meal. To reheat the pancakes, simply place them in a toaster oven until hot.**

Carrot Cake Muffins

Preparation time: 15 minutes to prepare, 40–45 minutes to bake
Yield: 1 dozen muffins

Imagine an orange-flavored carrot cake, lightly spiced with cinnamon, ginger, cloves, and nutmeg. These muffins are laced with pumpkin seeds, shreds of bright orange carrots, and plump, juicy raisins, and sensibly sweetened with orange juice, molasses, and honey. We often enjoy them in the morning as part of a nutritious breakfast.

2 cups shredded carrot

1½ teaspoons grated orange zest

½ cup raisins

½ cup pumpkin seeds

2½ cups whole-wheat pastry flour

2 teaspoons baking soda

1¼ teaspoons ground cinnamon

¾ teaspoon ground nutmeg

½ teaspoon sea salt

¼ teaspoon ground ginger

¼ teaspoon ground cloves

1 cup coarsely mashed banana

½ cup canola oil

½ cup orange juice

3 tablespoons honey

2 tablespoons molasses

2 teaspoons pure vanilla flavor

1. Preheat the oven to 375°F.

2. Line a 12-well muffin tin with paper baking cups. To prevent sticking, brush the cups lightly with a paste made from 1½ teaspoons each of canola oil and flour. Set aside.

3. In a medium bowl, toss together the carrot, orange zest, raisins, and pumpkin seeds until well combined. Set aside.

4. In a large mixing bowl, sift together the flour, baking soda, cinnamon, nutmeg, salt, ginger, and cloves. Whisk together until well combined. Set aside.

5. In a large mixing bowl, whisk together the banana, oil, orange juice, honey, molasses, and vanilla until well blended.

6. With a rubber spatula, gradually add the wet ingredients to the dry, making sure they are well blended before each addition. Scrape off any excess batter from the side of the bowl. Stir in the carrot mixture until well mixed.

7. Spoon the batter into the prepared muffin tin (the wells will be heaping full). Bake in the middle level of the preheated oven for 40–45 minutes. For uniformity in baking, rotate the tin from front to back halfway through the baking period.

8. The muffins are done when the center springs back when touched, or a tester inserted in the center comes

out clean. They will be golden brown. Remove the tin from the oven, let the muffins cool for 10 minutes in the tin, then transfer them to a wire rack until completely cool.

9. Serve the muffins by themselves, or with apple or peach butter and a cup of hot herbal tea.

NOTES

■ For those sensitive to wheat, an equal measure of either spelt or Lundberg brand brown rice flour can be used to replace the whole-wheat pastry flour.

■ For variety, the pumpkin seeds can be replaced with either sunflower seeds or coarsely chopped pecans.

Fantastic Fruit Salad

Preparation time: 10 minutes
Yield: 4 servings

The quality of a dish always depends on the freshness of the ingredients, which is one of the reasons I love springtime. That's when the farmers' markets are exploding with fresh, locally grown berries, and an abundance of other seasonal fruits, and I can make great salads like this one.

1 cup strawberries, hulled and quartered
1 cup blueberries
2 peaches, peeled, pitted, and diced
1 large banana, peeled and sliced
2 tablespoons freshly squeezed lime juice
Ground cinnamon to taste

In a large bowl, combine the strawberries, blueberries, peaches, and banana. Drizzle the lime juice onto the fruit and gently toss together until well coated. Sprinkle on the cinnamon, toss again, and serve.

NOTE

■ Other fruits can replace any in this recipe. Consider nectarines, honeydew melon, kiwifruit, grapes, apricots, papayas, and mangoes.

French Toast of the Town

Preparation time: 5 minutes to prepare, 5–7 minutes to cook 1 batch

Yield: 4 servings

French toast—golden crunchy on the outside and moist and rich on the inside—is a traditional breakfast fa-vorite. But think of it at snacktime too. It can be served with my kids' favorite—Maple Glazed Bananas (page 93)—or a wide variety of natural fruit toppings; let the children choose their own.

1 cup well-mashed ripe banana

2 cups soy milk, rice milk, or nut milk

2 teaspoons pure vanilla flavor

1 teaspoon ground cinnamon

8 slices whole-grain bread, sliced ½–¾ inch thick and with each slice cut into 4 pieces

1. In a medium mixing bowl, combine the banana, milk, vanilla, and cinnamon. Whisk together until well blended. Dip the bread in the banana mixture, turning to coat both sides.

2. Heat a griddle or large cast-iron frying pan over moderate to high heat, and brush lightly with oil.

3. Place the dipped bread—about 4 pieces—into the prepared pan, and cook over moderate to low heat until the underside is golden brown, about 3–4 minutes. Using a metal pancake turner, flip the French toast over, and cook on the other side an additional 2–3 minutes or until golden. Continue until the remaining 28 pieces of toast are made (you may need to re-oil the griddle between batches).

4. Serve topped with Maple Glazed Bananas (page 93), The Very Best Chunky Applesauce (page 100), pureed fresh fruit, or a little pure maple syrup.

NOTES

■ For those sensitive to wheat, try the many varieties of rice, millet, rye, or spelt breads that are found in health food stores.

■ For variety and fun, try adding the grated zest of 1 orange. For a thick French toast, you can cut homemade bread into 1-inch-thick slices. Another idea: Use breads loaded with nuts or raisins.

■ To keep warm, layer the finished slices in a baking dish (covered with aluminum foil) and place in an oven set at the lowest temperature.

Honey Cinnamon Toast

Preparation time: 1 minute to prepare, 6–8 minutes to toast
Yield: 4 servings

I have a daughter who loves cinnamon so much she often asks if she can eat it directly from the spice jar. She also enjoys toasted breads for breakfast, so I've combined the two.

8 slices whole-grain bread
¼ cup honey
1 teaspoon ground cinnamon

1. Toast the bread in a toaster oven for 5–6 minutes or until golden brown.

2. In a small ramekin or bowl, stir together the honey and cinnamon until well blended. Using a butter knife or spoon, evenly spread the cinnamon mixture onto the bread. Return to the toaster oven to warm for an additional 1–2 minutes. Slice into 16 halves and serve.

NOTE
■ **The bread can be toasted in a preheated 375°F oven for 10–12 minutes, then returned to the oven to warm for an additional 1–2 minutes.**

Hot Rye Muesli

Preparation time: 5 minutes to prepare, 10 minutes to cook
Yield: 4 servings

Creamy rye and oat flakes mixed with gooey dates, juicy raisins, and crunchy almonds—all are pieces of the puzzle for this hearty breakfast cereal. We often enjoy this treat drizzled with pure honey during the fall, winter, and early spring months.

4 cups pure water
1 cup rye flakes
½ cup rolled oats
¼ cup raisins or currants

¼ cup finely chopped dates
½ cup coarsely chopped almonds

1. In a medium saucepan, bring the water to a boil. With a wooden spoon, stir in the rye flakes, oats, raisins, and dates. Reduce the heat to low and simmer uncovered, stirring occasionally, for 7 minutes. Stir in the almonds and cook an additional 3 minutes, or until creamy.

2. Spoon into bowls and serve hot, topped with a little rice milk or soy milk and honey or apple juice.

NOTE

■ An equal measure of rolled oats can be used to replace the rye flakes.

Maple Glazed Bananas

Preparation time: 5 minutes to prepare, 15–20 minutes to broil
Yield: 4 servings

Originally these sweet golden bananas were a topping for French toast and pancakes. It wasn't long before I realized they could stand up on their own. As an extra-special dessert, try some with your favorite flavor nondairy frozen dessert.

6 ripe, firm, full-size bananas, peeled and cut into thirds (about 3½ pounds)
⅓ cup pure maple syrup
1 teaspoon freshly squeezed lemon juice
½ teaspoon pure vanilla flavor

1. Preheat the broiler for 5 minutes.

2. In a 9 x 11-inch baking dish, combine the bananas, maple syrup, lemon juice, and vanilla. Toss together until the bananas are well coated.

3. Slide the baking dish under the broiler with the top of the bananas about 2 inches from the heat source and broil for 15–20 minutes, turning them occasionally, or until golden brown.

4. Serve the bananas alone or accompanied by French Toast of the Town (page 91), Belgian Mochi Waffles (page 86), or vanilla nondairy frozen dessert.

NOTE

■ The quality of the bananas is important for this recipe. They should be firmly ripe; overripened or bruised bananas will produce mushy bananas when cooked.

Monkey Magic Muffins

Preparation time: 10 minutes to prepare, 45–50 minutes to bake
Yield: 1 dozen muffins

These moist banana muffins flavored with nutmeg are wonderful for breakfast or as a snack food. They are apple juice–sweetened, with just a little honey for flavor. The oat bran gives added whole-grain texture, and since these muffins are not overly sweet, your children may end up eating two or three at a time.

1¼ cups unbleached white flour
¾ cup whole-wheat pastry flour
¾ teaspoon baking soda
¾ teaspoon ground nutmeg
¾ teaspoon sea salt
1 cup plus 2 tablespoons oat bran
½ cup canola oil
3 tablespoons honey
1 cup apple juice
1½ teaspoons pure vanilla flavor
2¼ cups coarsely chopped bananas
1 cup coarsely chopped walnuts or sunflower seeds

1. Preheat the oven to 375°F.

2. Line a 12-well muffin tin with paper baking cups. To prevent sticking, brush the cups lightly with a paste made from 1½ teaspoons each canola oil and unbleached white flour. Set aside.

3. In a large mixing bowl, sift together the unbleached white flour, whole-wheat pastry flour, baking soda, nutmeg, and salt. Whisk in the oat bran until the texture is uniform. Set aside.

4. In a medium mixing bowl, whisk together the oil, honey, apple juice, and vanilla until well blended.

5. With a rubber spatula, gradually add the wet ingredients to the dry, making sure they are well blended be-

fore each addition. Scrape off any excess batter from the side of the bowl. Stir in the bananas and walnuts until well combined.

6. Spoon the batter into the prepared muffin tin (the wells will be heaping full). Bake in the middle level of the preheated oven for 45–50 minutes. For uniformity in baking, rotate the tin from front to back halfway through the baking period.

7. The muffins are done when the center springs back when touched, or a tester inserted in the center comes out clean. They will be golden brown. Remove the tin from the oven, let the muffins cool for 10 minutes in the tin, then transfer them to a wire rack until completely cool.

8. Serve plain or with hot herbal tea.

NOTES
- **The quality of the bananas is important for this recipe. They should be firmly ripe; overripe or bruised bananas will produce a loose batter and the muffins will not rise properly.**
- **For those sensitive to wheat, 2 cups of either spelt or Lundberg brand brown rice flour can be used to replace the unbleached white and whole-wheat pastry flours.**
- **To make banana bread, this muffin batter can be poured into two 9 x 4 x 2½-inch loaf pans, then baked for 50–55 minutes.**
- **For BLUEBERRY MUFFINS, replace the walnuts with an equal measure of blueberries and add ½ teaspoon finely grated orange zest.**

Pap's West Virginia Home Fries

Preparation time: 20 minutes to prepare, 50–60 minutes to cook
Yield: 4 servings

I can remember my tall, carved-out-of-a-mountain grandfather towering over a big black stove down on his West Virginia farm. He would cut up his home-grown potatoes, throw them into a cast-iron pan with a big scoop of bacon grease, and create the most crispy-golden home fries. Served with sunny-side-up eggs and white toast, they taught this 8-year-old, summer-vacation, New York City squirt a big lesson about good home-cooked country food. I know Pap won't mind if I make my version with just a bit of canola oil and serve it with scrambled tofu and whole-grain toast.

About 6 quarts pure water
4 pounds russet potatoes

5 tablespoons canola oil
1½ teaspoons sea salt
Freshly ground black pepper to taste

1. In a large pot, bring the water to a rolling boil. Stir the potatoes into the water, bring to a boil, and cook uncovered until just tender, about 20–25 minutes. Transfer to a colander, drain off excess water, and set aside until cool enough to handle. Using a small paring knife, remove and discard the peels, then cut the potatoes into ¾-inch squares. Set aside.

2. Heat a griddle or large cast-iron frying pan over moderate to high heat. Add the oil, potatoes, salt, and black pepper. Cook uncovered for 3–5 minutes or until the bottoms of the potatoes are golden. Sauté for 25–30 additional minutes, stirring occasionally, or until uniformly crisp and golden (use an angled-bottom spatula to scrape the bottom of the pan to prevent sticking).

3. Serve alone, with ketchup, or accompanied by Scrumptious Scrambled Tofu (page 97) and whole-grain toast.

NOTE

■ For Western-style flavors, sauté ¼ cup finely chopped red onion, ¼ cup finely chopped green bell pepper, and ¼ cup finely chopped yellow bell pepper in 1 tablespoon canola oil for 2–3 minutes or until the onion is translucent. Remove the pepper mixture from the pan and set aside. Continue with steps 1–2, then toss in the pepper mixture during the last 5 minutes of cooking time until heated through.

Pecan Oatmeal Waffles

Preparation time: 5 minutes to prepare, 2 hours to chill (or overnight), 4–5 minutes to cook 1 batch
Yield: 4 large waffles

Here's a new way to do the right thing. Some night before bed, whizz some oatmeal in the blender with soy milk, and the next morning you'll be 10 minutes away from a dynamite breakfast. Pecans boast the protein, minerals, and, of course, the crunch. No sweetener required.

2 cups rolled oats
2 cups soy milk or rice milk
1½ cups pecans (optional)
2 tablespoons pure maple syrup
2 tablespoons maple sugar
¼ teaspoon ground cinnamon

1. Combine the soy milk and oats in a blender. (You can do this the night before.) Blend on high speed for 1 minute or until smooth and creamy. Transfer to a medium mixing bowl and refrigerate for 2 hours or until thick and batter-like, Stir in the nuts, maple syrup, maple sugar, and cinnamon until well combined, and set aside.

2. To roast the pecans, preheat the oven to 375°F and line an 11 x 15-inch cookie sheet with parchment paper. Evenly spread the pecans on the prepared sheet and bake in the preheated oven for 8 minutes, or until the pecans are golden. Remove the sheet from the oven and set aside.

3. Lightly grease and preheat a Belgian waffle iron on a moderate to low setting until hot (it should not be smoking).

4. Spoon the batter—about ⅔ cup per waffle—into the prepared iron, spreading evenly with a spatula and gently allowing the top portion to close. Cook on a moderate to low setting until the steaming stops and the waffles are golden brown, about 4–5 minutes.

5. Serve alone, with hot apple topping (for The Very Best Chunky Applesauce, see page 100), or with a little maple syrup.

Scrumptious Scrambled Tofu

Preparation time: 2 minutes to prepare, 4–5 minutes to cook

Yield: 4 servings

My children never liked scrambled eggs, so I thought to myself, why not create a yummier, healthier option? I did, and combined with hash browns and toast, it's a big family hit. Try it once and I'm sure you'll understand why.

¼ cup lecithin granules (optional)
1 teaspoon onion powder
1 teaspoon dry mustard
½ teaspoon ground turmeric
½ teaspoon celery salt
¼ teaspoon sea salt
2 tablespoons canola oil
2 pounds extra-firm tofu, well drained and crumbled
1–2 tablespoons finely chopped fresh parsley (optional)

1. In a small mixing bowl, combine the lecithin, onion powder, mustard, turmeric, celery salt, and sea salt. Stir together until well combined and set aside.

2. In a large mixing bowl, toss together 1 tablespoon of the oil with the tofu and the spice mixture until well combined.

3. In a large frying pan, over moderate to high heat, sauté the tofu mixture in the remaining 1 tablespoon of oil for 4–5 minutes or until hot.

4. Serve hot, garnished with parsley, and accompanied by whole-grain toast or Pap's West Virginia Home Fries (page 95).

NOTE

■ For Western Scrambled Tofu, replace the canola oil with an equal measure of toasted sesame oil. Sauté ¼ cup finely chopped onion and ¼ cup finely chopped red bell pepper in 1 tablespoon toasted sesame oil for 2–3 minutes or until the onion is translucent. Set aside. Continue with steps 1–3, and add the tofu mixture to the reserved onion. Serve garnished with finely chopped fresh chives and a sprinkling of sesame seeds and cayenne pepper.

Strawberry Millet Cereal

Preparation time: 5 minutes to prepare, 13–15 minutes to cook
Yield: 4 servings

This mild-flavored grain is both rich in protein and highly digestible. However, since most children are unfamiliar with it, their first experience should be a delicious one. My suggestion: a satisfying cereal flavored with fresh strawberries, banana, and honey.

3 cups pure water
1 cup millet
1 large ripe banana, well mashed
½ cup diced strawberries
2 teaspoons honey
¼ teaspoon ground cinnamon
2 teaspoons pure vanilla flavor

1. In a medium saucepan, bring the water to a boil. With a wooden spoon, stir in the millet, banana, strawberries, honey, and cinnamon. Reduce the heat to low and simmer uncovered, stirring occasionally, for 13–15 minutes, or until all of the liquid has been absorbed. Remove from the heat and stir in the vanilla until well combined.

2. Spoon into bowls and serve hot, topped with a little nondairy milk or apple juice, and sliced bananas and strawberries.

NOTES

- **Do not overcook the millet; if you do, it will absorb all of the moisture as it cooks and continue to expand, giving you a drier cereal.**
- **Frozen strawberries can be used; just dice.**
- **This cereal can be cooked for 5 minutes less, then pureed for a creamy cereal.**

Sweet 'Taters and Spice

Preparation time: 10 minutes to prepare, 20 minutes to cook
Yield: 8 bruschettas

As a child I was always fond of the sweet potato pies that were a part of so many Southern meals. Unfortunately, these pies are usually loaded with sugar, butter, and eggs. On the other hand, these bruschettas are made from toasted whole-grain country bread spread with a heavenly spiced orange- and honey-flavored sweet potato "cream." Since this breakfast treat is low in fat and high in beta-carotene, it's the perfect morning send-off for your family.

**2 medium sweet potatoes or yams, scrubbed well and cut into 1-inch-thick slices, or 2 cups cooked
    sweet potato slices (about 1¼ pounds)**
⅓ cup freshly squeezed orange juice
3 tablespoons honey (optional)
½ teaspoon ground cinnamon
½ teaspoon ground nutmeg
¼ teaspoon ground allspice
8 slices whole-grain country bread or French bread, cut ½ inch thick

1. Place the sweet potato slices on a steamer set into a large pot filled with 1 inch of pure water. Cook covered over moderate to high heat until the potatoes are tender when a fork is inserted into their centers, about

15–20 minutes. Remove the steamer and run the potatoes under cool water until they can be handled comfortably. Using a small paring knife, remove and discard the peels.

2. In a food processor, using a metal blade, combine the sweet potatoes, orange juice, honey, cinnamon, nutmeg, and allspice. Process together until smooth and creamy, about 2 minutes. Set aside.

3. Lightly toast the bread on both sides. Spread bread slices with sweet potato "cream" and serve warm with hot tea, rice milk, soy milk, or almond milk.

NOTES

- I often bake the sweet potatoes rather than steam them. To bake, preheat the oven to 350°F. Scrub and dry the sweet potatoes, then prick the top and bottom surfaces of each 4 times with a fork. Place the potatoes on a cookie sheet lined with parchment paper, place on the center rack of the oven, and bake for about 1 hour or until tender.
- If a food processor is not available, you can use an electric mixer to beat the sweet potato "cream" ingredients.
- For those sensitive to wheat—rye, rice, and millet breads can be purchased in health food stores.

The Very Best Chunky Applesauce

Preparation time: 10 minutes to prepare, 15–20 minutes to cook
Yield: 4 servings

Every year for the holidays, I spoon this applesauce into large Mason jars, wrap it in ribbon, and give it to friends and family. Because this applesauce is chunky, it makes a perfect topping for breakfast items and desserts, as well as a great snack food on its own.

6 Golden Delicious apples, peeled, cored, and quartered (about 4 cups)
2 tablespoons freshly squeezed lemon juice
⅓ cup apple juice
⅔ cup pure water
1/16 teaspoon ground cinnamon

1. In a medium bowl, toss the apples together with the lemon juice, apple juice, water, and cinnamon until well combined.

2. Pour the apple mixture into a medium saucepan and bring to a boil. Reduce heat to moderate and simmer covered, stirring occasionally, for 15–20 minutes or until the apples are tender and a sauce has formed.

NOTE

■ **Any type of apple can be used; softer apples will require less cooking time.**

Walnutty Maple Granola

Preparation time: 5 minutes to prepare, 20–25 minutes to bake
Yield: 4 servings

I have fond childhood memories of summers in the mountains of upstate New York. We welcomed health-minded people into our home, and every morning the chefs would make a few types of granola. The sweet smells of roasting nuts and spices would waft over the grounds, and by 6 A.M. guests were heading toward the kitchen. These smells and the many others coming from that wonderful kitchen are what first sparked my interest in cooking. Besides, who wants to do early morning yoga when you can be around the food?

½ cup plus 2 tablespoons pure maple syrup
2 tablespoons canola oil
1 teaspoon pure vanilla flavor
4 cups rolled oats
½ cup coarsely chopped walnuts

1. Preheat the oven to 375°F. Line two 11 x 15-inch cookie sheets with parchment paper and set aside.

2. In a 1-cup capacity liquid measuring pitcher, combine the maple syrup, oil, and vanilla. Place the oats in a large mixing bowl. Drizzle the maple syrup mixture over the oats and, using your hands or a wooden spoon, incorporate until well combined.

3. Spread the mixture evenly on the two cookie sheets. Bake on the upper and middle racks of the preheated oven for 15 minutes. Remove the sheets from the oven and, with a wooden spoon, carefully stir the granola on the sheets, respreading evenly. Return the sheets to the oven to bake for an additional 5–10 minutes or until the granola is golden. For uniformity in baking, rotate the sheets from top to bottom and front to back. Re-

move the sheets from the oven, slide the granola onto a large flat sheet or baking pan, and cool completely, about 20 minutes.

4. Toss in the walnuts and serve with soy milk or rice milk, or store in an airtight container for up to 6 weeks.

NOTES

■ The granola will continue to cook on the hot sheets even after being removed from the oven, so do transfer to another sheet or pan to prevent burning.

■ For those sensitive to gluten, an equal measure of quinoa flakes (available in health food stores) can be used to replace the oats.

CHAPTER 8

SANDWICHES, SPREADS, AND SNACKS

Ants on Logs

Preparation time: 10 minutes
Yield: 4 servings

Ants on logs? What's that? A classic American snack for kids—celery sticks filled with cream cheese or nut butter, then topped with raisins. My daughter loves them, and I think your kids will too.

4 large celery stalks, washed and with ends trimmed
⅓–½ cup nut butter (almond, peanut, cashew, or pistachio)
⅓ cup raisins

1. Spread the concave portion of the celery pieces with the nut butter. Press the raisins into the nut butter. Use a sharp knife to cut each celery stalk into 2-inch pieces.

2. Transfer to a large serving platter or wrap tightly and refrigerate until needed.

NOTE
■ **For variety, try these sprinkled with toasted coconut, or replace the raisins with chopped dates or apricots.**

Bowl o' Crunch

Preparation time: 5 minutes
Yield: 4 servings

What happens when you take five of the most popular snack foods and combine them? You've got an easy kid-pleaser, that's what!

1 cup baked potato chips
1 cup baked blue corn chips
1 cup popped corn
1 cup rice crackers
1 cup unsalted pretzels

1. In a large mixing bowl, toss together the chips, popped corn, crackers, and pretzels until well combined.

2. Serve in lunch boxes, packed in plastic bags, or as party fare.

NOTE

■ **Blue corn chips and rice crackers are available in health food stores and supermarkets.**

Buttery White Bean Hummus

Preparation time: 10 minutes to prepare, 7–10 minutes to cook
Yield: 2 cups

Buttery beans creamed with extra-virgin olive oil, garlic, and fresh herbs to the point of pure delight—this hummus is perfect not only for sandwiches but also sent as a warm reminder of what love in food tastes like.

1 cup chopped yellow onion
4 large cloves garlic, peeled and coarsely chopped
3 tablespoons extra-virgin olive oil
One 15-ounce tomato, peeled, seeded, and chopped
Two 15-ounce cans white beans, rinsed and drained
¾ teaspoon sea salt
2 tablespoons finely chopped parsley
7 large basil leaves

1. In a medium saucepan, sauté the onion and garlic in the oil over moderate heat until soft, about 3–4 minutes. Stir in the tomato, beans, and salt and cook for 4–6 additional minutes or until thick.

2. In a food processor, using a metal blade, combine the bean mixture, parsley, and basil. Process for 2 minutes or until smooth and creamy.

3. Serve warm or chilled, with crackers, veggie sticks, or sandwiched with bread.

NOTE

■ **This dip can be refrigerated for up to 4 days.**

Carmela's Authentic Focaccia

Preparation time: 15–20 minutes to prepare, 2 hours to rise, 35–40 minutes to bake

Yield: 6–8 servings

When I decided to create a whole-grain version of focaccia, help arrived in the form of Carmela D'Lia, who had been making this kind of bread in the Bronx for decades. So off I went to discover her secrets, and this recipe was born. This focaccia is versatile enough to make a perfect addition to lunch boxes, family dinners, and parties too. The dough is unique—buttery and delicate on the inside, and crunchy on the outside.

DOUGH

2½ tablespoons extra-virgin olive oil, for oiling the pan, plus ¼ cup plus 1 tablespoon

2 tablespoons or 2 packages active dry yeast (½ ounce)

1½ cups plus 2 tablespoons lukewarm pure water (105°F/40°C)

3¼ cups unbleached bread flour or all-purpose flour, plus 1–3 tablespoons for rolling the dough

¾ cup whole-wheat flour

1½ teaspoons sea salt

OTHER COMPONENTS

12–13 large cloves garlic, peeled and quartered

2 tablespoons extra-virgin olive oil

½ teaspoon dried basil

½ teaspoon dried parsley

¼ teaspoon dried oregano

¼ teaspoon sea salt

1. Lightly oil a 10 x 15-inch baking pan with 2½ tablespoons olive oil. Set aside. Cover a wire rack with paper towels and set aside.

2. To prepare the dough, in a small bowl, combine the yeast and water. Stir together until well blended and set aside in a warm place for 10 minutes, or until slightly foamy.

3. In a large bowl, combine the 3¼ cups unbleached bread flour, ¾ cup whole-wheat flour, and sea salt. Whisk together until well mixed. Make a well in the center, and pour in the yeast mixture and remaining oil (¼ cup at a time). Starting from the center, stir with your hand until all the flour is incorporated into the dough.

4. Turn the dough out onto a slightly floured surface, and knead (using the heel of your hand) for about 8–10 minutes, or until the dough is pliable and elastic. Sprinkle a little flour as necessary to keep the dough from sticking to the surface. You should now have a soft, workable dough.

5. Place the dough into a lightly oiled medium bowl, turning it once so the surface is coated with oil. Cover the bowl with a kitchen towel, and let the dough rise in a warm place until it has doubled in bulk, about 1 hour.

6. Transfer the sticky, elastic dough to the prepared baking pan and stretch outward to cover as much of the bottom as possible. Cover the pan with a kitchen towel, and let the dough rise in a warm place until well puffed, about 45–55 minutes. Preheat the oven to 425°F.

7. Dimple the top all over vigorously with your index fingers. Press the garlic cloves about 1 inch into the dough (½ to 1 inch apart). Drizzle on the 2 tablespoons olive oil so that it will collect in pools on top of the dough. Evenly sprinkle with the basil, parsley, oregano, and salt.

8. Bake the focaccia on the lowest oven rack, for 35–40 minutes or until the crust is golden. For uniformity in baking, rotate the pan from front to back halfway through the baking period. The focaccia is done when the center springs back when touched, or a tester inserted in the center comes out clean. Remove the focaccia from the oven and immediately slide it out of the pan, placing it on the prepared paper towels to absorb any excess oil. Use cookie cutters to shape or a sharp knife to slice into pieces while still hot.

9. Serve hot or at room temperature, dipped in extra-virgin olive oil, soup, salad, or a vegetable or legume dish. You can also use this as sandwich bread.

NOTES

■ A KitchenAid electric mixer is always a good investment and makes steps 3 and 4 easy. Pour the flour mixture into the bowl and use the paddle attachment to combine the flour mixture, yeast mixture, and oil. Mix at speed #2 for 1 minute to distribute all the ingredients. Replace the paddle attachment with the dough hook, increase the mixture speed to #4, and knead the dough for 2–3 minutes, or until elastic and soft (the dough will pull completely away from the sides and bottom of the bowl; sprinkle additional flour as needed). If you do not have a heavy-duty electric mixer, a food processor can be used.

■ For those sensitive to wheat, an equal measure of spelt flour can be used to replace the unbleached white and whole-wheat flours.

■ I often make animal-shaped focaccia or pizzas as party fare. Use cookie cutters to press the baked focaccia into desired shapes. To make pizzas, spread with Joe's Marinara Sauce (page 166), sprinkle with grated Mozzarella-style nondairy cheese, and bake in a preheated 450°F oven for 8–10 minutes or until the cheese is melted.

■ For variety and crunch, add sunflower, sesame, poppy, or flaxseeds to the dough during the kneading process.

■ For some interesting foccacia sandwiches try: sautéed peppers, mushrooms, and onions with sun-dried tomato pesto; avocado, tomato, and sprouts, with basil vegan mayonnaise; white bean spread, roasted yellow peppers, sun-dried tomatoes, olives, fresh basil, and arugula; or simmered balsamic-marinated-tofu, tomatoes, and eggplant with fresh basil.

Cheese Panini with Salad Greens

Preparation time: 10 minutes

Yield: 4 sandwiches

Here's a way to take sandwich making to its highest level. Use the freshest possible ingredients, and make your sandwiches simple or complex, depending on your mood and your family's tastes. So have fun making this many different ways.

4 round rolls (5 inches in diameter), or 8 slices crusty whole-grain country bread

4 tablespoons extra-virgin olive oil

1½ tablespoons balsamic vinegar

12–16 oil-cured black olives, pitted and halved

16 large basil leaves, rolled and thinly sliced

1 large vine-ripened tomato, thinly sliced

8 ounces thinly sliced Mozzarella-style nondairy cheese

Sea salt to taste

Freshly ground black pepper to taste

4 small handfuls mixed baby lettuce leaves

For each sandwich, lightly brush bread with olive oil and vinegar. Arrange the olives, basil, tomato, and cheese on the bread. Season with salt and pepper. Top with lettuce leaves, cover with remaining bread, and press down lightly. Cut in halves or quarters, wrap tightly, and refrigerate until needed.

NOTES

- For those sensitive to wheat—rye, rice, and millet breads can be purchased in health food stores.
- The olive oil can be replaced by an equal measure of basil-flavored olive oil, pesto (sun-dried tomato or black olive), or egg-free mayonnaise.

Cinnamon Croutons

Preparation time: 5 minutes to prepare, 12–14 minutes to bake

Yield: 1 cup

These sweet, crunchy croutons taste a bit like cinnamon graham crackers. They are great for snacking, or as an accompaniment to sweet creamy soups or fruity salads.

1 cup cut-up whole-grain country or French bread, cut into ¼-inch cubes (about 2 slices)

1 tablespoon pure maple syrup

¼ teaspoon ground cinnamon

1. Preheat the oven to 425°F. Line an 11 x 15-inch cookie sheet with parchment paper and set aside.

2. In a medium mixing bowl, toss together the bread, maple syrup, and cinnamon until the cubes are well coated. Evenly spread the seasoned cubes on the prepared cookie sheet and bake in the preheated oven for 12–14 minutes, or until golden. Remove the sheet from the oven and cool the croutons completely.

NOTE

■ Although day-old bread will produce the crunchiest croutons, fresh bread can be used (it will require additional baking time). For those sensitive to wheat—millet and rice breads can be purchased in health food stores.

Croutons Deluxe

Preparation time: 5 minutes to prepare, 10–12 minutes to bake

Yield: 4 servings

These kid-pleasing croutons are a mouthful of garlic and crunch. They started out as part of my Little Caesar Salad (page 144), but made the jump into the snack section because of their popularity as munching foods. Do bake at least a few batches because they should disappear quickly.

2 cups cut-up whole-grain country or French bread, cut into ¾-inch cubes

2 tablespoons extra-virgin olive oil

2 large cloves garlic, peeled and pressed

1 teaspoon dried basil

1 teaspoon dried parsley

A pinch of sea salt to taste

1. Preheat the oven to 425°F. Line an 11 x 15-inch cookie sheet with parchment paper and set aside.

2. In a medium mixing bowl, toss together the bread, oil, garlic, basil, parsley, and salt until the cubes are well coated. Evenly spread the seasoned cubes on the prepared cookie sheet and bake in the preheated oven for

10–12 minutes, or until golden. For uniformity in baking, rotate the sheet from front to back halfway through the baking period. Remove the sheet from the oven and cool the croutons completely.

NOTE

■ **Although day-old bread will produce the crunchiest croutons, fresh bread can be used (it will require additional baking time). For those sensitive to wheat, millet and rice breads can be purchased in health food stores.**

Eggless Egg Salad

Preparation time: 10 minutes
Yield: 4 servings

Egg salad, the all-American favorite, has a new twist—no eggs. Try this tofu and veggie combo for a healthful spread that's completely delicious and completely cholesterol free.

About 2 quarts pure water
1 pound firm tofu, cut into 1-inch cubes
½ cup Nayonaise or eggless mayonnaise
1 tablespoon dehydrated minced onion (optional)
1 tablespoon finely chopped parsley
1½ teaspoons honey
1½ teaspoons Dijon mustard
1 teaspoon finely chopped dill
½ teaspoon sea salt
½ teaspoon ground turmeric
¼ teaspoon curry powder
¼ teaspoon apple cider vinegar
⅛ teaspoon freshly ground black pepper
¼ cup finely chopped celery

1. To blanch the tofu, in a large pot, bring the water to a rolling boil. Stir in the tofu and cook for 4–5 minutes or until firm. Strain the tofu from the water and plunge into a medium bowl of ice water for 2 minutes or until completely chilled. Drain thoroughly (squeeze out any excess liquid) and set aside.

2. In a food processor, using the metal blade, combine the Nayonaise, onion, parsley, honey, mustard, dill, salt, turmeric, curry powder, vinegar, and black pepper. Process for 30 seconds or until well combined. Add the tofu

and celery and process for 5 seconds or until the texture is egg-like. Remove the blade, and use a rubber spatula to scrape off any excess filling remaining on the blade or processor.

3. Serve accompanied by crackers, veggie sticks, or rice cakes, or sandwiched with bread.

NOTE

- **For people who like sunflower seeds, throw a handful in with the celery.**

"Gimme-More" Garlic Bread

Preparation time: 8–10 minutes to prepare, 7–10 minutes to bake
Yield: 4 servings

Having them eat garlic is an excellent way to boost your little ones' immune systems. And I cannot think of a better way to get this important food into children than in the form of that all-time favorite, garlic bread. Every time I make this my kids say the same thing: "Gimme more garlic bread, please." This bread does a real quick disappearing act, so you might want to serve the rest of the meal first.

1 loaf Italian bread
⅓ cup extra-virgin olive oil
1 large head garlic, peeled and coarsely chopped
¼ teaspoon sea salt (optional)

1. Preheat the oven to 350°F.

2. Using a large sharp knife, cut the bread in half lengthwise and scrape the inside lightly with a fork (this will allow for some additional indented surface area for the garlic to adhere to). Brush the indented surface with about ¼ cup of the oil. In a small bowl toss together the remaining oil, the garlic, and the salt until well combined. Using a small spoon, evenly spread the garlic mixture on the bread and place on a cookie sheet.

3. Bake in the preheated oven for 7–10 minutes or until hot and just golden. Remove the sheets from the oven, transfer the bread to a cutting board, and cut into 2-inch slices.

4. Serve immediately as a snack food or as an accompaniment to almost any meal.

■ For those sensitive to wheat, many spelt and other whole-grain Italian and French breads can be found in natural foods stores and bakeries.

■ This bread can be baked in a toaster oven. (You will need to cut the loaf in half widthwise so it will fit).

Golden Pumpkin-Seed Corn Bread

Preparation time: 10 minutes to prepare, 40–45 minutes to bake
Yield: 6–9 servings

Remember that boxed corn bread mix your mother used? Well, this is not only healthier, it tastes better too! It's golden yellow, slightly sweet, filled with fresh red peppers, and topped with roasted pumpkin seeds. Who can resist down-home, feel-good food?

1¼ cups cornmeal
1¼ cups spelt flour
4 tablespoons maple sugar
1 tablespoon baking powder
1½ teaspoons sea salt
1¼ cups soy milk
¾ cup well-mashed ripe banana
⅓ cup Spectrum Spread
⅓ cup diced red bell pepper
1 tablespoon finely diced jalepeño pepper
¼ cup roasted pumpkin seeds (optional)

1. Preheat the oven to 375°F. Oil and lightly flour a 10½-inch skillet. Set aside.

2. In a medium mixing bowl, sift together the cornmeal, flour, maple sugar, baking powder, and salt. Whisk together until well mixed. Set aside.

3. In another medium mixing bowl, combine the milk, banana, and Spectrum Spread. Whisk together until well blended.

4. With a rubber spatula, gradually add the wet ingredients to the dry, making sure they are well blended before each addition. Scrape off any excess batter from the side of the bowl. Stir in the peppers until well combined.

5. Pour the batter into the prepared skillet and distribute evenly. Sprinkle with the pumpkin seeds and bake in the middle level of the preheated oven for 40–45 minutes. For uniformity in baking, rotate the pan from front to back halfway through the baking period.

6. The corn bread is done when the center springs back when touched, or a tester inserted in the center comes out clean (the corn bread will be golden brown). Remove the corn bread from the oven and let cool for 5 minutes.

7. Serve hot or at room temperature, on its own or accompanied by apple butter, chili, baked beans, or a hearty soup.

NOTE
- **For those sensitive to spelt, an equal measure of Lundberg brand brown rice flour can be used.**

Good-Time Guacamole

Preparation time: 5–10 minutes
Yield: 4–6 servings

Whenever we go to Mexican restaurants my children eat the entire bowl of guacamole before the food even gets to the table! This mild version can be prepared smooth or chunky and is terrific on its own as a snack food or as part of the main meal, served with fajitas, burritos, or tacos.

3 medium Haas avocados, peeled, pitted, and quartered
2 tablespoons freshly squeezed lime juice
¼ teaspoon sea salt
3 tablespoons finely chopped tomato
One 8-ounce package mini baked corn or tortilla chips

1. In a medium mixing bowl, combine the avocados, lime juice, and salt. Use the back of a fork to mash the mixture together until chunky. Use a spatula to incorporate the tomato until well combined.

2. Spoon about ¼ cup of the guacamole into each of 4 small serving bowls. Place the bowls in the center of 4 plates and surround each with chips for dipping.

3. Serve at room temperature or chilled.

■ **Try adding these to the portions designated for the adults: a dash of cayenne pepper, 2 large cloves garlic (peeled and finely chopped), 2 teaspoons finely chopped cilantro, and ½ teaspoon finely chopped jalepeño peppers.**

Herbed Breadsticks

Preparation time: 10–15 minutes, 12–15 minutes to bake
Yield: 5 dozen breadsticks

For kids parties and special occasions—finger foods are always a big hit. I often make these golden delights for kids and adults alike, who love to crunch and munch on them.

1 tablespoon onion powder
1 tablespoon garlic powder
1 tablespoon dried basil
2 teaspoons dried savory
2 teaspoons dried marjoram
2 teaspoons sea salt
½ teaspoon dried oregano
Whole-Grain Pizza Dough (page 183, but shape into 2 flat rounds, not 4)
6 tablespoons extra-virgin olive oil

1. Preheat the oven to 450°F. Line two 11 x 15-inch cookie sheets with parchment paper.

2. In a small bowl, combine the onion powder, garlic powder, basil, savory, marjoram, salt, and oregano. Stir together until well mixed and set aside.

3. Roll out 1 dough round to a thickness of ⅛ inch, and shape into a rectangle. Brush the dough with the olive oil and sprinkle on half of the prepared spices. Gently press the herbs into the dough. Using a pizza wheel or long knife, cut the dough into long strips ⅛ inch wide. Pick up a strip, then fold it in half (herb-sides-in). Holding each end, twist the dough 3 or 4 times and then transfer it to the prepared baking sheet. Repeat with the remaining strips. Repeat the process with the second dough round to prepare the remaining breadsticks.

4. Bake the breadsticks on the upper and middle racks of the preheated oven for 12–15 minutes. For uniformity in baking, rotate the sheets from top to bottom and front to back halfway through the baking period. The breadsticks are done when golden in color. Remove the sheets from the oven and let the breadsticks cool for

10 minutes on the sheets; then, using an angled metal spatula or pancake turner, transfer them to a wire rack until completely cool.

5. Serve at dinner or snack times.

NOTES

- **For variety add sesame, caraway, or poppy seeds to the herbs.**
- **For plain breadsticks, brush with a little olive oil and omit the herbs.**

Home-Grown Tomato Sandwiches

Preparation time: 5–10 minutes
Yield: 4 sandwiches

People think of summertime, and what comes to mind? Grillin' outside, with burgers and hot dogs. Well, here's my favorite vegetarian spin on a quick and easy summer lunch. Organic beefsteak tomatoes, avocados, sprouts, fresh basil, and extra-virgin olive oil on toasted whole-grain bread.

2 medium Haas avocados, peeled, seeded, and quartered
2 tablespoons extra-virgin olive oil, or 6 tablespoons Nayonaise, plus 3–4 tablespoons extra-virgin olive oil, for brushing the bread
1 baguette, sliced into four 5-inch-wide sections, cut ¾ of the way through lengthwise, with the insides scraped lightly with a fork to remove a little dough
Herbamare seasoning salt to taste
Freshly ground black pepper to taste (optional)
One 14-ounce vine-ripened tomato, sliced ¼ inch thick
16 large basil leaves, stacked, rolled, and sliced into ribbons
3½ ounces alfalfa, broccoli, or clover sprouts

1. In a medium mixing bowl, combine the avocados and 2 tablespoons oil. Use the back of a fork to mash the mixture together until chunky. Set aside.

2. For each sandwich, lightly brush the bread with the remaining olive oil and toast for 4–5 minutes or until just the edges are golden. Spoon a fourth of the guacamole into each sub. Season with Herbamare and pepper. Top with tomato, basil, and sprouts, and cover with the bread. Press down lightly, cut in halves on the diagonal, and serve.

■ For those sensitive to wheat—rye, rice, and millet breads can be purchased in health food stores.
■ For FAKIN' BACON BLT'S the guacamole can be replaced with one 6-ounce package Fakin' Bacon (toasted until golden) and Nayonaise to taste. Layer each sandwich with 2 lettuce leaves.

Honey Crunch Granola Bars

Preparation time: 10 minutes to prepare, 25–30 minutes to bake
Yield: 16 bars

These bars make wholesome breakfast treats, lunch box stuffers, pick-me-up snacks, or desserts. If Pooh knew about these, he would have his paw in the cookie jar, since bears love the sweet smell of honey.

3 tablespoons almonds
2 tablespoons peanuts
1 tablespoon soy lecithin
1½ cups rolled oats
2 tablespoons maple sugar
¼ teaspoon sea salt
¼ teaspoon ground cinnamon
¼ teaspoon baking soda
3 tablespoons canola oil
3 tablespoons honey
1 tablespoon pure maple syrup

1. Preheat the oven to 325°F. Line an 11 x 15-inch cookie sheet with parchment paper, and set aside.

2. Using a mini food processor or coffee grinder, process the almonds, peanuts, and lecithin until powder-fine. Transfer to a medium mixing bowl and stir in the oats, maple sugar, salt, cinnamon, and baking soda until well combined. Set aside.

3. In a food processor, using the metal blade, combine the oil, honey, and maple syrup. Process until well blended, about 30 seconds. Add the dry ingredients and process until well combined. Set aside.

4. Cut an 8 x 8-inch square of parchment paper. Lay the paper on a cutting board and use it as a template to shape the dough. Pat out the dough to an 8 x 8-inch square with a thickness of ¼ inch (lightly oiling your hands will help). Score the dough into 8 strips lengthwise (each about 1 inch wide) and then crosswise into 2 strips (about 4 inches wide). Cut the dough through the scored lines. Use an angled metal spatula or pancake turner to place the dough bars 1 inch apart on the prepared cookie sheet.

5. Bake on the middle rack of the preheated oven for 25–30 minutes. For uniformity in baking, rotate the sheet from front to back halfway through the baking period. The bars are done when golden and firm. Remove the sheet from the oven and let the bars cool for 10 minutes on the sheet; then, using an angled metal spatula or pancake turner, transfer them to a wire rack until completely cool.

6. Serve with a glass of rice milk, soy milk, or nut milk.

NOTE

■ For those sensitive to peanuts, an equal measure of almonds can be used to replace the peanuts.

Hoppin' Frog Mix

Preparation time: 5 minutes
Yield: 4 servings

Animal crackers are one thing kids love. And the next three ingredients are three more things! Mix 'em all together, and you'll have some contented kids.

1 cup animal crackers
1 cup toasted whole-grain cold oat cereal (O-shaped)
1 cup mini rice cakes
½ cup dried, pitted sweet cherries, raisins, or dried bananas (cut into 1-inch pieces)

1. In a large mixing bowl, toss together the animal crackers, oat cereal, mini rice cakes, and cherries until well combined.

2. Pack into plastic bags and serve in lunch boxes or as party fare.

NOTE

■ Sugar-free animal crackers, toasted whole grain O-shaped oat cereals, and mini rice cakes can be purchased in most health food stores.

Lunchtime Hummus Sandwiches

Preparation time: 10 minutes

Yield: 4 sandwiches

These sandwiches really hit the spot, but if you're not in a sandwich-eating mood, try hummus with crackers or veggie sticks. Since hummus can be stored in the refrigerator for 4–5 days, it's ideal for those times when you need to make lunch in a hurry.

4 round rolls (5 inches in diameter), or 8 slices crusty, whole-grain country bread

1 cup hummus

12–16 oil-cured black olives, pitted and halved

1 large vine-ripened tomato, thinly sliced

4 green leaves Boston (butter) lettuce

Spread 4 slices of bread with the hummus. Top with olives, tomato, and lettuce. Cover with remaining bread and press down lightly. Cut in halves or quarters, and serve.

NOTES

- For those sensitive to wheat—rye, rice, and millet breads can be purchased in health food stores.
- For a good hummus recipe, see Main Course Hummus Plates (page 167).

Ma-Cheezmo Nachos

Preparation time: 5–10 minutes to prepare, 5 minutes to bake

Yield: 4 servings

When your family is ready for a major munchy experience, try this recipe. It's easy, fun, and nourishing. What more could you want from a snack?

4 cups baked tortilla chips

2 cups grated mild Cheddar-style nondairy cheese (about 8 ounces)

½ cup julienned romaine lettuce

½ cup finely chopped tomato

½ cup mild salsa (optional)

1. Preheat oven to 425°F. Line an 11 x 15-inch cookie sheet with parchment paper.

2. Distribute the chips in the center of the prepared cookie sheet and evenly sprinkle on the cheese. Bake on the upper rack of the preheated oven for 5 minutes or until the cheese is melted. Remove the sheet from the oven and, using a pancake turner, slide the nachos onto a serving platter. Serve hot topped with lettuce, tomato, and salsa.

NOTE

■ There are many organic mild-flavored salsas on the market, but for a homemade taste, see Sun-Sational Salsa (page 126).

Native Maize Trail Mix

Preparation time: 5 minutes
Yield: 4 servings

This crunchy, nutty snack mix is easy to prepare and versatile. Its indigenous North American ingredients make it perfect to serve before Thanksgiving dinner or as party fare.

⅔ cup sunflower seeds
⅔ cup pumpkin seeds
1⅓ cups Glad Corn Original A-Maizing Corn Snack

1. In a large mixing bowl, toss together the seeds and Glad Corn until well combined.

2. Pack into plastic bags and serve in lunch boxes or as party fare.

NOTES

■ I often roast the seeds by placing them on a cookie sheet in a preheated 375°F oven for 8–10 minutes or until golden. Remove from the oven and cool before continuing with the recipe.

■ Glad Corn is a healthy and delicious snack that I first discovered in a Texas natural foods store. It comes from a family-run company in Minnesota and is definitely worth trying. To order: Call (507) 427-2631 or write to G.E.F. Inc., Route 1, Box 91, Mount Lake, MN 56159.

■ For another recipe option, toss together ½ cup of each of the following: sunflower seeds, pumpkin seeds, dairy-free carob chips, and raisins.

Nightly Nut Mix

Preparation time: 5 minutes
Yield: 4 servings

Kids love dried fruit and nuts. This nutritious snack food is easy to prepare and perfect for munching at any time.

½ **cup dried sweet cherries or raisins**
¼ **cup raw cashews**
¼ **cup almonds**
¼ **cup pecans**
¼ **cup macadamia nuts or walnuts**

1. In a large mixing bowl, toss together the cherries, cashews, almonds, pecans, and macadamia nuts until well combined.

2. Pack into plastic bags and serve in lunch boxes or as party fare.

NOTE

■ **I often roast the nuts by placing them on a cookie sheet in a preheated 375°F oven for 10–15 minutes or until they have a roasted aroma. Let cool and continue with the recipe.**

Noah's Nuttyjam Jamborees

Preparation time: 5–10 minutes
Yield: 4 sandwiches

My son loved nut butter and jam sandwiches so much that he requested they be put in his lunch box for what seemed like years. Actually, it was years! Anyway, I decided to make the most of this sandwich romance by creating a different combination for every day. Maybe you have a child who is a peanut butter and jelly lover. If so, here are ideas for adding nutritional variety—and some yummy new flavors—to your child's sandwich plate.

8 **slices whole-grain bread (whole wheat, spelt, rice, millet, rye, or multigrain)**
½ **cup peanut, almond, cashew, sunflower, pistachio, or sesame butter**
½ **cup grape, strawberry, raspberry, boysenberry, or apricot jam, or honey**

To assemble the sandwiches, spread each of 4 slices of bread with about 2 tablespoons of nut butter, followed by 2 tablespoons of jam. Cover with the remaining bread slices and press down lightly. Cut in halves or quarters, wrap tightly, and refrigerate until needed.

NOTES

■ These combinations work especially well: cashew butter and raspberry jam on whole-wheat bread; peanut butter and grape jelly on spelt bread; almond butter and strawberry jam on rice bread; sesame tahini and apricot jam on millet bread; sunflower butter and boysenberry jam on rye bread; pistachio butter and honey on multigrain bread.

■ I often sprinkle a teaspoon or two of sunflower, pumpkin, sesame, or flaxseeds on top of the jam before sealing and slicing the sandwich.

■ Cookie cutters can be used to press sandwiches into fun shapes for exciting lunches or as interesting party fare.

"No-Cheat Chi-Enhancer" Treats

Preparation time: 5 minutes to prepare, 30 seconds to cook
Yield: 9 bars

This is for all you chocolaty-rich, gooey-caramel, creamy-peanut-butter-crunch-loving sinners. Check this out—it's vegan, sweetened with brown rice syrup (so the sugar enters the bloodstream slowly), and made with carob (no caffeine here). We've got a 100 percent bona-fide guilt-free deal goin' on, so go for it! Who ever said you can't be super-healthy, energetic, abundant with chi, and still have fun?!

5 cups unsalted crispy brown rice cereal
1 cup brown rice syrup
½ cup peanut butter, cashew butter, or almond butter
1 tablespoon pure vanilla flavor
½ teaspoon sea salt
½ cup dairy-free carob chips (optional)

1. Lightly oil an 8 x 8-inch baking pan and set aside. Pour the rice cereal into a medium mixing bowl and set aside.

2. In a small saucepan, bring the rice syrup and peanut butter to a rolling boil over moderate to high heat and stir constantly for 30 seconds. Remove from the heat and stir in the vanilla and salt until well blended. Pour the peanut butter mixture over the rice cereal and stir together until well combined.

3. Scrape half of the cereal mixture into the prepared pan and pat it to the edges, using a rubber spatula to coat the bottom evenly. Sprinkle on the chips, then top with the remaining cereal. Set aside to cool for 2 minutes; then pat and press down firmly. When completely cool, use a sharp knife and cut lengthwise into 3 strips, then crosswise into 3 strips. Use an angled metal spatula or pancake turner to dislodge the sides and remove bars from the pan.

4. Serve alone or with a glass of rice milk, soy milk, or nut milk.

NOTE
■ **An equal measure of toasted peanuts, almonds, sunflower seeds, or pumpkin seeds can be used to replace the carob chips. Flaked coconut or chopped, dried bananas or figs can also be used.**

Peanutty Neato Burritos

Preparation time: 5–10 minutes
Yield: 8 burritos

Children love to put together and eat these nutritious burritos. They make great lunch box or party fare because they've got 3 ingredients kids love—peanut butter, honey, and bananas.

1 cup peanut butter or almond butter
3 tablespoons honey
8 whole-wheat or corn tortillas
2 large bananas, thinly sliced
3 tablespoons sesame seeds (optional)

1. In a small bowl, cream together the peanut butter and honey until well combined.

2. To warm the tortillas, lightly oil and preheat a large cast-iron frying pan or griddle over moderate to high heat until a few drops of water sprinkled into the pan sizzle and bounce. Place the tortillas in the skillet, cover, and soften them for 1–2 minutes (do not crisp). Transfer tortillas to a flat surface.

3. To assemble the burritos, spread each tortilla equally with the nut butter mixture (leave a ½-inch edge free of mixture), top with the banana slices, and sprinkle with the sesame seeds. Roll up the tortillas, wrapping tightly, and serve or refrigerate for up to 2 days.

- An equal measure of finely chopped peanuts or almonds can be used to replace the sesame seeds.
- For variety, sprinkle each tortilla with 1–2 teaspoons of flaked coconut and a dusting of carob powder and cinnamon.

Perfect Party Popcorn Balls

Preparation time: 9–10 minutes
Yield: 16 balls

I originally thought of this recipe for parties, but these cool-looking finger-size popcorn treats turned out to be something much more. If you make a batch of these not-too-sweet protein-rich snacks, your kids will reap the benefits.

1 tablespoon peanut oil
¼ cup popping corn
½ cup brown rice syrup
¼ cup smooth or crunchy peanut butter, almond butter, or cashew butter
¼ teaspoon sea salt

1. In a large pot, combine the oil and popping corn. Cook covered over moderate to high heat for 5–7 minutes, or until the corn begins to pop. Using pot holders, lift the pot about 2 inches above the stove's flame, rotating or shaking it in a circular motion (this will prevent burning), and continue cooking until all of the corn is popped, about 1–2 minutes. Transfer to a large mixing bowl and set aside.

2. In a small saucepan, bring the rice syrup and peanut butter to a rolling boil over moderate to high heat and stir constantly for 30 seconds. Remove from the heat and stir in the salt until well blended. Pour the peanut butter mixture over the popcorn and stir together until well combined.

3. With your hands, shape the popcorn mixture into 2-inch balls (oil your hands slightly to prevent sticking). Set the popcorn balls onto a lightly oiled wire rack until completely cool.

NOTES
- Six cups air-popped or prepopped corn can be substituted for the fresh. Make sure to remove any unpopped kernels.
- A variation on this recipe, CRUNCHY SESAME POPCORN BALLS, is calcium rich and can be prepared by using ¼ cup sesame tahini to replace the peanut butter. After shaping the balls, roll them in 3 tablespoons sesame seeds.

Pigs in Blankets

Preparation time: 20 minutes to prepare, 60 minutes to rise, 15–20 minutes to bake
Yield: 4 servings

Kids love hot dogs, and these come in special little crispy dough packages. They're party perfect, but serve them anytime, because they're the good-for-you kind of hot dogs.

¼ recipe Carmela's Authentic Focaccia dough; follows steps 1–4 only (page 106)
1 package Yves Veggie Wieners, with each weiner cut into 2¼-inch cross sections

1. Line an 11 x 15-inch cookie sheet with parchment paper and set aside.

2. Using a rolling pin, roll out the dough to a thickness of ¼ inch and into a 12-inch circle. To do this, use even strokes and work from the center of the dough cake toward the edges, rolling in different directions. Using a 2-inch circular cookie cutter, cut the dough into 12 circles. Place the weiners in the center of each dough circle. To seal the pigs in their blankets, fold the uncovered portions over the weiners, gently stretching them to cover the weiners completely, forming half-circles. Firmly press and crimp the edges together to seal securely. Evenly distribute the weiners, crimp-side-down, onto the prepared sheet. Cover the weiners with a kitchen towel, and let the dough rise in a warm place for 60 minutes or until well puffed.

3. Bake on the middle rack of a preheated 425°F oven for 15–20 minutes or until the crusts are golden and crisp. For uniformity in baking, rotate the sheet from front to back halfway through the baking period. Remove the sheet from the oven and let the pigs in blankets cool for 5 minutes on the sheet; then, using an angled metal spatula or pancake turner, transfer them to a serving platter.

4. Serve warm, accompanied by a dish of ketchup or mustard.

NOTES
- Remember, when preparing Carmela's Authentic Focaccia dough, follow steps 1–4 only.
- If you are running short of time, omit the focaccia dough altogether and make **Pigs on Sticks**. Slice each weiner into ½-inch cross sections, spear with a small stick pretzel, arrange on a cookie sheet, and bake in a preheated 375°F oven for 5–6 minutes or until warm.

Seemingly Sinful Sour Cream

Preparation time: 10 minutes

Yield: 4–8 servings

This sour cream seems sinful because it's filled with the characteristic richness of full-fat, dairy sour cream. We have, however, used silken tofu and a small amount of extra-virgin olive oil in just the right proportions to obtain this creamy, delicious alternative.

1 pound silken tofu, well drained

3 tablespoons extra-virgin olive oil

1 tablespoon plus 1 teaspoon freshly squeezed lemon juice

1 tablespoon umeboshi plum paste (see Notes page 144)

1 teaspoon finely chopped chives

¾ teaspoon sea salt

¼ teaspoon garlic powder

¼ teaspoon celery root powder

1. In a food processor, using the metal blade, combine the tofu and oil. Process until creamy, about 1 minute. Pour in the lemon juice, plum paste, chives, salt, garlic powder, and celery root powder. Process until well blended.

2. Serve with julienned vegetables, crackers, chips, toasted bread, or baked potatoes.

NOTES

■ For Herbed Sour Cream, add 1 tablespoon finely chopped cilantro, dill, or parsley.

■ I like to present this dip in a round loaf of crusty whole-grain country bread as party fare. Using a serrated knife, slice 1 inch from the top of the loaf (cut this piece into 1 x 3-inch pieces and toast for dipping), remove about 2½ cups of dough from the center portion of the loaf, creating a hollow space, and fill with dip. Slice removed dough into 1 x 3-inch pieces and toast for dipping.

Sun-Sational Salsa

Preparation time: 5–10 minutes

Yield: 4 servings

Northern California has some of the best restaurants in the country. One reason is that they use organically grown produce from local farms. On my last trip there, I had the pleasure of visiting numerous organic farms and sampling their fine fruits and vegetables. I also enjoyed some of the great restaurant fare. This recipe was inspired by a salsa I had at a local eatery in Carmel.

1 large ripe tomato, peeled, seeded, and finely chopped

1 tablespoon finely chopped red onion

2 tablespoons finely chopped yellow bell pepper

½ teaspoon finely chopped fresh garlic

1 teaspoon finely chopped fresh parsley

1 teaspoon freshly squeezed lemon juice

½ teaspoon apple cider vinegar

¼ teaspoon sea salt

⅛ teaspoon chili powder

1. In a medium bowl, toss together the tomato, onion, pepper, garlic, and parsley. In a 1-cup-capacity liquid measuring cup, stir together the lemon juice, apple cider vinegar, salt, and chili powder until well mixed. Drizzle over the tomato mixture and toss the salsa until well coated.

2. Serve immediately or chilled, with chips or as an accompaniment to fajitas, nachos, quesadillas, burritos, or tacos.

NOTE

■ **In the summer months when exotic varieties of tomatoes are available, I use yellow tomatoes instead of red ones, and red peppers to replace the yellow peppers.**

Tomato and Basil Crostini

Preparation time: 10 minutes to prepare, 15–20 minutes to bake
Yield: 20–24 crostini

Crostini are small golden toasts. Topped with creamy spreads, freshly chopped tomatoes and herbs, or melted cheese, they are great beginners to any meal, or quick anytime snacks.

2 large vine-ripened tomatoes, cored and diced (about 1¼ pounds)
2 cloves garlic, peeled and crushed
20 large fresh basil leaves, washed, patted dry, and thinly sliced
2 tablespoons extra-virgin olive oil, plus more for brushing the bread
2½ teaspoons balsamic vinegar
½ teaspoon sea salt
Freshly ground black pepper to taste
1 whole-grain baguette, sliced into ½-inch-thick bread rounds

1. Preheat the oven to 400°F.

2. In a medium mixing bowl, combine the tomatoes, garlic, and basil. Toss together until well combined. Drizzle on the 2 tablespoons olive oil and the vinegar, and sprinkle on the salt and pepper. Stir together until well blended and set aside.

3. Lightly brush both sides of the bread rounds with a little olive oil. Evenly distribute them on an 11 x 15-inch baking sheet. Bake on the top rack of the preheated oven for 15–20 minutes, or until crisp and golden. Remove the sheet from the oven; then, using an angled metal spatula or pancake turner, transfer the toasted rounds to a wire rack until cool enough to handle.

4. Use a small spoon to top each round with 2 teaspoons of the prepared tomato mixture and serve immediately. (Drizzle any leftover tomato juices on top of the crostini.)

NOTES
■ **For variety, forgo the tomato-basil option and try these golden toasts topped with hummus, scrambled tofu, sautéed peppers and onions or mushrooms, bean dip, melted soy cheese, or any variety of pesto.**
■ **For those sensitive to wheat—rye, rice, and millet breads can be purchased in health food stores. Use cookie cutters to press into rounds or decorative shapes, then bake as directed.**

CHAPTER 9

SOUPS

Denise's Mediterranean Bean Soup

Preparation time: 10 minutes to prepare, 40–50 minutes to cook

Yield: 4 servings

Denise Barbara is a fantastic cook who prepares the most delicious meals for her family every day. I was moved by the tender love and care she put into her cooking. She often makes this wonderful soup for her grandchildren, who eat every drop! It's light but satisfying, centered around beans, and a takeoff on the fresh vegetable or pistou soup so popular in the French Mediterranean region.

2 cups chopped yellow onions

4 large cloves garlic, peeled and coarsely chopped

3 tablespoons extra-virgin olive oil

2 cups peeled, seeded, and finely chopped ripe tomatoes

1 cup white beans, soaked overnight, rinsed, and drained

1 sprig fresh sage, or ¼ teaspoon dried

4 cups pure water

1½ teaspoons sea salt

⅓ cup packed, thinly sliced fresh basil leaves

¼ cup finely chopped fresh parsley

1. In a 4-quart or larger pressure cooker, sauté the onions and garlic in the oil over high heat until soft, about 3–4 minutes. Stir in the tomatoes, beans, sage, and water. Close the lid and bring the pressure to high. Reduce the heat to moderate to low, and cook for 25 minutes.

2. Remove from the heat and let sit for 5 minutes. Using a long-handled spoon, depress the valve on the pressure cooker lid and release the steam. Stir in the salt, basil, and parsley until well combined. Return to the heat and continue cooking uncovered for 5–10 additional minutes or until hot. Ladle into soup bowls and serve with a loaf of crusty, whole-grain bread and a mixed green salad.

NOTES

■ **Although dried beans provide a nicer flavor than canned ones do, if you have to, you can replace the dried soaked beans with 3 cups of canned beans. Decrease the water in the recipe to 3 cups. Then simmer covered in a large saucepan for 15 minutes.**

■ **I often throw in ¼ cup uncooked quinoa with the beans before pressure-cooking for a tasty bonus.**

Fresh Vegetable Stock

Preparation time: 5 minutes to prepare, 20–25 minutes to cook

Yield: 2 quarts

This is a basic vegetable stock designed to be quickly thrown together using ingredients already in your refrigerator. Store-bought bouillon cubes and mixes just do not provide the freshest possible building blocks necessary to prepare a homemade soup or main meal. Furthermore, it is often impossible to find one that both tastes good and is good for you.

2 small yellow onions, peeled and thinly sliced

2 small leeks, roughly chopped

4 cloves garlic, peeled and crushed

2 tablespoons extra-virgin olive oil

2 small carrots, scrubbed well and cut into thirds

1 medium potato, scrubbed well and thinly sliced

6 sprigs fresh parsley

2 large celery stalks, cut into 2-inch lengths

6 large mushrooms, quartered

2 bay leaves

10 fresh basil leaves, or ½ teaspoon dried basil

3 sprigs fresh savory, or ½ teaspoon dried winter savory

1 teaspoon sea salt

8 black peppercorns

2 quarts pure water

1. In a large pot, sauté together the onions, leeks, and garlic in the oil over moderate to high heat for 5 minutes. Stir in the carrots, potato, parsley, celery, mushrooms, bay leaves, basil, savory, salt, peppercorns, and water. Cover and bring to a boil over high heat. Reduce the heat to moderate, and simmer covered for 15–20 minutes.

2. Remove from the heat and strain the stock through a fine sieve (press as much liquid as possible from the vegetables and discard any solids). You can use now, refrigerate, or freeze the remaining stock.

NOTE

- **The recipe can easily be doubled and frozen in ice-cube trays or plastic containers for future use.**

Hearty Vegetable Lentil Soup

Preparation time: 10 minutes to prepare, 65–70 minutes to cook

Yield: 4 servings

My kids have decided this easy-to-make, great-tasting soup is their current favorite. A fine meal-base for a winter's day, this hearty vegetable soup is nutritionally complemented by the addition of legumes and whole grains.

1 small yellow onion, peeled and chopped

2 large cloves garlic, peeled and coarsely chopped

1 small celery stalk, diced

2 medium tomatoes, peeled, seeded, and finely chopped

3 tablespoons extra-virgin olive oil

4 quarts pure water

1 cup green lentils, rinsed and drained

¼ cup wild rice

1 small carrot, diced

1 small yellow squash, finely chopped

1 tablespoon finely chopped fresh parsley

1 teaspoon dried parsley

½ teaspoon dried basil

2 bay leaves

2 teaspoons sea salt

2½ cups packed, chopped spinach (about ¾ pound)

1. In a large pot, sauté the onion, garlic, celery, and tomatoes in the oil over moderate heat for 3–4 minutes or until the onion is translucent. Pour in the water, increase the heat to high, cover, and bring to a boil. Stir in the lentils, rice, carrot, squash, parsley, basil, bay leaves, and salt. Cook partially covered over moderate to high heat for 55–60 minutes, or until the rice is tender. Stir in the spinach, cover, and simmer for 5 additional minutes or until the spinach is tender.

2. Serve hot, alone, or accompanied by a loaf of crusty, whole-grain bread and a tossed green salad.

NOTE

■ An equal measure of long-grain brown, brown basmati, or brown texmati rice (American brown basmati) can be used to replace the wild rice.

Italian Red Lentil Soup

Preparation time: 10 minutes to prepare, 25–30 minutes to cook

Yield: 4 servings

Recently I needed a nutritious 1-pot dinner in a real hurry. I had only 30 minutes to pick my kids up from school and get to a play date with dinner for everyone. This delicious creamy soup was my solution! It took only 6 minutes to prepare in the pressure cooker, and was sufficiently nourishing to satisfy a small army of hungry children. Note that even if you cook this the traditional way, you only need a half hour.

¼ cup chopped yellow onion

2 large cloves garlic, peeled and finely chopped

2 tablespoons extra-virgin olive oil

6 cups pure water

¾ cup diced carrot

1 cup red lentils, rinsed and drained

2 teaspoons sea salt

2 tablespoons small pasta shapes (alphabet, stars, or rings)

2 tablespoons chopped parsley

1. In a large pot, sauté the onion and garlic in the oil over high heat for 3–4 minutes. When the onion becomes translucent, pour in the water, cover, and bring to a boil. Stir in the carrot, lentils, and salt. Simmer partially covered over moderate heat for 10 minutes. Stir in the pasta shapes and continue to cook an additional 10–15 minutes or until creamy. Remove from the heat and stir in the parsley until well combined.

2. Serve hot on its own or with a loaf of whole-grain bread and a salad.

NOTES

- For those sensitive to wheat, an equal measure of white basmati rice or white texmati rice (American white basmati) can be used in place of the pasta.
- This is a relatively speedy recipe; but to make it even faster—in 6 minutes—you can use a pressure cooker.

Magical Minestrone Soup

Preparation time: 10 minutes to prepare, 25–30 minutes to cook

Yield: 4–6 servings

For generations the making of minestrone soup has been a tradition in many Italian families. This lightly flavored tomato broth is laden with pasta and a cornucopia of fresh vegetables in every spoonful. Serve this soup with a crusty loaf of whole-grain bread and your family will be enjoying a dinner-table visit to the Mediterranean.

1 small yellow onion, peeled and diced

2 large cloves garlic, peeled and coarsely chopped

1 small celery stalk, diced

¼ cup chopped green cabbage

3 medium tomatoes, peeled, seeded, and finely chopped

3 tablespoons extra-virgin olive oil

2 tablespoons tomato paste

8 cups pure water

1 small carrot, diced

¾ cup fresh or frozen corn kernels

1 medium white potato, diced

¼ cup diced yellow squash

¾ cup chopped green beans

¼ cup small pasta shapes (alphabet, stars, or rings)

¼ cup chopped fresh parsley

1 teaspoon dried parsley

½ teaspoon dried basil

1 bay leaf

2½ teaspoons sea salt

1 cup cooked white beans (cannelini, navy, or great northern)

1. In a large pot, sauté the onion, garlic, celery, cabbage, and tomatoes in the oil over high heat for 4–5 minutes or until the onion is translucent. Using a wooden spoon, dissolve the tomato paste in the water until well combined. Add the water to the pot, cover, and bring to a boil. Stir in the carrot, corn, potato, squash, green beans, pasta, fresh and dried parsley, basil, bay leaf, and salt. Simmer partially covered over moderate heat for 15–20 minutes, or until the carrots are tender. Stir in the white beans, and cook for an additional 5 minutes.

2. Serve alone or garnished with a drizzle of extra-virgin olive oil and accompanied by a loaf of crusty, whole-grain bread and a tossed green salad.

- For those sensitive to wheat, an equal measure of white basmati rice or white texmati rice (American white basmati) can be used in place of the pasta.

Mellow Miso Soup

■▪▪▪

Preparation time: 5 minutes to prepare, 10 minutes to cook
Yield: 4 servings

This mild, nourishing broth with cubed tofu and sliced scallions is perfect for those times when comfort food is needed. It's a great vegan alternative to chicken soup and takes only minutes to prepare.

½ cup mellow white miso
6 cups pure water
¾ cup extra-firm tofu, cut into ½-inch cubes
2 tablespoons thinly sliced scallions

1. In a medium saucepan, dissolve the miso in the water using a wooden spoon or whisk. Stir in the tofu, then bring to a gentle simmer over low to moderate heat.

2. Spoon into bowls and serve garnished with scallions.

NOTES

- When heating, do not allow the soup to boil. Boiling diminishes the beneficial properties of the miso.
- For a great SEA VEGETABLE SOUP, sauté ½ medium yellow onion (thinly sliced) in 2 teaspoons canola oil until translucent. Add the water, 4 large shiitake mushrooms (sliced), and 1 medium carrot (chopped). Simmer for 10 minutes, then stir in the miso until completely dissolved. Add ½ ounce Laver (Wild Atlantic Nori) rinsed and coarsely chopped with the tofu. Bring to a gentle simmer, garnish with scallions, and serve.

Mushroom Barley Soup

Preparation time: 15 minutes to prepare, 50–55 minutes to cook

Yield: 4 servings

This memorable mushroom barley soup is delicious, simple to prepare, filling, and good for you too!

¾ cup pearled barley

8 cups pure water

3 tablespoons extra-virgin olive oil

3 large leeks, thinly sliced, then chopped, white parts only (about 1½ cups)

1 large yellow onion, peeled and chopped (about 1¼ cups)

1 pound mushrooms, thinly sliced

1 tablespoon finely chopped fresh dill

1½ teaspoons celery salt

1¼ teaspoons sea salt

¼ teaspoon freshly ground black pepper

2 tablespoons finely chopped parsley

1. To cook the barley, bring a small saucepan filled with 2 cups of pure water to a boil. Stir in the barley and simmer covered for 30–35 minutes or until tender. Set aside.

2. In a large pot, sauté the leeks, onion, and mushrooms in the oil over moderate heat for 7–8 minutes. When the onion becomes translucent, add the remaining 6 cups of pure water. Increase the heat to high, cover, and bring to a boil. Stir in the barley, dill, salts, and pepper. Simmer covered over moderate heat for 10 minutes. Remove from the heat and stir in the parsley.

3. Ladle into bowls and serve accompanied by a loaf of whole-grain bread and a salad.

NOTE

■ **For an immune-boosting soup try SHIITAKE MUSHROOM QUINOA SOUP. Replace the mushrooms with 21 ounces shiitake mushrooms (stems removed) and replace the barley with 2 cups cooked quinoa (page 37).**

New-Spin-on-Spinach Soup

Preparation time: 15 minutes to prepare, 35–40 minutes to cook

Yield: 4 servings

This hearty soup, flavored mildly with curry, is great for fall or winter days when kids need a warm, filling meal. It's one of my favorite recipes, and one that you can serve at parties or any large festive event where a winning recipe is needed.

1 cup chopped yellow onion

1 tablespoon extra-virgin olive oil

½ cup crushed canned tomatoes with their liquid

7 cups pure water

1½ teaspoons curry powder

2½ teaspoons sea salt

⅓ cup white basmati rice

3 cups packed, chopped spinach (about 1 pound)

1. In a large pot, sauté the onion in the oil over moderate heat for 3–4 minutes. When the onion becomes translucent, add the tomatoes, water, curry powder, and sea salt. Increase the heat to high, cover, and bring to a boil. Stir in the rice and simmer covered over moderate heat for 30 minutes, or until the rice is cooked. Stir in the spinach, and cook for an additional 2–3 minutes.

2. Serve hot by itself or accompanied by a salad and a loaf of whole-grain bread.

NOTE

■ **For small children, decrease the curry powder measurement by ½ teaspoon.**

Roasted Autumn Squash Soup

Preparation time: 20 minutes to prepare, 30–40 minutes to cook

Yield: 4–6 servings

Butternut squash, carrots, and sweet potatoes are colorful, naturally sweet, and carotenoid rich. So why not use them to make a creamy, delicious soup? I often serve this bright orange treat flavored with ginger and cinnamon croutons at breakfast time, but it's a great addition to any meal. During those fall and winter months when comfort food is of high value, this soup does the job. It keeps so well in the fridge that you can make a big batch in advance and serve it for a few days.

2 large celery stalks, cut into ¼-inch pieces

1 medium leek, thinly sliced, then chopped, white part only (about 3 ounces)

1 small white onion, peeled and diced

4 cloves garlic, peeled and coarsely chopped

1 tablespoon plus 1½ teaspoons finely grated, peeled fresh ginger

2 bay leaves

5 tablespoons extra-virgin olive oil

2 pounds butternut squash, halved, seeds and fibers removed, peeled, and cut into ½-inch pieces

2 medium carrots, cut into ½-inch pieces (about ½ pound)

2 medium parsnips, peeled and cut into ½-inch pieces (about ½ pound)

1 medium sweet potato, peeled and cut into ½-inch pieces (about 1 pound)

1 teaspoon ground coriander

2 teaspoons sea salt

8 cups pure water

Cinnamon Croutons (page 108)

Cinnamon to taste

1. In a large pot, sauté together the celery, leek, onion, garlic, 1 tablespoon ginger, and bay leaves in the oil over moderate heat for 5–7 minutes, or until the onion is soft. Stir in the squash, carrots, parsnips, potato, coriander, and salt. Increase the heat to high and sauté for 10–12 additional minutes until the root vegetables are slightly carmelized. Add the water, cover, and bring to a boil. Reduce the heat to moderate, and simmer covered for 10–15 minutes, or until the root vegetables are tender. Remove and discard the bay leaves.

2. Remove half the mixture and puree in a food processor. Return it to the pot, add the remaining 1½ teaspoons ginger, and stir well. Cover, and bring to a boil over high heat. Reduce the heat and simmer uncovered over moderate heat for 5–6 minutes or until heated through.

3. Pour into soup bowls, top with Cinnamon Croutons, and sprinkle with cinnamon.

NOTE

■ Sometimes I serve this soup in hollowed-out squash shells—the shells of sweet dumpling, acorn, carnival, or delicata squash make ideal bowls—and accompanied by Golden Pumpkin-Seed Corn Bread (page 112).

Spinach Wonton Soup

Preparation time: 50–60 minutes to prepare, 30–40 minutes to cook

Yield: 4 servings

Want to try something great that you've probably never made at home? This may fill the bill. Actually, I have to admit that I made this recipe for myself. As a child, I had always loved wonton soup. When I became a vegetarian, I needed an alternative that would satisfy my wonton craving. As it turned out, this recipe is better than the pork-filled restaurant versions. Delicate handmade wonton skins filled with sautéed spinach and shiitake mushrooms are what make this soup a super hit!

FRESH WONTON STOCK

2 small leeks, roughly chopped

1 large-leaf Napa cabbage (or bok choy), quartered and roughly chopped

1 small carrot, scrubbed well and cut into thirds

Three ½-inch cubes peeled ginger

6 small shiitake mushrooms, destemmed and quartered

¼ cup packed, finely chopped fresh spinach

2 tablespoons canola oil

2¼ teaspoons sea salt

1 teaspoon tamari soy sauce

3 quarts pure water

WONTON FILLING

1 tablespoon thinly sliced scallions

2 teaspoons peeled, finely chopped ginger

1 large clove garlic, peeled and crushed

2 tablespoons canola oil

2 cups packed, finely chopped fresh spinach

1 cup destemmed, finely chopped shiitake mushrooms

¼ teaspoon sea salt

OTHER COMPONENTS

Twenty-four 3¼ x 3¼-inch wonton wrappers

¼ pound or 1 cup baby spinach leaves

1 tablespoon plus 1 teaspoon thinly sliced scallions

1. To prepare the stock, in a large pot, sauté the leeks, cabbage, carrot, ginger, mushrooms, and spinach in the oil over moderate to high heat for 5 minutes. Stir in the salt, tamari, and water. Cover and bring to a boil over high heat. Reduce the heat to moderate, and simmer covered for 15–20 minutes. Remove from the heat and

strain the stock through a fine sieve (press as much liquid as possible from the vegetables). Return the stock to the pot, cover, and set aside.

2. To prepare the wonton filling, in a medium saucepan, sauté the scallions, ginger, and garlic in the oil over moderate heat for 3–4 minutes. When the scallions become translucent, stir in the spinach, mushrooms, and salt. Continue cooking uncovered, stirring occasionally, for 3–5 minutes or until the spinach is soft. Remove from the heat, transfer to a fine sieve, and drain off any excess liquid.

3. To assemble the wontons, set a wrapper in front of you in a diamond orientation and place 1 teaspoon of the filling slightly above the center. With your finger, moisten the exposed edges of the wrapper (with water) and bring the bottom of the wrapper up over the filling, pressing it gently to seal and eliminating any air pockets. The wonton will now be triangular in shape. Bring the two side points of the triangle up over the filling, overlap the points in a twisting motion, and seal with a bit of water by pinching the ends firmly together. Repeat with remaining wonton skins until all the ingredients are used. Place the wontons onto parchment-paper-lined cookie sheets, and cover with a dish towel. Set aside and reheat the stock until simmering.

4. To cook the wontons, slide the wontons into the pot, stir gently, and simmer uncovered for 2–3 minutes or until they float to the surface and are cooked. Ladle into soup bowls, garnish with a few spinach leaves and a sprinkling of scallions, and serve.

NOTES
- The wontons can be prepared the day before, then refrigerated wrapped in an airtight plastic bag. Or make them several weeks ahead and freeze.
- Wonton wrappers can be purchased in 1-pound packages (75–80 wonton skins) at specialty markets and health food stores. If you are not able to find wonton skins, use 8-inch-square egg roll sheets cut into quarters. (Be careful to read the ingredients on these premade wonton skins since many contain preservatives.)
- The recipe for fresh wonton stock can easily be doubled. Freeze some in ice-cube trays or plastic containers for future use.
- For a quick NOODLE SOUP À LA VEGGIE, replace the wontons with 3.5 ounces Bifun Japanese Rice pasta, add 1 cup sliced shiitake mushrooms, and simmer for 8–10 minutes.

Sweet Corn Chowder

Preparation time: 15 minutes to prepare, 15–20 minutes to cook

Yield: 4 servings

Here's a soup whose sweet flavor comes from the natural sugars present in onions, corn, and red bell pepper. My kids love this creamy, colorful soup, and I love to make it during the summer and fall months when sweet corn is in season. Then I extend the enjoyment into the winter with frozen corn I've saved from those in-season months.

3 tablespoons canola oil

2 cups chopped yellow onions

2 cups fresh corn kernels (3–4 ears)

½ cup diced red bell pepper

½ cup chopped red potato

¾ teaspoon onion powder

¾ teaspoon sea salt

¼ teaspoon garlic powder

½ teaspoon celery salt

⅛ teaspoon ground cumin

1 tablespoon lecithin granules (optional)

3 cups pure water

2 tablespoons finely chopped parsley

1. In a medium saucepan, combine the oil, onions, corn, red pepper, potato, onion powder, salt, garlic powder, celery salt, and cumin. Sauté over moderate to high heat for 5–7 minutes, or until the onions are soft.

2. In a blender, combine 1½ cups of the sautéed vegetables with the lecithin granules and water. Blend on low speed for about 10 seconds or until smooth (try not to overblend or the mixture will become frothy). Stir the blended mixture back into the pan, and simmer covered over moderate heat for 10 minutes. Remove from the heat and stir in the parsley until well combined.

3. Ladel into soup bowls and serve hot with biscuits or corn bread and a mixed green salad.

NOTE

■ **Frozen corn can be substituted for the fresh.**

A Bronx Salad

Preparation time: 10 minutes

Yield: 4–6 servings

I recently spent a Saturday afternoon in New York City's North Bronx exploring the Italian markets and restaurants of Arthur Avenue. With so many eateries to choose from, I asked a couple of neighborhood women for their recommendation. They sent me right to a local family-owned restaurant with no menu and long picnic tables filled to capacity. I instantly knew that these women were wise when I started my meal with one of the best salads ever. Crisp lettuce, cucumbers, bell peppers, vine-ripened tomatoes, thinly sliced onions, and the best olives I had ever tasted were tossed together with a simple, yet delicious, Italian dressing. This is my version, and one that's established itself as a family favorite.

ZESTY ITALIAN DRESSING

½ cup extra-virgin olive oil

2 tablespoons freshly squeezed lemon juice

1 tablespoon balsamic vinegar

½ teaspoon apple cider vinegar

½ teaspoon dried basil

½ teaspoon dried parsley

½ teaspoon sea salt

¼ teaspoon dried oregano

SALAD

2 heads fresh, young romaine lettuce (about 1½ pounds)

1 large yellow bell pepper, cored, seeded, and sliced

1 large cucumber, halved, seeded, and thinly sliced

1 large vine-ripened tomato, cored and sliced into 6–8 wedges

1 small red onion, peeled and very thinly sliced (optional)

½ cup pitted Kalamata olives (see Note)

1. To prepare the dressing, use a blender to combine the oil, lemon juice, vinegars, basil, parsley, salt, and oregano. Blend for 1 minute or until the dressing emulsifies. Set aside.

2. Trim the bases of the romaine lettuce and discard any bruised outer leaves. Use the tender inner leaves, keeping the small leaves whole and cutting or tearing the larger outer leaves crosswise into halves or thirds. Wash and dry the greens in a spinner.

3. In a large bowl, combine the lettuce, pepper, cucumber, tomato, onion, and olives. Drizzle the dressing onto the salad, gently toss together until well coated, and serve immediately.

NOTE

▪ **Pitted black olives can be used to replace the Kalamata olives.**

Garden's Gift Salad

Preparation time: 10–15 minutes

Yield: 4 servings

During the summer months I enjoy an abundance of fresh lettuces, tomatoes, cucumbers, and herbs from my garden. Last summer, this salad and dressing combination turned out to be a big hit. The dressing in particular is delicious, with fresh lime juice, sweet honey, and fragrant herbs all complementing one another to enhance this garden-grown treat.

ROSEMARY-BASIL VINAIGRETTE

1 tablespoon plus 1 teaspoon freshly squeezed lime juice

1 tablespoon balsamic vinegar

1 tablespoon honey

¼ cup tightly packed fresh basil leaves (about 24 medium leaves)

1 teaspoon finely chopped fresh rosemary leaves, or ½ teaspoon dried

¾ teaspoon sea salt

⅔ cup extra-virgin olive oil

SALAD

8 ounces mixed baby lettuces or mixed red and green lettuce leaves (about 4 large handfuls)

4 ounces sunflower sprouts (about 2 large handfuls) (see Note)

8 cherry tomatoes, halved (about 1 cup)

1 large cucumber, peeled, seeded, and thinly sliced

1 ripe Haas avocado, peeled, halved, pitted, and sliced

1. To prepare the vinaigrette, combine the lime juice, vinegar, honey, basil, rosemary, and salt in a blender and puree. With the motor running, slowly add the oil until emulsified. Set aside.

2. Wash and dry the lettuces and sprouts in a spinner and transfer to a large bowl. Add the cucumbers, tomatoes, and avocado. Drizzle the dressing onto the salad and gently toss together until well coated. Serve immediately.

NOTE

■ **An equal measure of mixed baby lettuces can be used to replace the sunflower sprouts.**

Little Caesar Salad

Preparation time: 10–15 minutes

Yield: 4–6 servings

This salad is an absolute family favorite. The plum paste adds a unique flavor to the delicious egg-free dressing, while the crunchy texture of herbed croutons is the crowning glory to a salad fit for a king, or in this case, a Roman emperor.

MISO-PLUM DRESSING

½ cup extra-virgin olive oil

¼ cup canola oil

¾ cup silken tofu

1 tablespoon plus 2 teaspoons umeboshi plum paste (see Notes)

1 tablespoon sweet white miso

1 tablespoon apple cider vinegar

1 teaspoon balsamic vinegar

1 tablespoon freshly squeezed lemon juice

1 large clove garlic, peeled and finely chopped

SALAD

2 heads fresh, young romaine lettuce (about 1½ pounds)

2 cups Croutons Deluxe (page 109)

1. To prepare the dressing, use a blender to combine the oils and tofu. Blend on medium speed for 1 minute or until creamy. Add the plum paste, miso, vinegars, lemon juice, and garlic. Blend on high speed until smooth, about 2 minutes. Set aside.

2. Trim the bases of the romaine lettuce and discard any bruised outer leaves. Use the tender inner leaves, keeping the small leaves whole and cutting or tearing the larger outer leaves crosswise into halves or thirds. Wash and dry the greens in a spinner, and transfer to a large bowl.

3. Drizzle about two thirds of the dressing onto the salad and gently toss together until well coated. Toss briefly with the croutons and serve immediately. Set aside remaining dressing for those who cannot resist adding more to their plate.

NOTES

■ **Both umeboshi plum paste and miso can be purchased in health food stores. My favorite brand is Miso Master.**

■ **To boost the nutritional content of this recipe, top with julienned strips of sushi nori.**

Mashed Red Potato Salad

Preparation time: 10 minutes to prepare, 15–20 minutes to cook

Yield: 4 servings

This is potato salad the way it should be—healthful, delicious, no-fuss. In fact, I'd call this dish—made from delicate red potatoes tossed with extra-virgin olive oil, black olives, celery, and fresh parsley—a perfect meal.

3 pounds peeled red potatoes, cut into ¾-inch pieces
½ cup diced celery
¾ cup black olives, pitted and sliced
¼ cup finely chopped fresh parsley
¾ cup extra-virgin olive oil
1½ teaspoons sea salt
Freshly ground black pepper and paprika to taste

1. In a large pot with 1 inch of water and a steamer, steam the potatoes over high heat for 15–20 minutes or until tender when poked with a fork. Drain and cool slightly.

2. Transfer to a large mixing bowl, and stir in the celery, olives, parsley, oil, salt, and black pepper until well combined.

3. Sprinkle each serving evenly with paprika and serve hot, warm, or at room temperature, alone or accompanied by a mixed green salad or Glorious Garlicky Greens (page 163).

NOTES
- **My kids like the above version, but I will often throw in some finely chopped fresh chives and yellow bell pepper.**
- **Yukon Gold potatoes can be used to replace the red.**

Quick Cuke Can't-Miss Dish

Preparation time: 5 minutes
Yield: 4 servings

This fresh salad with its tangy sesame dressing is simple and easy to prepare. It's a perfect complement to a Far Eastern meal featuring vegetable fried rice, norimaki, or spinach wonton soup. But serve it anytime you like; your family will appreciate the refreshing taste as an accompaniment to many different dishes. Best of all, it takes less than 5 minutes to prepare.

¼ cup canola oil
1 teaspoon toasted sesame oil
3 tablespoons apple cider vinegar
2 tablespoons tamari soy sauce
2 large cucumbers, peeled, seeded, halved, and sliced paper-thin
1 teaspoon sesame seeds

1. To prepare the dressing, use a mini food processor to combine the oils, vinegar, and tamari. Process for 30 seconds or until emulsified. Set aside.

2. Arrange the cucumber slices equally among 4 plates. Drizzle each salad with dressing to taste. Sprinkle with seeds, and serve.

NOTE

■ When purchasing cucumbers, look for firmness. Soft spots indicate older vegetables. If you can find them, European cucumbers are great in this salad (they do not have to be peeled, seeded, or halved— just thinly sliced).

Razz-Matazz-Berry Green Salad

Preparation time: 10–15 minutes
Yield: 4 servings

This is, on one level, a salad. But on another level it's an experience because its vibrant colors—bright green, red, yellow, and orange—practically jump out at you. Your family will give this salad the thumbs-up on taste because it's topped with a dressing made from fresh raspberries.

CREAMY RASPBERRY DRESSING

¼ cup pure water

¼ cup Dijon mustard

2 tablespoons apple cider vinegar

6 raspberries, fresh or frozen

½ cup canola oil

SALAD

1 large head Bibb lettuce (about ½ pound)

1 large yellow bell pepper, cored, seeded, and thinly sliced

1⅓ cups fresh raspberries (see Note)

2 large carrots, grated

2 tablespoons sesame seeds (optional)

1. To prepare the dressing, combine the water, mustard, vinegar, and raspberries in a blender and puree. With the motor running, slowly add the oil until emulsified. Set aside.

2. Trim the base of the lettuce and discard any bruised outer leaves. Use the tender inner leaves, keeping the small leaves whole and cutting or tearing the larger outer leaves crosswise into halves or thirds. Wash and dry the greens in a spinner.

3. Divide the lettuce equally among 4 plates and drizzle each salad with dressing to taste. Arrange the pepper slices and raspberries around the lettuce, giving each plate an equal portion. Sprinkle each salad with a fourth of the carrot and seeds and serve.

NOTE

■ **In off-season months, the fresh raspberries can be replaced by 1 small beet (peeled and grated).**

Rebuilt Waldorf Salad

Preparation time: 10 minutes
Yield: 4 servings

Traditional Waldorf salad, usually loaded with mayonnaise, is both heavy on the palate and unhealthy for the body. This fresh, light alternative is the perfect way to get children to eat salad. Organic baby greens are topped with apples, bright orange carrots, juicy grapes, and sunflower seeds, then drizzled with a delicious strawberry dressing. The natural sweetness of the fresh fruit and the kid-popular ingredients will make this salad a hit.

8 ounces mixed baby lettuces or mixed red and green lettuce leaves (about 4 large handfuls)

2 medium Golden Delicious apples, peeled, cored, julienned, and then tossed in 1 tablespoon freshly squeezed orange juice

1 large carrot, grated

1 cup seedless red grapes, halved

¼ cup sunflower seeds (optional)

STRAWBERRY DRESSING

One 10-ounce package frozen strawberries, thawed

1½ large oranges, squeezed with pulp discarded (about ½ cup)

2 tablespoons brown rice syrup

1. Wash and dry the lettuces in a spinner, and then refrigerate them.

2. To make the dressing, use a blender to combine the strawberries, orange juice, and rice syrup. Blend for 30 seconds until homogenous. Set aside.

3. Divide the lettuces equally among 4 plates and top each portion with a fourth of the apples, carrot, and grapes. Drizzle each salad with dressing to taste. Sprinkle with seeds, and serve on its own—or accompanied by a smile!

NOTE

- Try using Red Delicious, Gravenstein, or Cortland apples in place of Golden Delicious.

Salad Supreme

Preparation time: 20–25 minutes
Yield: 4 servings

No one sitting at your table will be able to resist this crisp, colorful, full-of-everything salad. By the way, when I made the celery dressing, it turned out that it was used not only for the salad, but for the entree as well. Enjoy!

CREAMY CELERY DRESSING

¾ cup extra-virgin olive oil

½ cup silken tofu

2 large celery stalks, cut into 1-inch lengths

⅓ cup pure water

1 tablespoon apple cider vinegar

2 teaspoons balsamic vinegar

1 tablespoon dried basil

½ teaspoon sea salt

SALAD

8–10 ounces mixed red and green lettuce leaves (about 4–5 large handfuls)

1 cup tightly packed alfalfa sprouts

1 cup thinly sliced red cabbage

1 cup thinly sliced green cabbage

1 large carrot, grated

1 medium daikon radish, grated

¼ cup sunflower seeds (optional)

1. To prepare the dressing, use a blender to combine the oil, tofu, celery, and water. Blend on medium speed for 1 minute or until creamy. Add the vinegars, basil, and salt. Blend on high speed until smooth, 1–2 additional minutes. Set aside.

2. Trim the base of the lettuce and discard any bruised outer leaves. Use the tender inner leaves, keeping the small leaves whole and cutting or tearing the larger outer leaves crosswise into halves or thirds. Wash and dry the greens in a spinner, and transfer to a large bowl.

3. Divide the lettuce equally among 4 plates and top each portion with a fourth of the sprouts. Arrange the cabbage, carrots, and daikon around the sprouts, giving each plate an equal portion. Drizzle each salad with dressing to taste. Sprinkle with seeds, and serve.

NOTE

■ **This delicious dressing brings simple meals to life, so try it drizzled over cooked grains, legumes, or vegetables.**

Sea Salad Delight

Preparation time: 20 minutes to prepare, 15 minutes to cook

Yield: 4 servings

This salad is a must-try! It's both fun and nutritious. Arame is a sweet, mild sea vegetable that is second to none in nutrition. The salad colors—bright green, orange, red, and black—are vivid, and the sweet, pungent dressing is delicious.

SALAD

1 cup dry arame (about 1 ounce)

½ lemon, squeezed and with pulp discarded

4 cups pure warm water

8 ounces mixed red and green lettuce leaves (about 4 large handfuls)

9 ounces sunflower sprouts (see Note)

1 large red bell pepper, cored, seeded, and thinly sliced

3 large oranges, peeled and sectioned (threads, membranes, and seeds removed)

1 tablespoon plus 1 teaspoon sesame seeds

SWEET GINGER-SOY DRESSING

⅓ cup plus 2 tablespoons balsamic vinegar

4 tablespoons tamari soy sauce

2 tablespoons honey

1 teaspoon peeled, grated, and finely diced fresh ginger

2 cloves garlic, peeled and pressed

½ cup canola oil

¼ cup toasted sesame oil

1. To prepare the arame, use a medium mixing bowl to combine the arame, lemon juice, and 4 cups warm water. Let soak for 15 minutes, transfer to a colander, and rinse well. In medium saucepan, bring the arame and enough pure water to cover to a boil over moderate heat and simmer for 15 minutes. Return the arame to the colander, and run under cold water for 2 minutes, until cool. Drain well and set aside.

2. Wash and dry the lettuces and sprouts in a spinner, and then refrigerate them (discarding any black shells).

3. To prepare the dressing, combine the vinegar, tamari, honey, ginger, and garlic in a blender and puree. With the motor running, slowly add the oils until emulsified. Set aside.

4. Divide the greens equally among 4 plates and top each portion with a fourth of the arame. Arrange the red pepper and orange slices around the sprouts, giving each plate an equal portion. Drizzle each salad with dressing to taste. Sprinkle with sesame seeds, and serve.

NOTE

■ **An equal measure of mixed baby lettuces can be used to replace the sunflower sprouts.**

Totally Terrific Quinoa Tabbouleh Salad

Preparation time: 20 minutes

Yield: 4 servings

Children just love raw parsley. They also like plunging things into cold water and working salad spinners. So enlist your child's help with this one. You just may be inspiring a future culinary artist!

½ pound fresh parsley (curly-leafed preferred)

¾ cup cooked quinoa (page 37), completely cooled

1 small vine-ripened tomato, cored and sliced into ¼-inch cubes

¼ cup finely chopped yellow onion

¼ plus ⅛ teaspoon sea salt

Freshly ground black pepper to taste

¼ cup extra-virgin olive oil

1 tablespoon plus 2 teaspoons freshly squeezed lemon juice

1. To prepare the parsley, discard any yellow sprigs and trim off any brown ends from the stems. Plunge the parsley into a large bowl filled with cold water. Swish the sprigs around and allow any grit to sink to the bottom. Spin in a salad spinner until completely dry. Realign so all the ends are together, roll up firmly in paper towels, and set aside to dry for 5 minutes. To chop, hold the bunch together tightly (aligning the sprigs so that the leaves are all at the same level) and discard all but 1 inch of the stalks. Chop the parsley as if you were slicing it.

2. In a large bowl, toss together the parsley, quinoa, tomato, onion, salt, and black pepper until well combined. Drizzle on the oil and lemon juice and gently toss together until well coated. Serve immediately.

NOTE

■ **For a traditional tabbouleh salad, an equal measure of cooked bulgur wheat can be used to replace the quinoa.**

Turkish Coban Salad

Preparation time: 10 minutes

Yield: 3–4 servings

From the time my children were old enough to eat solid food, our family has frequented numerous Middle Eastern restaurants because of the abundant vegetarian options. We have always been fond of Turkish food, especially this salad made from fresh garden vegetables tossed in a light lemony dressing. Purely simple, purely delicious!

½ pound vine-ripened tomatoes, seeded and cut into ½-inch "dice"

½ pound cucumbers, seeded and cut into ½-inch "dice"

½ cup finely chopped curly-leafed parsley

⅓ cup diced red onion

⅓ cup diced green bell pepper

1 tablespoon plus 1 teaspoon freshly squeezed lemon juice

1 tablespoon extra-virgin olive oil

1½ teaspoons apple cider vinegar

½ teaspoon sea salt

½ teaspoon ground paprika

Freshly ground black pepper to taste

In a large bowl, combine the tomatoes, cucumbers, parsley, onion, and pepper. Drizzle the lemon juice, oil, and vinegar onto the vegetables and gently toss together until well coated. Sprinkle with salt, paprika, and black pepper. Toss again, and serve.

NOTE
- **This salad is best made minutes before serving.**

CHAPTER 11

ENTREES

Authentic "Sausage" and Peppers

Preparation time: 15 minutes to prepare, 25–30 minutes to cook

Yield: 4 sandwiches

So here's the question: Where are we? South Philly? No. The Jersey shore boardwalk? No. The San Genaro Festival in New York's Little Italy? No again. All right, here's the answer: We're in your very own kitchen, whipping up an authentic favorite for the whole family. I developed this recipe almost by accident when I had some extra peppers and onions. I sautéed them in olive oil, threw in some tempeh, added some leftover marinara sauce, and sandwiched it all between a loaf of Italian bread. Some time when you feel like remembering the old neighborhood, sit down and dig in.

1 pound quinoa sesame tempeh, cut into 1-inch cubes and seasoned with ¼ teaspoon sea salt

¾ cup extra-virgin olive oil plus 3–4 tablespoons for brushing the bread

2 large yellow onions, peeled and thinly sliced into half-moons (about 1 pound)

10 sweet Italian peppers or yellow bell peppers, cored, seeded, and sliced (about 10 ounces)

8 large cloves garlic, peeled and coarsely chopped

1 teaspoon fennel seeds (optional)

1 cup marinara sauce

2 tablespoons finely chopped parsley

Sea salt to taste

Freshly ground black pepper to taste

1 long loaf Italian bread, sliced into four 5-inch-thick sections, cut ¾ of the way through lengthwise, and with the insides scraped lightly with a fork to remove a little dough

1. In a large frying pan, sauté the tempeh in ½ cup oil over moderate to low heat for 10–12 minutes, or until golden on all sides. Transfer to a plate and set aside.

2. In the same frying pan, sauté the onions, peppers, garlic, and fennel seeds in the remaining ¼ cup oil over moderate to high heat for 10–12 minutes. When the onions become translucent, stir in the marinara sauce, tempeh, parsley, salt, and black pepper until well combined. Simmer uncovered for 1–2 minutes or until heated through. Cover and set aside.

3. Set the toaster oven on toast and preheat to 475°F. For each sandwich, lightly brush the bread with the olive oil and toast for 4–5 minutes or until just the edges are golden. Spoon a fourth of the tempeh mixture into each sub and press down lightly. Cut in halves on the diagonal and serve.

NOTES

- For Joe's Marinara Sauce, see page 166.
- For those sensitive to wheat—rye, rice, and millet breads can be purchased in health food stores.
- For variety, try this saucy tempeh dish over cooked short-grain brown rice.

Shiitake Butternut Subs

Preparation time: 15 minutes to prepare, 20–25 minutes to broil

Yield: 4 sandwiches

Although this might seem like an adult-type meal, kids love it too! I almost always have shiitake mushrooms in my fridge because of their immune-boosting properties. Combined with squash, and sandwiched between whole-grain bread, they form the base of a healthy, hearty sandwich.

1¼ cups butternut squash, seeds and fibers removed, peeled, and cut into ½-inch cubes

1 pound shiitake mushrooms, destemmed and sliced into ¾-inch strips

¼ cup extra-virgin olive oil, plus 3–4 tablespoons for brushing the bread

6 large cloves garlic, peeled and coarsely chopped

1 tablespoon balsamic vinegar

3 tablespoons chopped parsley

1 teaspoon chopped fresh rosemary leaves (optional)

1 teaspoon sea salt

Freshly ground black pepper to taste

1 baguette, sliced into four 5-inch-thick sections, cut ¾ of the way through lengthwise, and with the insides scraped lightly with a fork to remove a little dough

1. Set the toaster oven on toast and preheat to 475°F.

2. To cook the butternut squash, place the squash onto a steamer set into a medium pot filled with 1 inch of water. Cook covered over high heat until the squash pieces are tender when a fork is inserted into their centers, about 8–10 minutes. Set aside.

3. In a medium mixing bowl, toss together the mushrooms, squash, ¼ cup oil, garlic, vinegar, parsley, rosemary, salt, and pepper until well combined. Transfer the mushroom mixture to an 8-inch-square baking dish and distribute evenly. Broil in the preheated toaster oven for 10–12 minutes or until the mushroom edges are golden. Remove from the oven and let cool for 2 minutes.

4. For each sandwich, lightly brush the bread with the remaining olive oil and toast for 4–5 minutes or until just the edges are golden. Spoon a fourth of the roasted squash and mushroom mixture into each sub and press down lightly. Cut in halves on the diagonal and serve.

NOTES

- **For super-subs the olive oil for brushing the bread can be replaced with Buttery White Bean Hummus (page 105) or Glorious Garlicky Greens (page 163).**
- **For those sensitive to wheat—rye, rice, and millet breads can be purchased in health food stores.**
- **A conventional oven can be used for cooking instead of a toaster oven.**

Basmati Rice Pilaf

Preparation time: 10 minutes to prepare, 30–35 minutes to cook
Yield: 4 servings

Children enjoy this buttery rice dish because it is delicate and nutty-tasting. Basmati rice, which often comes from India and Pakistan, is a staple for many people in Asia. Try the Spanish-inspired saffron and pea version as well (see Note).

2 tablespoons finely minced yellow onion
2 tablespoons canola oil
1¼ cups white basmati rice
1 bay leaf
2⅔ cups pure water
1¼ teaspoons sea salt

1. In a large saucepan or skillet, sauté the onion in the oil over moderate heat for 1–2 minutes. When the onion becomes translucent, stir in the rice and bay leaf. Sauté until just golden, about 5 minutes.

2. Stir in the water and salt. Bring to a boil, reduce heat to low, and simmer covered for 20–25 minutes or until all of the water is absorbed. Fluff rice with a fork, cover, and let stand for 5 minutes. Remove and discard bay leaf before serving.

3. Serve hot by itself or accompanied by legume, vegetable, chicken, or seafood dishes.

■ For a delicious Yellow Rice and Pea Pilaf, add 1 teaspoon saffron plus ⅔ cup frozen peas after the salt in step 2, or for kids who don't like the flavor of saffron try 2 tablespoons annatto-infused oil.

Bite-Size Nori Rolls

Preparation time: 15–20 minutes
Yield: 4 servings

Norimaki, or nori rolls, have come to my rescue on more than one occasion. Since they make great finger foods, I often pack them into lunch boxes, along with little containers of tamari purchased from my local Chinese restaurant. Also, we enjoy having these for dinner, accompanied by miso or wonton soup and a light cucumber salad.

DIPPING SAUCE

¼ cup plus 1 tablespoon brown rice vinegar
2 tablespoons plus 2 teaspoons toasted sesame oil
1 tablespoon plus 1 teaspoon freshly squeezed lemon juice
2 teaspoons tamari soy sauce

NORI ROLLS

8 sheets of nori seaweed
6 cups cooked short-grain brown or sushi rice (see Note)
1 tablespoon umeboshi plum paste (see Notes page 144) (optional)
¼ cup sesame seeds
Eight 8-inch-long vegetables (2 pieces avocado, 2 pieces red bell pepper, cucumber, or blanched carrots), julienned

1. To prepare the dipping sauce, combine the vinegar, oil, lemon juice, and tamari in a small bowl. Stir together until well combined and set aside.

2. Toast each nori sheet by holding it over a flame for a few seconds or by spreading it out in a 250°F oven for 2 minutes. The nori is done when it crisps and turns green. Set out a small bowl filled with cold water, and a bamboo mat for rolling. (As an alternative, you can use a paper towel or a piece of waxed paper.)

3. Take a sheet of nori and flatten it on the bamboo mat. Wet your hands in cold water to prevent the rice from sticking to them. Evenly spread a thin layer of rice (about ½ cup) on the nori sheet, covering all but a 1-inch-

strip along the edge farthest from you. Brush or spread about ⅓ teaspoon of plum paste across the center of the rice layer, sprinkle on 1 teaspoon sesame seeds, and top with julienned vegetables.

4. Roll the mat forward tightly (do not roll the mat into the rice layer) with your thumbs while holding the filling in place with your fingers. When all but 1 inch has been rolled, lightly moisten the remaining edge of nori with water and continue rolling to seal. Completely roll up the norimaki by pressing lightly with both hands to seal the edge and firm the roll. Remove the mat and slice the roll into 5–6 equal pieces (use a very sharp knife and rinse it in water if the rice begins to stick). Repeat with each nori sheet until all the ingredients are used.

5. To serve, pour about 3 tablespoons dipping sauce into a ramekin and place in the center of a salad plate. Stand 10–12 pieces (or 2 cut-up rolls) on their ends, arranging them around the ramekin. Proceed this way for the remaining 3 plates.

NOTES

- Remember, making perfect nori rolls takes time and practice. At first you may feel a little awkward and your rolls might not be perfect. But, with perseverance, your technique will improve.
- To cook rice, in a medium saucepan, bring 2½ cups pure water to a boil. Stir in 1 cup short-grain brown or sushi rice, reduce heat to low, and simmer covered for 25 minutes or until all of the water is absorbed.
- Although Wasabi mustard may be a little spicy for most children, my kids love it and it's an excellent accompaniment to this dish. The powder can be purchased in health food stores and specialty shops.

Build-Your-Own Burritos

Preparation time: 5 minutes to prepare, 8–10 minutes to cook
Yield: 4 burritos

Here's your chance to become a burrito artiste. You can get creative and make them in many different ways, varying the type of bean, tortilla, and salsa. This will provide enough variety to keep the entire family happy and well fed. Here is the recipe for a basic, no-fail burrito. Feel free to build on it to suit your family's tastes.

4 whole-wheat or corn tortillas
2 cups finely chopped onions
8 large cloves garlic, peeled and coarsely chopped
4 tablespoons extra-virgin olive oil
1 pound vine-ripened tomatoes, peeled, seeded, and finely chopped
Two 15-ounce cans pinto beans, rinsed and drained

1 teaspoon cumin powder

1 teaspoon chili powder

1½ teaspoons sea salt

½ cup fresh corn kernels (optional)

1 cup grated Cheddar-style nondairy cheese (optional)

1. To warm the tortillas, wrap them in a damp towel and place them in a preheated 350°F oven for about 10 minutes.

2. In a large saucepan, sauté the onions and garlic in the oil over moderate to high heat for 3–4 minutes. When the onions become translucent, stir in the tomatoes, beans, cumin powder, chili powder, and salt until well combined. Cook uncovered over moderate heat for 3–4 minutes. Using a potato masher, slightly mash the beans until the mixture is almost refried in consistency. Then stir in the corn until well blended. Cover, remove from the heat, and set aside.

3. To assemble the burritos, spread about 1 cup of the bean mixture along the middle of the lower two thirds of each tortilla. Evenly distribute about ¼ cup cheese on top of the beans. Fold the right and left sides of the tortilla over the filling and roll up the tortilla away from you, resting on top of the seam. Place seam side down on plates.

4. Serve hot, alone or accompanied by guacamole, salsa, and nondairy sour cream and a salad.

NOTES

■ **Some ideas for variety: Add sautéed peppers and onions, guacamole, saffron-flavored rice, or nondairy sour cream along with the bean mixture during the burritos' assembly.**

■ **To make enchiladas: Tightly roll each bean-stuffed tortilla into a cylinder and place it seam side down in a large baking dish. Top each with ½ cup tomato sauce and ½ cup grated cheese, and bake uncovered in a preheated 375°F oven for 20 minutes.**

■ **For Sun-Sational Salsa, see page 126; for Good-Time Guacamole, see page 113; and for Seemingly Sinful Sour Cream, see page 125.**

Children's-Choice Chili

Preparation time: 20–25 minutes to prepare, 40 minutes to cook

Yield: 4–6 servings

Here's a new twist on Texas chili. Did you know that Texas is the state that sets the rules on how to make chili? The thing is, in making this dish, I wasn't playing by the rules, because adding beans to your chili is practically illegal in the Lone Star State. Nevertheless, this vegetarian version was a hit there, and hopefully it will be a hit with your family. It's light and soup-like—not muddy or heavy—and children go for the colors and the crunch of the peppers added at the end.

2 medium red onions, peeled and finely chopped (about 12 ounces)

1 large green bell pepper, cored, seeded, and finely chopped

4 large cloves garlic, peeled and coarsely chopped

4 tablespoons canola oil

1½ cups dried pinto, kidney, or red beans, soaked overnight, rinsed, and drained

4 large ripe tomatoes, peeled, seeded, and chopped (about 2½ pounds)

12 ounces seitan, rinsed and finely chopped (optional)

1 tablespoon chili powder

¾ teaspoon ground cumin

½ teaspoon ground cinnamon

¼ teaspoon ground paprika

¼ teaspoon ground allspice

2 cups pure water

¼ cup freshly squeezed lemon juice

1 tablespoon sea salt

¼ cup finely chopped parsley

1 large yellow bell pepper, cored, seeded, and finely chopped

1. In a 4-quart or larger pressure cooker, sauté the onions, green pepper, and garlic in the oil over moderate to high heat until soft, about 5 minutes. Stir in the beans, tomatoes, seitan, chili powder, cumin, cinnamon, paprika, allspice, and water. Close the lid and bring the pressure to high. Reduce the heat to moderate to low, and cook for 30 minutes until the beans are tender.

2. Remove from the heat and let sit for 5 minutes. Using a long-handled spoon, depress the valve on the pressure cooker lid and release the steam. Stir in the lemon juice, salt, parsley, and yellow pepper until well combined. Cook uncovered for an additional 5 minutes or until the yellow pepper is heated through.

3. Ladle into soup bowls and serve with a dollop of nondairy sour cream, corn bread, and a mixed green salad.

NOTES

■ If a pressure cooker is not available you will need to cook the chili in a large pot, covered, over moderate heat for 1¼ to 1½ hours. Water will evaporate, so add additional water as it does.

■ Although dried beans provide a nicer flavor than canned ones do, if you have to, you can replace the dried soaked beans with two 15-ounce cans of beans (rinsed and drained). Decrease the water to 1 cup and simmer covered for 30 minutes.

■ For Seemingly Sinful Sour Cream, see page 125, and for Golden Pumpkin-Seed Corn Bread, see page 112.

Creamy Curried Potatoes and Peas

Preparation time: 20 minutes to prepare, 55–60 minutes to cook

Yield: 4–6 servings

I developed a love for Indian food one summer while working at a restaurant on Manhattan's Upper West Side. This recipe is a dairy-free takeoff on my favorite dish from that summer, matar paneer. *It's filled with kid-friendly veggies (potatoes and peas) bathing in a to-die-for sauce. My son has decided that this is his favorite way to eat potatoes, so how could the book be complete without it? Serve it over saffron pilaf (see Note), and we've got something to talk about.*

2 quarts plus 2¾ cups pure water

1½ pounds Yukon Gold potatoes, quartered

One 1-inch piece fresh ginger, peeled and quartered

6 large cloves garlic, peeled and coarsely chopped

4 tablespoons canola oil

3 cardamom pods

1 pound tomatoes, peeled, seeded, and finely chopped

2½ teaspoons sea salt

1¼ teaspoons ground cumin

½ teaspoon ground turmeric

½ teaspoon ground coriander

½ teaspoon garam masala

¼ teaspoon ground cayenne pepper (optional)

One 10-ounce package frozen peas (washed and drained)

1 tablespoon chopped fresh cilantro

1. In a medium pot with 2 quarts of pure water, boil the potatoes over high heat for 15–20 minutes or until tender when poked with a fork. Drain and peel the potatoes, then slice into 1-inch cubes and set aside.

2. In a mini food processor, fitted with a metal blade, combine the ginger, garlic, and ¼ cup of the water. Process until creamy, about 30 seconds. Set aside.

3. In a large pot, sauté the potatoes in the oil over moderate to high heat for 8–10 minutes or until just golden. Using a slotted spoon, transfer the potatoes to a small bowl and set aside. Add the cardamom pods to the pot and sizzle for 3–4 seconds. Stir in the tomatoes, ginger mixture, salt, cumin, turmeric, coriander, garam masala, and cayenne pepper. Sauté over moderate heat for 3–4 minutes or until thick. Add the remaining 2½ cups

water, the potatoes, and the peas. Cook uncovered over moderate to high heat for 20–25 minutes, or until a thick, creamy sauce forms.

4. Serve garnished with cilantro and accompanied by saffron pilaf.

NOTE
- **For Basmati Rice Pilaf, see page 156.**

Create-Your-Own Pizzas

Preparation time: 10–15 minutes to prepare, 12–15 minutes to bake
Yield: 8 pizzas

Kids love to be part of the creative cooking process and this easy-to-make meal is the perfect opportunity for them to do so. There are only a few ingredients and the mess is minimal. Remember this one for parties!

8 pocketless or whole-wheat pitas
¼ cup extra-virgin olive oil
2 cups marinara sauce
3 cups grated Mozzarella-style nondairy cheese (about 12 ounces)

1. Preheat the oven to 400°F. Line two 11 x 15-inch cookie sheets with parchment paper.

2. Place pitas, concave side up, onto the prepared sheets. Brush each pita with 1 teaspoon oil, spread on 2 heaping tablespoons sauce (leave ½-inch edge free of sauce), sprinkle on about ⅓ cup cheese, and drizzle ½ teaspoon oil over the top.

3. Bake on the upper and middle racks of the preheated oven for 12–15 minutes. Halfway through the baking period, rotate the sheets from top to bottom and front to back. The pizzas are done when the cheese is melted. Remove the sheets from the oven and let the pizzas cool for 1 minute on the sheets; then, using an angled metal spatula or pancake turner, transfer them to a cutting board. Using a sharp knife or cutting wheel, slice each into 4 equal wedges.

4. Serve accompanied by julienned veggie sticks.

- For those sensitive to wheat, try the many varieties of rice, millet, rye, or spelt breads that are found in natural foods stores.
- For variety, try this pizza with sautéed vegetables (spinach, red onions, yellow bell peppers, mushrooms, or zucchini).
- For Joe's Marinara Sauce, see page 166.

Glorious Garlicky Greens

Preparation time: 10–15 minutes to prepare, 15–20 minutes to cook

Yield: 4 servings

Fortunately, my children love just about every type of green vegetable. As soon as they were old enough to chew, I started making numerous varieties of sautéed greens for them. As long as I present a variety, they never seem to tire of them. I sometimes serve them with baked sweet potatoes or a whole grain such as millet, brown rice, or barley. Or I make a whole meal out of the greens by adding sliced black olives, and either garbanzo or white beans, and a few Italian herbs. Either way, it's a simple solution for those times when a quick, super-healthy meal is needed.

2 pounds Italian kale, escarole, spinach, or green chard
About 6 quarts pure water
10 large cloves garlic, peeled and chopped
¼ cup extra-virgin olive oil
½ teaspoon sea salt

1. Separate the leaves of the greens and trim the bases, discarding any yellow or bruised leaves. If the leaves are small, keep them whole. If they are large, layer 5 leaves together, roll them up, and slice them into wide ribbons. Wash and dry the greens in a spinner, and set aside.

2. To blanch the greens, in a large pot, bring the water to a rolling boil. Stir half the greens into the water and cook for 4–5 minutes or until just tender. Strain the greens and plunge them into a large bowl of ice water for 5–10 seconds, then drain thoroughly (squeeze out any excess liquid), coarsely chop, and set aside. To blanch the remaining greens, repeat the above process.

3. In a large sauté pan or wok, sauté the garlic in the oil over moderate heat for 2 minutes or until the edges are just golden. Toss in the prepared greens, sprinkle on the salt, and sauté over moderate heat for 5–7 minutes or until the greens are heated through.

4. Serve hot accompanied by a whole grain or baked sweet potato.

■ The cooking time will vary depending on the thickness of the greens. Spinach does not need to be blanched first. Escarole and some varieties of kale have thicker leaves and need a greater cooking time, while spinach and green chard have thinner leaves and therefore need less cooking time.

Healthy-Style Tater Skins

Preparation time: 10–15 minutes to prepare, 5–8 minutes to bake
Yield: 4–6 servings

As a rebellious teenager, I used to love to go to T.G.I. Friday's and eat potato skins with bacon, melted cheese, and sour cream. I always felt terrible afterward, and this is my attempt as a fully reformed adult to create a healthy version of this dish. This recipe is dairy free and low fat, so it should leave you feeling great. And your kids—while they may not care about nutritional virtues—will love it too.

4 large baked russet potatoes
1 tablespoon canola oil
¾ teaspoon sea salt
½ teaspoon Cajun seasoning
2 cups grated Cheddar-style nondairy cheese
½–⅔ cup nondairy sour cream
2–3 tablespoons finely chopped chives
Paprika to taste

1. Preheat the oven to 425°F. Line two 11 x 15-inch cookie sheets with parchment paper and set aside.

2. Split the potatoes in half lengthwise and use a spoon to carefully scoop out the potato pulp, but leave about a ½-inch layer of the potato in the skin. Cut each half into quarters, and brush skin sides lightly with the oil. Place the potato shells, skin side down, on the prepared cookie sheets. Evenly sprinkle each shell with salt, Cajun seasoning, and cheese. Bake on the upper rack of the preheated oven for 5–8 minutes, or until the cheese is melted.

3. Remove the sheets from the oven and, using a pancake turner, slide the potato skins onto a serving platter. Serve hot topped with nondairy sour cream, chives, and paprika.

NOTES

■ To bake the potatoes, preheat the oven to 425°F. Scrub and dry the potatoes, then prick the surface of each 4 times with a fork and rub each with ½ teaspoon of canola oil. Place the potatoes on a cookie sheet lined with parchment paper, place on the center rack of the oven, and bake for about 1 hour or until tender.

■ Try these with Seemingly Sinful Sour Cream (page 125).

Hungarian Country Potatoes

Preparation time: 15–20 minutes to prepare, 40–45 minutes to cook

Yield: 4 servings

My mom used to take me downhill skiing on the weekends; we would venture into snowy upstate New York and stay at bed-and-breakfast inns. One in particular comes to mind, an establishment operated by a Hungarian family, where meals were brought to the table in one large pan and tasted incredibly delicious. I was not so fond of the skiing, but dinnertime made it all worthwhile. These potatoes, inspired by those memories, are simmered in tomatoes and fresh herbs until they are so tender that they melt in your mouth. In short, this is a comforting meal that you and the family will never be disappointed with.

¼ cup extra-virgin olive oil

2 pounds yellow-fleshed potatoes, peeled and cut into 1-inch pieces

2 cups chopped yellow onions

4 large cloves garlic, peeled and coarsely chopped

2 cups canned whole tomatoes with their liquid, pureed in a blender for 5–10 seconds

2 tablespoons chopped parsley

1 bay leaf

1 sprig fresh sage, or ¼ teaspoon dried

1 sprig fresh thyme, or ¼ teaspoon dried

1 teaspoon ground paprika

1 teaspoon sea salt

¼ teaspoon freshly ground black pepper

2 cups pure water

¼ cup fresh basil leaves, washed, patted dry, and thinly sliced

1. Heat the oil in a large saucepan; then brown the potatoes in the oil over moderate to high heat for about 3–4 minutes on each side. Transfer to a plate, cover, and set aside.

2. Sauté the onions and garlic in the oil remaining in the pan. When the onions become soft, after about 2–3

minutes, stir in the tomatoes, parsley, bay leaf, sage, thyme, paprika, salt, pepper, and water. Place the prepared potatoes in the pan, and simmer partially covered over moderate heat, stirring occasionally, for about 30–35 minutes, or until the potatoes are tender and a rich sauce has formed. Stir in the basil until well combined. Remove and discard the bay leaf.

3. Serve hot on top of flat noodles tossed in a little extra-virgin olive oil, finely chopped parsley, and salt; or serve atop Basmati Rice Pilaf (page 156). Accompany by a mixed green salad.

NOTE

- **To make Hungarian Country Beans use two 15-ounce cans white beans in place of the potatoes.**

Joe's Marinara Sauce

Preparation time: 5 minutes to prepare, 25 minutes to cook
Yield: 4–6 servings

This light and delicious tomato sauce is perfect for pasta, pizza, or just about any entree that needs added pizzazz. It takes only minutes to prepare, and it never fails to satisfy a serious eater.

Two 28-ounce cans whole peeled tomatoes with their liquid
6 large cloves garlic, peeled and finely chopped
1 tablespoon plus 1 teaspoon finely minced onion
4 tablespoons extra-virgin olive oil
½ teaspoon sea salt
½ teaspoon dried basil
1 tablespoon plus 1 teaspoon finely chopped parsley

1. In a blender, blend the tomatoes on low speed for about 10 seconds or until smooth (try not to overblend or they will become frothy). Set aside.

2. In a medium saucepan, sauté the garlic and onion in the oil over moderate to low heat for 1–2 minutes or until just golden. Stir in the tomatoes, salt, basil, and parsley. Reduce the heat to low and simmer uncovered for 20 minutes, stirring occasionally.

3. Serve hot atop pasta, whole grains, or vegetables.

NOTE

■ The secret to an excellent marinara is the tomatoes: Good-quality Italian tomatoes are ideal for this purpose, or use tasty organic tomatoes with basil.

Main Course Hummus Plates

Preparation time: 10 minutes

Yield: 4 servings

We often serve hummus as our main course at the dinner table because we love the happy mingling of sesame, chickpeas, and garlic. There is nothing like pressure-cooking your own organic beans, then making this dish while the beans are still warm. My kids will always eat hummus served with either toasted whole-wheat flat bread or baked tortilla chips.

HUMMUS

3 cups cooked garbanzo beans

¾ cup sesame tahini

1 large clove garlic, peeled

¾ teaspoon ground cumin

1½ teaspoons sea salt

¾ cup pure water

¼ cup plus 1 tablespoon freshly squeezed lemon juice

2 tablespoons extra-virgin olive oil

OTHER COMPONENTS

1 tablespoon plus 1 teaspoon extra-virgin olive oil

1 tablespoon plus 1 teaspoon chopped curly-leafed parsley

1 tablespoon plus 1 teaspoon finely chopped tomato (optional)

½–1 teaspoon Hungarian paprika

One 8-ounce bag whole-wheat chapati, or one 8-ounce bag baked tortilla chips

1. In a food processor, using the metal blade, combine the beans, tahini, garlic, cumin, and salt. Pulse together until coarse, about 10 seconds. Restart the food processor, pour in the water, lemon juice, and olive oil through the feed tube, and run until smooth and creamy, about 5 minutes. Remove the blade, and use a rubber spatula to scrape off any excess hummus remaining on the blade or processor.

2. Assemble each of 4 plates: For each, spoon about ½ cup hummus onto a small serving plate. Using a spoon, make a circular well in the center of the hummus. For each plate, drizzle 1 teaspoon of oil into the well and top

with 1 teaspoon of tomato. Sprinkle the plate evenly with 1 teaspoon parsley followed by ⅛–¼ teaspoon paprika.

3. Serve warm or chilled with the whole-wheat chapati, toasted for a few minutes, or with tortilla chips for dipping, and a mixed green salad.

NOTE

■ **To prepare dried beans, soak 1 cup garbanzo beans overnight, rinse and drain. Pressure-cook in 4 cups pure water for 12 minutes. Remove from the heat, let sit for 5 minutes, then use a long-handled spoon to depress the valve on the pressure cooker lid and release the seam. Canned beans can be used, although cooking your own provides the best taste.**

Mama Palma's Pizza

Preparation time: 10–15 minutes to prepare, 10–15 minutes to bake per batch
Yield: four 10-inch pizzas

Palma Riti was born in America, but the pizza recipe that follows traveled many miles from Italy with her mother, Angelina. In this country, Palma was known as the best cook in town and over the years her pizza pleased many. This recipe was shared with me by her son Joseph, who makes it at least once a week for his three children (who eat up every bit!).

2 pounds fresh plum tomatoes, peeled, seeded, and halved
16 fresh basil leaves, washed and patted dry
½ teaspoon sea salt
Whole-Grain Pizza Dough (page 183)
12 ounces Mozzarella-style nondairy cheese, cut into 3 x 1-inch slices (about ¼-inch thick)
1½ tablespoons grated Parmesan-style nondairy cheese
1 tablespoon plus 2 teaspoons extra-virgin olive oil
16 Kalamata olives (optional)

1. Preheat the oven to 450°F. (If you are using tiles or a baking stone, place them on the oven's lowest rack now.)

2. To prepare the tomato sauce, use a blender to combine the tomatoes, basil, and salt. Blend on medium speed for 1 minute or until smooth. Set aside.

3. Roll out the first flat round of pizza dough and place it on a lightly oiled pizza pan or a well-floured or cornmeal-dusted wooden peel, if you are using it.

4. Evenly spread on the sauce (about ⅓–½ cup poured in the center, then spread with the bottom of the ladle in a circular motion toward the edges, leaving ½ inch free of sauce). Evenly cover with a fourth of the mozzarella, sprinkle on 1–2 teaspoons Parmesan, and drizzle 1¼ teaspoons oil over the top.

5. Bake in the pan or on the preheated tiles, on the lowest rack, for 10–15 minutes or until the crust is golden and crisp. (To prevent sticking, sprinkle the baking stone with cornmeal just before putting the pizzas in the oven.) While baking repeat step 4 to prepare the remaining pizzas. Remove the pizzas from the oven and let cool for 2–3 minutes. Top each pizza with 4 olives and, using a sharp knife or cutting wheel, slice each into 8 equal wedges.

6. Transfer to plates and serve accompanied by a mixed green salad.

NOTES

■ This pizza dough can be shaped into 3-inch hors d'oeuvre-sized rounds for parties or snacks.

■ For variety, try this pizza with or without the cheese plus sautéed spinach, red onions, yellow bell peppers, eggplant, mushrooms, or zucchini.

Mjadara

Preparation time: 5 minutes to prepare, 90–95 minutes to cook
Yield: 6 servings

Along the banks of the Raritan River in the college town of New Brunswick, New Jersey, sits an ever-popular, family-run Lebanese restaurant. It was here, where Mom does the cooking herself, that I was first inspired to develop a recipe for mjadara, a warm lentil and rice dish. Carmelized onions provide a sweet taste to this simple, delicious meal that the entire family will gobble up!

4 cups chopped yellow onions
½ cup extra-virgin olive oil
3 quarts pure water (12 cups)
1½ cups green lentils
½ cup white basmati rice
2 teaspoons sea salt

1. In a large pot, sauté the onions in the oil over moderate to high heat for 5 minutes. When the onions become translucent, pour in the water, cover, and bring to a boil. Stir in the lentils, rice, and salt. Simmer covered over moderate to low heat, stirring occasionally, for 60 minutes.

2. Remove the cover and continue to simmer slowly, stirring every 5–10 minutes, for an additional 25–30 minutes until the mjadara is thick and creamy. Remove from the heat and whisk vigorously for 1 minute. Ladle into six 4 x 7-inch heatproof ceramic casserole dishes or 2 heatproof glass pie pans and set aside for 5–10 minutes or until the top is firm to the touch.

3. Serve alone, accompanied by a salad, or topped with finely chopped tomatoes and parsley.

NOTE

■ **This dish can easily be frozen for quick future meals.**

Paella Valencia

Preparation time: 10 minutes to prepare, 60–65 minutes to cook
Yield: 4 servings

Here is a vegetarian version of a traditional Spanish dish that has Moorish roots. The yellow saffron rice is flavored with sweet onion, tomato, and red peppers, and complemented with tender baby lima beans. It's a great choice for kids since the veggies are in tiny nonthreatening pieces, imparting bright colors. This paella is a family favorite; we enjoy it served as a wholesome meal with tabbouleh or coban salad on the side (see pages 151–152).

½ **cup diced red bell pepper**
½ **cup peeled, seeded, and finely chopped tomato**
¼ **cup chopped onion**
2 large cloves garlic, peeled and finely chopped
3 tablespoons extra-virgin olive oil
8 cups pure water
1½ cups short-grain brown rice or Arborio rice
One 10-ounce package frozen baby lima beans, rinsed and drained
1 tablespoon finely chopped parsley
½ **teaspoon saffron (about .016 ounces)**
2 teaspoons sea salt

1. In a large saucepan or skillet, sauté the red pepper, tomato, onion, and garlic in the oil over moderate heat for 5 minutes. Pour in the water, cover, and bring to a boil over high heat. Reduce the heat to moderate and stir in the rice, beans, parsley, saffron, and salt until well combined. Cover and cook for 55–60 minutes or until all of the water is absorbed (don't stir, or the paella will become mushy). Remove from the heat, and let sit covered for 5 minutes.

2. Serve hot by itself or accompanied by a salad.

NOTE

■ An equal measure of frozen peas can be used to replace the lima beans.

Quesadillas Olé

Preparation time: 10 minutes to prepare, 5–8 minutes to cook
Yield: 8 quesadillas

What kid, big or small, doesn't love melted cheese on lightly toasted bread? Quesadillas are a way of experiencing this flavor combo with Mexican flair. These special treats are great at snacktime, as a whole meal, or as party fare.

16 whole-wheat or corn tortillas
4 cups grated Cheddar-style nondairy cheese
1 cup diced red bell pepper (optional)
2 teaspoons thinly sliced chives (optional)
Sea salt to taste

1. To warm the tortillas, lightly oil and preheat a large cast-iron frying pan or griddle over moderate to high heat until a few drops of water sprinkled into the pan sizzle and bounce. Place 2 tortillas in the skillet, cover, and soften them for 1–2 minutes (do not crisp). Reduce the heat to low, and transfer the tortillas to a flat surface.

2. To assemble a quesadilla, on one of the tortillas place ½ cup cheese (keeping the cheese close to the center, allowing for a ¼-inch cheeseless border) followed by a sprinkling of 2 tablespoons red pepper, ¼ teaspoon chives, and salt. Top with a second tortilla, and press together. Return to the pan, and cook covered over moderate to high heat for 2–3 minutes, or until the cheese has melted. Using a pancake turner, flip the quesadilla over, and cook on the other side an additional 2–3 minutes or until done.

3. Remove from the heat, and, using a sharp knife, slice into 6 equal pizza-like wedges. Transfer to a plate and serve topped with salsa, guacamole, or a little nondairy sour cream. Proceed this way for the remaining seven quesadillas.

NOTE

■ For Sun-Sational Salsa, see page 126; for Good-Time Guacamole, see page 113; and for Seemingly Sinful Sour Cream, see page 125.

Rockin' Roasted Oven Fries

Preparation time: 5 minutes to prepare, 35–40 minutes to roast
Yield: 4–6 servings

We've all had those nights when the kids are feeling extra finicky. The next time that happens, whip up this recipe, serve it as a main dish with salad or soup, or use it to liven up any entree. You'll soon be enjoying the family's compliments as they gobble up this quick, easy, healthy, and delicious version of that age-old classic, French fries. Right on for the Rockin' Roasteds!

4 pounds large Yukon Gold or russet potatoes, cut lengthwise into ½-inch-thick slices, then into ½-inch-long x ½-inch-thick strips, and dried well on a dish towel
5 tablespoons extra-virgin olive oil
1 tablespoon Cajun seasoning
1½ teaspoons sea salt
½ teaspoon garlic salt
½ teaspoon paprika
½ teaspoon dried marjoram
½ teaspoon dried oregano
Freshly ground black pepper to taste

1. Preheat the oven to 500°F.

2. In a large mixing bowl, combine the potatoes and oil. Toss together until well combined. Sprinkle on the Cajun seasoning, salt, garlic salt, paprika, marjoram, oregano, and black pepper. Toss again until the potatoes are well coated.

3. Evenly distribute the potatoes on two 11 x 15-inch baking sheets. Roast on the top and middle racks of the

preheated oven, turning them occasionally, until golden brown and crisp on all sides, about 35–40 minutes. For uniformity in baking, rotate the sheets from top to bottom and front to back halfway through the baking period.

4. Serve with a mixed green salad.

NOTE

■ **For ROASTED SWEET POTATO FRIES use an equal measure of sweet potatoes in place of the Yukon Gold.**

Rosendale Café Stroganoff

Preparation time: 20 minutes to prepare, 70–85 minutes to cook
Yield: 4–6 servings

Imagine this: ribbony noodles topped with tender morsels of tofu swimming in a smooth creamy sauce, seasoned with mushrooms and fresh herbs. If you're going to be visiting upstate New York, the Rosendale Café is a must. Not only do they have a delicious homestyle vegetarian menu but they've become a bastion of culture in a small mountain village. Folk, jazz, and eclectic music on the weekends, and good conversation with friends are staples, and the hospitable owners and welcoming staff create an atmosphere that is kind to the soul as well as the stomach.

2 pounds extra-firm tofu, well drained
1¼ cups plus 1 tablespoon canola oil
2 teaspoons tamari soy sauce
5 quarts plus 1 cup pure water
¼ cup freshly squeezed lemon juice
1 tablespoon ground mustard powder
4 large yellow onions, peeled and sliced into ¼-inch-thick half-moons (about 2½ pounds)
2 pounds mushrooms, thinly sliced
¾ cup red wine
½ cup Bragg Liquid Aminos all-purpose seasoning
Freshly ground black pepper to taste
2 tablespoons plus 1 teaspoon finely chopped parsley
2 tablespoons plus 1 teaspoon finely chopped dill
1 pound ribbon-style pasta

1. To prepare the tofu, preheat the oven to 400°F. Line an 11 x 15-inch cookie sheet with parchment paper and set aside. Slice 1 pound of the tofu into ¼-inch cubes. In a medium bowl, toss together the tofu, 1 tablespoon

of the oil, and the tamari until well combined. Evenly spread the tofu on the prepared sheet and bake on the middle rack of the preheated oven, turning occasionally, until golden brown and crisp on all sides, about 35–40 minutes. For uniformity in baking, rotate the sheet from top to bottom and front to back halfway through the baking period. Remove the sheet from the oven and slide the parchment paper onto a wire rack to cool.

2. To prepare the nondairy sour cream, in a food processor, using the metal blade, combine the remaining pound of tofu, ¾ cup of the oil, 1 cup of water, the lemon juice, and the mustard powder. Process for 2 minutes or until smooth and creamy and set aside.

3. To prepare the filling, sauté together the remaining ½ cup oil, the onions, and the mushrooms in a large pot over high heat for 12–15 minutes or until the onions are translucent. Pour the wine and Bragg Liquid Aminos into the pot with the vegetables and cook for 5 more minutes. Stir in the prepared sour cream, tofu, and black pepper. Simmer until thick and creamy, about 10–15 minutes. Toss in the parsley and dill until well combined, cover, and set aside.

4. In a large pot, bring about 5 quarts of water to a rolling boil. Stir the noodles into the water and cook until the pasta is just tender, but not soft, about 8–10 minutes. Transfer to a colander, and drain. Reheat the tofu mixture over moderate heat until hot and pour on top of the prepared noodles.

5. Serve hot, accompanied by a mixed green salad.

NOTES
- **Bragg Liquid Aminos all-purpose seasoning can be purchased in health food stores.**
- **For variety, the ribbon-style pasta can be replaced by cooked short-grain brown rice.**

Savory Quiche with Mushrooms and Greens

Preparation time: 20–25 minutes to prepare, 55–60 minutes to bake
Yield: 4–6 servings

This wonderful Swiss chard and pine nut tart is flavored with caramelized leek, mushrooms, and fresh basil. It has the delicate texture of quiche without all the fat and cholesterol. I have replaced the dairy products with just the right amount of silken tofu. Along with this classic pesto version I make a saffron and nutmeg one for Easter and Mother's Day (see Notes). So when you have to cook for a special occasion, trust me on this one.

2 tablespoon pine nuts
1 pound green chard

About 4 quarts pure water

2 tablespoons plus ¾ teaspoon sea salt

1 large leek, thinly sliced, then chopped, white part only

1 medium yellow onion, peeled and finely chopped

½ pound mushrooms, thinly sliced

4 large cloves garlic, peeled and coarsely chopped

4 tablespoons extra-virgin olive oil

1½ cups silken tofu, well drained

18–20 large, fresh basil leaves

1 tablespoon finely chopped fresh parsley

Freshly ground black pepper to taste

½ recipe Healthy Pie Crust dough (page 208), rolled into a 9-inch tart shell and prebaked for 15–20 minutes

1. Preheat the oven to 375°F. Evenly spread the pine nuts on an 11 x 15-inch cookie sheet and bake in the preheated oven for 5 minutes, or until the edges are just golden. Remove the sheet from the oven and transfer the nuts to a plate. Cool completely.

2. Separate the leaves of the chard and trim the bases and cut away the fleshy stalks, discarding any yellow or bruised leaves. If the leaves are small, keep them whole. If they are large, layer 5 leaves together, roll them up, and slice them into wide ribbons. Wash and dry the greens in a spinner, and set aside.

3. To blanch the chard, in a large pot, bring the water and 2 tablespoons of sea salt to a rolling boil. Stir the chard into the water and cook until just tender, about 2 minutes. Plunge the chard into a large bowl of ice water for 5–10 seconds, then drain thoroughly (squeezing out any additional liquid). Chop coarsely and set aside.

4. In a large pot, sauté together the leek, onion, mushrooms, and garlic in 3 tablespoons of the olive oil over moderate heat for 5–8 minutes, or until the onion is translucent. Toss in the chard, and sauté covered over moderate heat for 1 minute or until the greens are warm and well combined.

5. In a food processor, using the metal blade, combine the tofu and the remaining tablespoon of oil. Process until creamy, about 1 minute. Add the basil, parsley, remaining ¾ teaspoon salt, and black pepper. Process until well blended. Remove the blade, and use a rubber spatula to scrape off any excess filling remaining on the blade or processor.

6. In a large bowl, combine the chard mixture and tofu mixture. Stir together until well mixed. Pour the filling into the prepared tart shell and distribute evenly with a spatula. Evenly sprinkle on the pine nuts.

7. Bake in the middle level of the preheated oven for 35–40 minutes, or until the top is golden and firm. For uniformity in baking, rotate the pan from front to back halfway through the baking period. Remove the pan

from the oven, transfer to a wire rack, and let the tart cool in the pan for 10 minutes. Carefully push up the bottom and slide the tart off the disk and onto a cutting board. Using a sharp knife, slice the tart into 4–6 equal wedges.

8. Serve alone or accompanied by a mixed green salad.

NOTES

■ For Spinach & Red Pepper Quiche, use 1 pound fresh spinach in place of the green chard (1 pound fresh spinach will yield about 3 cups chopped). The spinach does not need to be blanched first; just sauté for 3 minutes, then squeeze out any excess liquid. Use ½ pound red bell peppers (roasted, peeled, seeded, and diced) to replace the mushrooms. To roast the peppers, preheat the oven to 350°F. Rub the peppers with olive oil, place them on a baking sheet, and roast for 25 minutes. Remove from the oven and place them in a brown paper bag for 5 minutes to steam. Cut the peppers in half, remove the stems and seeds, peel off the skin, and dice.

■ Adults love the flavors of saffron and nutmeg, so try replacing the basil with ½ teaspoon saffron (soaked in 2 teaspoons hot water) and ¼ teaspoon ground nutmeg.

Sesame Hijiki

Preparation time: 20 minutes to prepare, 18–20 minutes to cook
Yield: 4–6 servings

Hijiki is one of the richest sources of potassium on the planet, and one of the best sources of calcium as well. So this super food is too valuable to be passed over. It is, however, a food that smart parents will introduce early, so children can acquire a taste for it. Here's a delicious way to do so.

1 package hijiki (2.1 ounces) (see page 43)
7 cups pure water
1 large lemon, squeezed and with pulp discarded
1 large yellow onion, peeled and diced
3 tablespoons toasted sesame oil
2 large carrots, julienned
4–5 tablespoons tamari soy sauce
3 tablespoons sesame seeds

1. Place the hijiki into a large bowl and, using the bottom of a glass, crush it into ¼-inch pieces. Pour in 4 cups of the water and the lemon juice. Let soak for 20 minutes. Transfer to a colander, rinse, and drain well.

2. In a large saucepan, sauté the onion in the oil over moderate to high heat for 2–3 minutes. When the onion becomes translucent, stir in the hijiki, carrots, tamari, and the remaining 3 cups of water. Simmer covered over moderate heat for 15 minutes or until the carrots are tender.

3. Serve hot topped with sesame seeds, accompanied by any whole-grain or legume-based entree.

NOTES
- **Two-thirds cup dry crushed hijiki is equal to 2.1 ounces**
- **Arame can be used to replace the hijiki.**
- **For those sensitive to wheat, be sure to use tamari labeled "wheat-free" and not shoyu tamari, which contains wheat.**

Stir-Fried Sesame Broccoli

Preparation time: 15–20 minutes to prepare, 8–10 minutes to cook
Yield: 4 servings

This dish is on the menu of almost every Chinese restaurant for one simple reason: It's delicious! But it's also nutritious, which is another reason you'll want to make it a part of your family-meal repertoire. Vitamin- and mineral-rich vegetables are lightly cooked to crunchy perfection and tossed with tender morsels of tofu. Covered with an aromatic sesame sauce, this flavorful delicacy will have your family coming back for more.

1¼ cups pure water

3 tablespoons tamari soy sauce

2 tablespoons pure maple syrup

2 teaspoons brown rice vinegar or freshly squeezed lemon juice

3 cups broccoli florets with stems, cut into 1-inch pieces (about 6 ounces)

12 ounces firm tofu, cut into ½-inch cubes

About 3 quarts pure water

1 tablespoon plus 1 teaspoon toasted sesame oil

1 tablespoon canola oil

¾ cup thinly sliced, then chopped, leeks, white parts only

8 large cloves garlic, peeled and finely chopped

1 teaspoon finely chopped, peeled ginger

1 medium yellow squash, cut into ¼-inch cubes (about 6 ounces)

6 ounces shiitake mushrooms, destemmed and sliced

3 tablespoons arrowroot powder or cornstarch, dissolved in ¼ cup water
1 large red bell pepper, cored, seeded, and cut into ½-inch cubes
1½ tablespoons black sesame seeds

1. In a small mixing bowl, combine the water, tamari, maple syrup, and vinegar. Whisk together until well blended and set aside.

2. To blanch the broccoli and tofu, in a large pot, bring about 3 quarts of water to a rolling boil. Stir the broccoli and tofu into the water and cook until the broccoli is tender-crisp, about 2–3 minutes. Strain the broccoli and tofu from the water and plunge into a large bowl of ice water for 5–10 seconds, then drain thoroughly, and set aside.

3. Heat a wok or large cast-iron frying pan over high heat, until hot enough to evaporate a bead of water on contact. Add the oils, swirl to glaze the pan, and reduce the heat to moderate. When the oil is hot enough to sizzle a piece of ginger, add the leeks, garlic, and ginger. Stir-fry for 30–45 seconds, or until aromatic. Toss in the squash and mushrooms (turning the vegetables in a folding motion so that they heat evenly and do not stick to the pan). Cook for 1–2 additional minutes. Add the maple syrup mixture to the wok. Raise the heat to high, cover the pan, and bring the sauce to a simmer. Stir the arrowroot mixture to recombine, add it to the wok, and stir-fry until the sauce turns glossy, 10–20 seconds. Add the broccoli, tofu, and red pepper and stir-fry for 3–4 additional minutes, or until heated through.

4. Serve over brown rice and garnish with a sprinkling of sesame seeds.

NOTES
- **For those sensitive to wheat, be sure to use tamari labeled "wheat-free" and not shoyu tamari, which contains wheat.**
- **For Stir-Fried Broccoli and Tempeh, use one 8-ounce package of tempeh (cut into ½-inch cubes and pan-fried until crunchy and golden) to replace the blanched tofu.**

Tamari Mushroom Brown Rice

Preparation time: 10 minutes to prepare, 30 minutes to cook
Yield: 4 servings

This mild-flavored rice enhanced with caramelized onion and golden mushroom slices is always a big hit with children and adults alike. I have made this dish for my friends seemingly forever. They are always amazed that something so tasty can be so simple to prepare.

2½ cups pure water
1 cup short-grain brown rice
½ cup chopped yellow onion
1½ cups sliced mushrooms
1 tablespoon canola oil
2 teaspoons tamari soy sauce
2 tablespoons sesame seeds (optional)

1. In a medium suacepan, bring the water to a boil. Stir in the rice, reduce the heat to low, and simmer covered for 25 minutes or until all of the water is absorbed.

2. In a large frying pan, over high heat, sauté the onion and mushrooms in the oil for 5–7 minutes or until just golden. Stir in the cooked rice, drizzle with tamari, and mix with a large wooden spoon until well combined.

3. Garnish with sesame seeds and serve alone or accompanied by sea vegetables, steamed vegetables, legumes, or a salad.

NOTE
■ For those sensitive to wheat, be sure to use tamari labeled "wheat-free" and not shoyu tamari, which contains wheat.

Teepee Tacos

Preparation time: 5–10 minutes to prepare, 8–12 minutes to cook
Yield: 8 tacos

I've never met a kid who didn't like to create and consume hard-shell tacos. Mine are no exception, and I'm sure yours will be the same. Even if you don't have children, the kid in you will find them irresistible too.

8 taco shells
¼ cup finely chopped onion
2 tablespoons canola oil
Two 15-ounce cans pinto beans, rinsed and drained
½ cup pure water
1 teaspoon sea salt
½ teaspoon onion powder
¼ teaspoon cumin powder

¼ teaspoon chili powder

¼ teaspoon garlic powder

1¼ cups grated Cheddar-style nondairy cheese (about 5 ounces)

1½ cups green leaf, iceberg, or Boston (butter) lettuce, sliced into thin ribbons

1 small, vine-ripened tomato, seeded and chopped (optional)

½ cup salsa or taco sauce

1. Preheat the oven to 350°F. Evenly arrange the taco shells on an 11 x 15-inch cookie sheet and bake in the preheated oven for 5–7 minutes, or until they are warm. Remove the sheet from the oven and set aside.

2. While the shells are baking, use a large pan to sauté the onion in the oil over moderate heat for 1–2 minutes. When the onion becomes translucent, stir in the beans, water, salt, onion powder, cumin powder, chili powder, and garlic powder until well combined. Using a potato masher, mash the beans until they are almost refried in consistency. Simmer uncovered over high heat for 2–3 minutes, or until thick and creamy. Cover, remove from the heat, and set aside.

3. To assemble the tacos, spread about 2 tablespoons of the hot refried beans into each taco shell. Top each taco with cheese, lettuce, tomato, and salsa.

4. Serve alone or accompanied by guacamole and corn chips.

NOTE

- For Sun-Sational Salsa, see page 126; and for Good-Time Guacamole, see page 113.

Vegetable Fried Rice

Preparation time: 15 minutes to prepare, 45–50 minutes to cook

Yield: 4 servings

This is one menu item from the local Chinese restaurant my kids always enjoy. I can remember more than one occasion when they vigorously negotiated possession of the baby corn and water chestnuts. Fortunately, this homemade version has no unhealthy additives and plenty of the good stuff to go around, so everyone is happy.

6 cups pure water

⅓ cup diced carrot

2 cups short-grain brown rice

2 tablespoons canola oil

1 small yellow onion, peeled and finely chopped

¼ cup finely chopped leek

1 scallion, thinly sliced

2 large cloves garlic, peeled and finely chopped

½ teaspoon finely grated ginger

½ cup thinly sliced Napa cabbage (or bok choy)

⅔ cup baby corn, drained and cut into ¼-inch half-sections (optional)

½ cup frozen peas, thawed and drained

¼ cup diced water chestnuts (optional)

1 tablespoon toasted sesame oil

1 tablespoon tamari soy sauce

1 teaspoon sea salt

¼ cup black sesame seeds

1. In a medium saucepan, bring the water to a boil. Stir the carrot into the water and cook for 4–5 minutes or until just tender. Strain the carrot from the water and run under cold water for 5–10 seconds, then drain thoroughly and set aside. Stir the rice into the water, reduce the heat to moderate, and simmer uncovered for 35 minutes or until all of the water is absorbed. Cover and set aside for 5 minutes.

2. Heat a wok or large cast-iron frying pan over high heat, until hot enough to evaporate a bead of water on contact. Add 1 tablespoon of the canola oil, swirl to glaze the pan, and reduce the heat to moderate. When the oil is hot enough to sizzle a piece of ginger, add the onion, leek, scallion, garlic, and ginger. Stir-fry for 2–3 seconds, or until aromatic. Toss in the carrot and cabbage, and continue cooking for 1–2 additional minutes. Toss in the corn, peas, and water chestnuts until well combined. Remove the ingredients from the pan, and set aside.

3. Heat the wok over high heat, until hot enough to evaporate a bead of water on contact. Add the remaining tablespoon of canola oil and the sesame oil, and swirl to glaze the pan. Add the rice and stir-fry to heat through (turning rice in a folding motion so that it heats evenly and does not stick to the pan). Toss the vegetables into the rice, drizzle on the tamari, sprinkle on the salt, and toss until well mixed.

4. Spoon into bowls and garnish with a sprinkling of sesame seeds.

NOTE

■ For those sensitive to wheat, be sure to use tamari labeled "wheat-free" and not shoyu tamari, which contains wheat.

West Virginia Chili Dogs

Preparation time: 10 minutes to prepare, 10 minutes to cook
Yield: 6 chili dogs

When I was little, the high point of a summer's day would be an outing to Betty Davis's drive-in. We would pull up in my grandfather's pickup and order root beer floats and foot-long hotdogs with sauce and onions. You might think that such a treat could be nothing more than a memory for a person eating a sensible diet. Wrong! Here's my healthy version, and believe me, the kids will not know these hotdogs are soy-based if you don't tell.

CHILI SAUCE

¼ cup finely chopped yellow onion
2 large cloves garlic, peeled and finely chopped
1 tablespoon plus 1 teaspoon canola oil
1 cup peeled, seeded, and finely chopped ripe tomato
4 ounces seitan, rinsed, drained, and finely chopped (about ¾ cup)
2 teaspoons honey
1 teaspoon chili powder
1 teaspoon sea salt

OTHER COMPONENTS

About 6 cups pure water
1 package Yves Veggie Wieners
6 whole-grain hotdog rolls
⅔ cup grated Cheddar-style nondairy cheese (about 3½ ounces)
⅔ cup finely chopped yellow onion (optional)

1. In a medium saucepan or skillet, sauté the onion and garlic in the oil over moderate heat for 1–2 minutes. When the onion becomes translucent, stir in the tomato, seitan, honey, chili powder, and salt. Simmer covered about 7–8 minutes or until a sauce has formed. Set aside.

2. In a medium saucepan, bring the water to a rolling boil. Add the wieners and simmer uncovered for 3 minutes or until hot. Place the wieners into the rolls and top with chili sauce, cheese, and onion. Serve with a salad.

NOTES

▪ **For those sensitive to wheat, 1 cup of coarsely chopped pinto beans can be used to replace the seitan. Also, spelt hotdog rolls are available in most health food stores.**
▪ **For Sloppy Joes, try this chili sauce sandwiched between burger buns.**

Whole-Grain Pizza Dough

Preparation time: 15–20 minutes to prepare, 1 hour to rise
Yield: four 10-inch crusts

Whole grains and whole-grain flours still contain their nutritious germ and bran. This pepped-up version of pizza dough is easy to prepare, and there is nothing like pizza made from homemade dough. Who says pizza has to be unhealthy?

½ teaspoon honey
1½ cups plus 2 tablespoons plus 2 teaspoons lukewarm water (105°F/40°C)
2 tablespoons or 2 packages active dry yeast (¼-ounce each), rapid-rise preferred
3 cups unbleached bread flour, plus 1–3 tablespoons additional for rolling the dough
1 cup whole-wheat flour
2 teaspoons sea salt
1 tablespoon extra-virgin olive oil
Cornmeal, for dusting the wooden peel, if you are using it

1. In a small bowl, combine the honey, water, and yeast. Stir together until well blended and set aside in a warm place for 10–12 minutes, or until slightly foamy.

2. In a large bowl, combine 3 cups bread flour, the whole-wheat flour, and the salt. Whisk together until well mixed. Make a well in the center, and pour in the oil and the yeast mixture. Starting from the center, stir with a spoon or with your hand until all the flour is incorporated into the dough. You should now have a soft, workable dough.

3. Turn the dough out onto a lightly floured surface, and knead (using the heel of your hand) for about 5–8 minutes, or until the dough is pliable and elastic. Sprinkle a little flour as necessary to keep the dough from sticking to the surface.

4. Form the dough into a ball, and place it into a lightly oiled bowl, turning it once so the surface is coated with oil. Cover the bowl with a kitchen towel, and let the dough rise in a warm place until it has doubled in bulk, about 1 hour.

5. To shape the pizza, turn the dough out onto a lightly floured surface. Using a dough scraper, divide the dough into 4 equal pieces. Shape the dough into 4 flat rounds (wrap 3 of the flat rounds tightly in plastic wrap or plastic sandwich bags). Lightly sprinkle the unwrapped round with unbleached white flour. Using a rolling pin, roll out the dough to a thickness of ⅛ inch, and into a 10-inch round. To do this, use even strokes, and work from the center of the dough cake toward the edges, rolling in different directions. To produce an even round shape

and to keep it from sticking to the work surface, move the dough, reflour the surface, and reposition the dough. (If you have a little experience you can pat and press or fling and twirl the dough until it is the size and shape you need.) To form a crust, lift the edge of the pizza to form a slight rim or press 3 fingers around the perimeter ½-inch toward the center into the dough. Repeat the process to prepare the remaining crusts.

6. Lay the rolled-out dough on an oiled pizza pan, cornmeal-dusted wooden peel, or baking sheet. Cover with topping (according to the individual recipe) and bake the pizza on its pan or quickly slide it onto a heated pizza stone or tiles. (To prevent the pizza from sticking, sprinkle the baking stone with cornmeal just before putting the pizza in the oven.)

NOTES

■ A KitchenAid electric mixer is always a good investment and makes steps 2 and 3 easy. Pour the flour mixture into the bowl and use the paddle attachment to combine the flour mixture, yeast mixture, and oil. Mix at speed #2 for 1 minute to distribute all the ingredients. Replace the paddle attachment with the dough hook, increase the mixture speed to #4, and knead the dough for 2–3 minutes, or until elastic and soft (the dough will pull completely away from the sides and bottom of the bowl). If you do not have a heavy-duty electric mixer, a food processor can be used.

■ For those sensitive to wheat, an equal measure of spelt flour can be used to replace the unbleached white and whole-wheat flours. All-purpose flour can be used to replace the unbleached bread flour.

■ For variety and crunch, add sesame or poppy seeds or flaxseeds to the dough during the kneading process.

■ This dough can be stored wrapped airtight in plastic bags and refrigerated for a few hours or frozen up to 1 week.

CHAPTER 12

PASTA

Creamy Spinach and Pine Nut Fusilli

Preparation time: 10 minutes to prepare, 15–18 minutes to cook

Yield: 4 servings

Remember parsley, sage, rosemary, and thyme? They're all in this delicious dish. Try it; your taste buds may well feel like singing.

5 tablespoons pine nuts

¾ pound baby spinach

2 cups unsweetened soy milk

1½ teaspoons sea salt

Freshly ground black pepper to taste

About 5 quarts pure water

1 pound whole-wheat semolina fusilli (see Notes)

6 tablespoons extra-virgin olive oil

1 medium yellow onion, peeled and finely chopped (about 1 cup)

6 large cloves garlic, peeled and finely chopped

1 pound mushrooms, sliced

2 tablespoons finely chopped parsley

1 teaspoon sage

½ teaspoon thyme

¼ teaspoon rosemary

¼ cup grated Parmesan-style nondairy cheese (optional)

1. To toast the nuts, in a small frying pan, sauté over low heat for 3–4 minutes or until just golden. Transfer them to a plate and set aside.

2. In a food processor, using the metal blade, combine the spinach, soy milk, salt, and pepper. Process until creamy, about 2 minutes, and set aside.

3. In a large pot, bring the water to a rolling boil. Stir the fusilli into the water and cook until the pasta is just tender, but not soft, about 8–10 minutes. Transfer to a colander, drain, cover, and set aside.

4. While the pasta is cooking, use a large pot to sauté together the oil, onion, and garlic over moderate heat for 4–5 minutes, or until the onion is translucent. Add the mushrooms, increase the heat to moderate to high, and sauté for 3–4 additional minutes or until the mushrooms are tender. Stir in the spinach mixture, parsley, sage, thyme, and rosemary until well combined. Reduce the heat to low, cover, and simmer for 5 minutes or until a rich sauce forms. Toss the cooked fusilli into the spinach sauce and cook until heated through.

5. Spoon into bowls, garnish with the pine nuts and nondairy cheese, and serve with a mixed green salad.

- For those sensitive to wheat—try rice- or quinoa-based pastas, available in health food stores.
- Ziti, penne, or rotelli can be used to replace the fusilli.

Gnocchi and Sweet Pepper Tomato Coulis

Preparation time: 10–15 minutes to prepare, 35–40 minutes to cook

Yield: 4 servings

A coulis is a smooth, rich, and creamy sauce. The first time I had it, my friends took me out to eat in New York. I was totally hooked on the velvet-like tomato delicacy. Combined with sweet peppers, garlic, and herbs, it makes a wonderful topping for warm potato gnocchi.

About 5 quarts plus ¼ cup pure water

2 medium white onions, peeled and sliced (about ½ pound)

½ cup extra-virgin olive oil

1¼ pounds vine-ripened tomatoes, coarsely chopped

1¼ pounds red bell peppers, cored, seeded, and sliced

4 large cloves garlic, peeled and sliced

2 bay leaves

8 large fresh basil leaves

1 sprig fresh thyme

1 sprig fresh parsley

1 teaspoon sea salt

Freshly ground black pepper to taste

1 pound fresh gnocchi (see Notes)

¼ cup grated Parmesan-style nondairy cheese (optional)

1. In a large pot fitted with a metal colander, bring the water to a rolling boil.

2. To prepare the coulis, in a large pot, over moderate to low heat, cook the onions in the oil, covered, until they are translucent, about 10–15 minutes. Add the tomatoes, peppers, garlic, bay leaves, basil leaves, thyme, parsley, salt, black pepper, and ¼ cup water. Cook covered over moderate heat, stirring occasionally for 20 minutes. Remove from the heat and discard the bay leaves and thyme sprig. Put the mixture through the fine disk of a food mill, or puree it in a blender or food processor for 1 minute (then press it through a fine strainer to remove the remaining seeds). Return the coulis to the pot and cover.

3. Stir the gnocchi into the boiling water and cook until just tender, but not soft: They will all float to the top when done, about 1–2 minutes. Drain through the colander.

4. Spoon into bowls, garnish with the cheese, and serve with a mixed green salad.

NOTES

- **If your tomatoes are not vine-ripened and lack flavor, try adding 2 tablespoons of tomato paste.**
- **For those sensitive to wheat, try rice- or quinoa-based pastas to replace the gnocchi, available in health food stores.**
- **Cavatelli, ravioli, or tortellini can be used to replace the gnocchi. The coulis also makes a great sauce for polenta!**

Grandma's Macaroni and Cheese

Preparation time: 5 minutes to prepare, 15 minutes to cook
Yield: 4 servings

I wasn't much more than 3 years old the first time I tasted Grandma's macaroni and cheese. I was standing alongside her, trying to convince her that the good stuff came in a cardboard box with a foil packet of powdered cheese. It was then that she stopped what she was doing and spoke a few words of kindness. I went from hungry and distraught to calm and reassured. I knew then that her version would be the best ever. On that day, as always, my grandma cooked with the spirit of love.

About 5 quarts pure water
2 cups elbow-style pasta
2 teaspoons canola oil
2½ cups unsweetened soy milk
¼ cup unbleached white flour
2 cups grated Cheddar-style nondairy cheese
1½ teaspoons sea salt
¼ teaspoon freshly ground black pepper
1 tablespoon finely chopped parsley (optional)

1. In a large pot, bring the water to a rolling boil. Stir the pasta into the water and cook until the pasta is just tender, but not soft, about 8–10 minutes. Transfer to a colander, drain off excess water, and set aside.

2. In a medium saucepan, whisk together the oil, milk, and flour until the flour is dissolved. Bring to a simmer

over moderate to low heat. Stir in the cheese, salt, and pepper. Reduce the heat to low, and simmer uncovered (stirring occasionally) for an additional 2–3 minutes or until smooth and creamy.

3. Gently toss the pasta into the melted cheese mixture until well combined. Spoon into large serving bowls and garnish with parsley. Serve alone or accompanied by a mixed green salad.

NOTES

- **This dish is best made minutes before serving.**
- **For those sensitive to wheat, try rice-, quinoa-, or corn-based pasta, available in health food stores. An equal measure of Lundberg brand brown rice flour can be used to replace the unbleached white flour.**

Mario's Stuffed Shells

Preparation time: 40–45 minutes to prepare, 15–20 minutes to bake
Yield: 20–24 shells or 4–6 servings

You can't do much better than stuffed shells and garlic bread for dinner. This low-fat, cholesterol-free version of the shells has all the flavor of its traditional counterpart; the only difference is that you actually feel good after eating. The first time I tried it I couldn't believe the taste. I should have known that a guy whose family comes from the province of Salerno would be right on the mark when it comes to pasta. Try it with A Bronx Salad (page 142) on the side.

1 pound silken tofu, well drained
2 tablespoons plus 2 teaspoons extra-virgin olive oil
1¼ teaspoons onion powder
¼ teaspoon sea salt
1 large clove garlic, peeled and finely minced
1 tablespoon plus 1 teaspoon finely chopped parsley
About 5 quarts pure water
One 8-ounce package large shells
3 cups marinara sauce (see Notes)

1. To prepare the filling, in a food processor, using the metal blade, combine the tofu, onion powder, and salt. Pulse together until well combined, about 10 seconds. Add the garlic and parsley and process until well blended, about 30 seconds. Remove the blade, and use a rubber spatula to scrape off any excess filling remaining on the blade. Cover with plastic wrap and refrigerate until ready to use.

2. Preheat the oven to 450°F, and lightly oil a 9 x 13-inch baking dish. To prepare the shells, in a large pot, bring the water to a rolling boil. Stir the shells into the water and cook until the pasta is just tender, but not soft, about 8–10 minutes. Transfer to a colander and drain. Using a small spoon, carefully spoon the filling into the shells (about 2 heaping teaspoons per shell; do not overstuff). Place the stuffed shells, seam side up, next to one another in the prepared dish. Cover evenly with 2 cups marinara sauce, cover with aluminum foil, and bake in the preheated oven for 15–20 minutes or until hot. In a small saucepan, bring the remaining sauce to a simmer over moderate to low heat. Serve the shells topped with extra sauce, and accompanied by garlic bread and a tossed salad.

NOTES

■ **For Joe's Marinara Sauce, see page 166.**

■ **The filling can be prepared 1 or 2 days in advance and stored in the refrigerator in airtight containers. Or prepare the shells and freeze until a quick, yummy meal is needed. Then just thaw and follow the baking step.**

■ **For those sensitive to wheat, try Ener-G Foods rice cannelloni or stuffable rice-, quinoa-, or corn-based pastas, available in health food stores.**

Maria's Peanut Noodles

Preparation time: 10 minutes to prepare, 8–10 minutes to cook
Yield: 4 servings

Here's a dish that my friend Maria makes for her children. The first time my children tasted it, they would not let me forget how much they loved it. Now we regularly take turns making it for lunch or dinner. Try it, make extra, and bring it to your friends.

½ cup peanut butter

¼ cup canola oil

2 tablespoons plus 2 teaspoons pure maple syrup

2 tablespoons tamari soy sauce

2 tablespoons toasted sesame oil

2 tablespoons brown rice vinegar

1 tablespoon plus 1½ teaspoons freshly squeezed lime juice

½ teaspoon finely grated ginger

About 5 quarts pure water

1 pound udon noodles

2 large scallions, thinly sliced

2 tablespoons finely chopped cilantro (optional)
2 teaspoons black sesame seeds or finely chopped roasted peanuts

1. To prepare the peanut sauce, in a food processor, using the metal blade, combine the peanut butter, canola oil, maple syrup, tamari, sesame oil, vinegar, lime juice, and ginger. Process until smooth and creamy, about 2 minutes. Set aside.

2. To prepare the noodles, in a large pot, bring the water to a rolling boil. Stir the noodles into the water and cook until the pasta is just tender, but not soft, about 8–10 minutes. Transfer to a colander, rinse under cold water, and drain thoroughly.

3. Transfer the noodles to a large mixing bowl, drizzle with the prepared sauce, and gently toss together until well coated. (You can use your fingers to help coat and separate the individual strands.)

4. Twirl the noodles into bowls and serve at room temperature or chilled, garnished with scallions, cilantro, and sesame seeds.

NOTES
■ For those allergic to peanuts, make SESAME NOODLES by using ½ cup sesame tahini in place of the peanut butter and increase the maple syrup measurement to 5 tablespoons.
■ For those sensitive to wheat, be sure to use tamari labeled "wheat-free" and not shoyu tamari, which contains wheat. Also, try some of the rice-based pastas that can be found in health food stores.

Penne and Spring Vegetables

Preparation time: 10 minutes to prepare, 9–12 minutes to cook
Yield: 4 servings

Springtime, with its abundance of nutritious, brightly colored vegetables, is a great season to try this light, fragrant dish. Penne is a great pasta for children since no twirling is involved—just pure eating pleasure.

About 5 quarts pure water
1 pound whole-wheat semolina penne
¾ cup finely chopped onion
6 large cloves garlic, peeled and finely chopped
4 tablespoons extra-virgin olive oil
2 large red bell peppers, cored, seeded, and cut into ¼-inch strips

1 large yellow squash, halved, seeds removed, and thinly sliced

1 pound tomatoes, peeled, seeded, and finely chopped

1 cup sliced black olives

1 tablespoon balsamic vinegar

½ teaspoon sea salt

32 large basil leaves, thinly sliced (about ½ cup)

⅓ cup finely chopped parsley

¼–½ cup grated Parmesan-style nondairy cheese (optional)

1. In a large pot, bring the water to a rolling boil. Stir the penne into the water and cook until the pasta is just tender, but not soft, about 8–10 minutes. Transfer to a colander, drain, and set aside.

2. While the pasta is cooking, use a large saucepan to sauté together the onion and garlic in the oil over moderate heat for 1–2 minutes or until translucent. Stir in the peppers and squash and cook for 5–6 additional minutes or until tender. Add the tomatoes, olives, vinegar, and salt. Continue cooking for 3–4 minutes or until saucy. Add the penne and toss together until heated through. Remove from heat and stir in the basil and parsley until well combined.

3. Spoon into bowls, garnish with cheese, and serve with a crusty loaf of whole-grain bread.

NOTES

- For those sensitive to wheat, try rice-, or quinoa-based pastas, available in health food stores.
- Ziti, rigatoni, or bow ties can be used to replace the penne.

Pesto Bow-Tie Pasta

Preparation time: 10 minutes to prepare, 16–20 minutes to cook

Yield: 4 servings

I have often prepared bow-tie pasta at parties and other events because it's loved by kids and requested by parents. This colorful pesto dish geared to the little ones is low on garlic but is still loaded with flavor. What's more, it's not too oily, and can be prepared with or without cheese.

About 5 quarts pure water

¼ cup sun-dried tomatoes (8 large slices)

½ cup walnuts or pine nuts

2 cloves garlic, peeled

½ cup extra-virgin olive oil

1 teaspoon sea salt

1¼ cups washed, patted dry, and packed fresh basil leaves

¼ cup washed, patted dry, and packed fresh flat-leaf parsley

One 12-ounce package bow-tie pasta

¼ cup pine nuts

Nondairy Parmesan-style cheese to taste (optional)

1. In a large pot, bring the water to a rolling boil. Ladle enough boiling water over the tomatoes to cover, and let sit for 5 minutes or until soft. Drain off the excess water and set aside.

2. In a food processor, using the metal blade, combine the tomatoes, walnuts, garlic, oil, and salt. Pulse together until coarse, about 10 seconds. Add the basil and parsley, processing until well blended, about 1 minute. Remove the blade and scrape off any excess pesto remaining on the blade or processor.

3. Stir the bow ties into the boiling water and cook until the pasta is tender, but not soft, about 8–10 minutes. Transfer to a colander and drain. Return to the pan, add the pesto, and gently toss until well combined.

4. Spoon into large serving bowls, and garnish with pine nuts and cheese.

NOTE

■ For those sensitive to wheat, try Mrs. Leeper's multicolored rice vegetable twists, or rice-, quinoa-, or corn-based pastas, available in health food stores.

Ribbony Noodles with Parsley and Peas

Preparation time: 2 minutes to prepare, 5–8 minutes to cook

Yield: 4 servings

This pasta dish is perfect for times when a quick meal is needed, since it takes only minutes to make. It's simple, buttery, and delicious. For a healthy dinner combination, serve with salad.

About 5 quarts pure water

1 pound ribbon-style pasta

1 cup frozen peas, rinsed and drained

3 tablespoons extra-virgin olive oil

2 tablespoons finely chopped fresh parsley

1½ teaspoons sea salt or to taste

¼ cup Parmesan-style nondairy cheese (optional)

1. In a large pot, bring the water to a rolling boil. Stir the noodles into the water and cook until the pasta is just tender, but not soft, about 5–8 minutes. Stir in the peas and continue cooking for an additional 30 seconds. Transfer to a colander, drain, and return to the pan. Sprinkle on the oil, parsley, and salt. Toss together until well combined.

2. Spoon into bowls and garnish with cheese.

NOTE

- **For children with wheat sensitivities, try rice-, quinoa-, or corn-based pastas, available in health food stores.**

Spaghetti and Fresh Tomato Sauce

Preparation time: 20 minutes to prepare, 35–40 minutes to cook

Yield: 4 servings

Here's a dish that's simple and easy, but very delicious when it's made with fresh vine-ripened tomatoes and basil. The basil adds lightness to the sauce, while the garlic, onion, and olive oil deliver a characteristic Italian richness that you can't find in a jar.

About 5 quarts pure water

¼ cup finely chopped yellow onion

7 large cloves garlic, peeled and sliced

4 tablespoons extra-virgin olive oil

6 pounds vine-ripened tomatoes, peeled, seeded, and finely chopped

½ teaspoon sea salt

1 pound spaghetti

16 fresh basil leaves, washed, patted dry, and thinly sliced

2 tablespoons finely chopped parsley

¼–½ cup grated Parmesan-style nondairy cheese (optional)

1. In a large pot, bring the water to a rolling boil.

2. In a large pot, sauté together the onion and garlic in the oil over moderate heat for 3–4 minutes or until the

edges are just golden. Add the tomatoes and salt and simmer partially covered for 30–35 minutes or until a thick sauce has formed. Begin cooking the spaghetti about 10 minutes before the sauce is done.

3. Stir the spaghetti into the boiling water and cook until the pasta is just tender, but not soft, about 8–10 minutes. Transfer to a colander, and drain. Add the spaghetti, basil, and parsley to the prepared sauce, then toss together until well combined and heated through.

4. Twirl into bowls, garnish with cheese, and serve with a mixed green salad.

NOTES
- **For children with wheat sensitivities, try rice- or quinoa-based pastas, available in health food stores.**
- **Vermicelli, capellini, or linguine can be used to replace the spaghetti.**

Tamari Tossed Shells

Preparation time: 1 minute to prepare, 8–12 minutes to cook
Yield: 3–4 servings

I asked a friend of mine who does the cooking for an after-school program what dishes were real kid-pleasers, and she gave me this recipe. She reported that even little kids get a real kick out of these shells.

About 5 quarts pure water
1 pound small shells
2 tablespoons canola oil
2 tablespoons tamari soy sauce
2 tablespoons sesame seeds (optional)

1. In a large pot, bring the water to a rolling boil. Stir in the shells and boil until the pasta is tender, but not soft, about 8–12 minutes. Transfer to a colander and drain. Return to the pan, add the oil, tamari, and seasame seeds, and stir until well combined.

2. Serve with julienned vegetables.

NOTE
- **For those sensitive to wheat, try quinoa-, corn-, or rice-based pastas, available in health food stores. And be sure to use tamari labeled "wheat-free" and not shoyu tamari, which contains wheat.**

All-American Rice Pudding

Preparation time: 5 minutes to prepare, 55–65 minutes to cook
Yield: 4–6 servings

My grandma Null's rice pudding was famous. It was always the first to disappear from the picnic table at many a summertime Sunday church barbecue on the mighty Ohio River. Today, this creamy-sweet pudding flavored with raisins and cinnamon is my children's favorite, and one that I'm sure your children will enjoy too!

6 cups soy milk
⅓ cup pure maple syrup
2 cups cooked short-grain brown rice
¼ cup raisins (optional)
¼ cup pure vanilla flavor
½ teaspoon ground cinnamon

1. In a medium saucepan, combine 4 cups of the milk and the maple syrup. Cover and bring to a simmer over moderate heat. Stir in the rice and raisins, reduce the heat to low, and simmer partially covered, stirring frequently with an angled-bottom wooden spoon, for 40–45 minutes or until thick and creamy. Add the remaining 2 cups milk and cook for an additional 15–20 minutes or until creamy. Remove from the heat and stir in the vanilla until well combined.

2. Pour the pudding into a medium shallow baking dish and set aside to cool for 15–20 minutes. Evenly sprinkle on the cinnamon, cover with plastic wrap, and refrigerate for 1 hour or until chilled.

3. Spoon into bowls and serve.

NOTES
■ **To cook the rice, bring 2½ cups pure water to a boil in a medium saucepan. Stir in 1 cup rice, reduce the heat to low, and simmer covered for 25 minutes or until all of the water is absorbed.**
■ **For best results, use Vitasoy Creamy Original soy milk. Remember, this pudding will thicken as it chills, so it should be a bit looser than you would like when hot.**

Animal Honey Grahams

Preparation time: 10 minutes to prepare, 1 hour to chill, 10–12 minutes to bake
Yield: 2 dozen cookies

These fun-to-make cookies are a perfect family activity with a tasty bonus. Kids love to select their own animal cutter shapes and cut the dough. They love to smell these treats baking in the oven, and—best of all, of course—to eat them when they're done.

2 cups plus 2 tablespoons spelt flour
2 teaspoons baking soda
1 teaspoon ground cinnamon
¼ teaspoon sea salt
½ cup canola oil
¼ cup well-mashed ripe banana
⅓ cup honey
1 teaspoon pure vanilla flavor

1. Preheat the oven to 375°F. Line two 11 x 15-inch cookie sheets with parchment paper and set aside.

2. In a medium mixing bowl, sift together the flour, baking soda, cinnamon, and salt. Set aside.

3. In a food processor, using the metal blade, combine the oil and banana. Process until creamy, about 1 minute. Pour in the honey and vanilla, then process until well blended. Pulse in the dry ingredients until just incorporated. Scrape the dough into a bowl, cover with plastic wrap, and refrigerate for at least 1 hour or until well chilled.

4. Place the dough on a large piece of waxed or parchment paper and top with another sheet of paper. Roll the dough out to a thickness of ¼ inch. Remove the paper and cut out the cookies using animal-shaped cookie cutters (about 2½ inches in diameter). Use a small metal spatula to transfer the cookies onto the prepared cookie sheets (12 cookies per sheet).

5. Bake on the upper and middle racks of the preheated oven for 10–12 minutes. For uniformity in baking, rotate the sheets from top to bottom and front to back halfway through the baking period. The cookies are done when firm to the touch. Remove the sheets from the oven and let the cookies cool for 10 minutes on the sheets; then, using an angled metal spatula or pancake turner, transfer them to a wire rack until completely cool.

6. Serve with a glass of rice milk, soy milk, or nut milk.

NOTES

- For those sensitive to wheat, an equal measure of Lundberg brand brown rice flour can be used to replace the spelt flour.
- 1 cup unbleached white flour plus 1⅛ cups whole wheat pastry flour can be used to replace the spelt flour.
- For Cinnamon Grahams, combine ⅓ cup maple sugar and ¾ teaspoon ground cinnamon and gently pat into the pressed cookies before baking.
- For Carob Grahams, omit the cinnamon and replace ⅓ cup plus 2 tablespoons spelt flour with an equal measure of carob powder, then pat ⅓ cup maple sugar into the pressed cookies.

Brownie Blastoff

Preparation time: 10 minutes to prepare, 45–50 minutes to bake
Yield: 9 brownies

These wheat-free brownies are delicious but light, and actually good for you. Rich in fiber and minerals from carob, bananas, and pecans, they are completely vegan and have no cocoa at all. So forget caffeine, food allergies, and headaches, because you're safe here. Enjoy!

1½ cups oat flour
½ cup carob powder
1½ teaspoons baking powder
¼ teaspoon sea salt
⅓ cup canola oil
½ cup well-mashed banana
½ cup soy milk or rice milk
½ cup pure maple syrup
1 teaspoon pure vanilla flavor
¼ cup dairy-free carob chips
½ cup coarsely chopped pecans

1. Preheat the oven to 375°F. Oil and lightly flour an 8 x 8 x 2-inch baking pan. Set aside.

2. To make the brownies, in a large mixing bowl, sift together the flour, carob powder, baking powder, and salt. Whisk together until well mixed. Set aside.

3. In a food processor, using the metal blade, combine the oil and banana. Process until creamy, about 1 minute. Pour in the soy milk, maple syrup, and vanilla. Process until well blended.

4. With a rubber spatula, gradually add the wet ingredients to the dry, making sure they are well blended before each addition. Scrape off any excess batter from the side of the bowl. Stir in the chips and pecans until well mixed. Pour the batter into the prepared pan and distribute evenly.

5. Bake in the middle level of the preheated oven for 45–50 minutes. For uniformity in baking, rotate the pan from front to back halfway through the baking period.

6. The brownies are done when a tester inserted in the center comes out clean. Remove the brownies from the oven and let cool completely, about 15–20 minutes. Slice into 9 brownies.

NOTE

■ Oat flour can be purchased in most health food stores or made at home with a food processor by using the metal blade to process 1½ cups rolled oats for 3 minutes, or until powder-fine. For children with gluten sensitivities, an equal measure of Lundberg brand brown rice flour can be used to replace the oat flour.

Chewy Oatmeal Chip Cookies

Preparation time: 10 minutes to prepare, 15–20 minutes to bake
Yield: 2–3 dozen cookies

Every Christmas I enjoy making gift baskets filled with holiday treasures, including homemade chunky applesauce, kitchenware, and these delicious cookies. If you like your cookies to be crunchy and chewy, and chock full of surprises, then this recipe is for you.

1½ cups pecans
2½ cups rolled oats
1½ cups raisins
1 cup dairy-free carob chips
1⅔ cups spelt flour
1 teaspoon baking soda
1 teaspoon baking powder
½ teaspoon sea salt
1 cup Spectrum Spread
½ cup well-mashed banana
1¾ cups maple sugar
1 teaspoon pure vanilla flavor

1. Preheat the oven to 375°F.

2. Line two 11 x 15-inch cookies sheets with parchment paper. Evenly spread the pecans and oats on the prepared sheets and bake in the preheated oven for 8 minutes, or until the pecans are golden. Remove the sheet from the oven and cool completely.

3. In a medium mixing bowl, toss together the pecans, oats, raisins, and chips until well combined. Set aside.

4. In a large mixing bowl, sift together the flour, baking soda, baking powder, and salt. Whisk together until well mixed. Set aside.

5. In a medium bowl, cream together the Spectrum Spread, banana, maple sugar, and vanilla until well blended.

6. With a wooden spoon, gradually add the wet ingredients to the dry, making sure they are well blended before each addition. Scrape off any excess batter from the side of the bowl. Stir in the pecan mixture until well combined.

7. Using heaping tablespoons or a lightly greased 1½-inch scoop, drop the dough 2 inches apart onto the prepared cookie sheets (12 cookies per sheet). Then, with a lightly greased palm or the bottom of a glass, press down each cookie and flatten to a thickness of ¼ inch.

8. Bake on the upper and middle racks of the preheated oven for 15–20 minutes. For uniformity in baking, rotate the sheets from top to bottom and front to back halfway through the baking period. The cookies are done when golden in color. Remove the sheets from the oven and let the cookies cool for 10 minutes on the sheets; then, using an angled metal spatula or pancake turner, transfer them to a wire rack until completely cool.

9. Serve with a glass of either rice milk, soy milk, or nut milk.

NOTES

- 1 cup unbleached white plus ¾ cup whole-wheat pastry flour can be used to replace the spelt flour, or, for those sensitive to wheat, equal measures of Lundberg brand brown rice flour can be used to replace the spelt flour.
- If you like, you can make the dough ahead of time, and freeze it.

Chief Cloud's Cupcakes

Preparation time: 30–35 minutes to prepare, 30–35 minutes to bake

Yield: 1 dozen cupcakes

These moist banana- and coconut-flavored cupcakes topped with a creamy "chocolate" pudding frosting are lucious and easy to prepare—perfect for school birthday parties when parents are asked to bring in cupcakes.

ALL-OCCASION YELLOW CUPCAKES

2 cups whole-wheat pastry flour

1 tablespoon baking powder

¼ teaspoon sea salt

¾ cup Spectrum Spread

⅔ cup pure maple syrup

½ cup well-mashed banana

1 teaspoon pure vanilla flavor

½ cup soy milk or rice milk

1 cup flaked coconut (optional)

"CHOCOLATE" PUDDING FROSTING

1 pound silken tofu, well drained

One 10-ounce package dairy-free carob chips (1¼ cups)

¼ cup honey

1 tablespoon pure vanilla flavor

1. Preheat the oven to 375°F.

2. Line a 12-well muffin tin with paper baking cups. To prevent sticking, brush the cups lightly with a paste made from 1½ teaspoons each of canola oil and flour. Set aside.

3. In a large mixing bowl, sift together the flour, baking powder, and salt. Whisk together until well combined. Set aside.

4. To make the cupcakes, in a medium mixing bowl combine the Spectrum Spread, maple syrup, banana, and vanilla. With a handheld electric mixer on medium speed, beat until creamy, about 1 minute. Gradually pour in the milk, increase to high speed, and beat for 30 seconds. Reduce the mixer speed to low, and gradually add the banana mixture (in 2 batches) to the flour mixture, beating for 20 seconds after each addition to incorporate the ingredients. When the ingredients are fully incorporated, increase the mixer speed to high, and beat for 1 minute to aerate. Pour in the coconut and beat for 10 seconds or until well combined. Scrape off any excess batter from the side of the bowl. Spoon the batter evenly into the prepared muffin tin (the wells will be full).

5. Bake on the middle level of the preheated oven for 30–35 minutes. For uniformity in baking, rotate the tin from front to back halfway through the baking period.

6. The cupcakes are done when the center springs back when touched, or a tester inserted in the center comes out clean. They will be golden brown. Remove the tin from the oven, let the cupcakes cool for 10 minutes in the tin, then transfer them to a wire rack until completely cool.

7. To prepare the frosting, in a food processor, using the metal blade, process the tofu for 2 minutes or until smooth. In a double boiler over very hot water, or with a heavy small saucepan over moderate to low heat, combine the chips, honey, and vanilla. Stir frequently with a wooden spoon until the chips are a fudgy consistency, about 5–6 minutes. Restart the food processor, quickly add the melted chip mixture through the feed tube, and run until smooth and creamy, about 2 minutes. Scrape off any excess frosting from the sides of the processor, then transfer to a medium mixing bowl. Cover the surface directly with plastic wrap and chill for 1 hour or until firm enough to spread.

8. Spread the frosting on the cupcakes and serve immediately. Transfer to a large serving platter with the birthday candle cupcake in the center if this is for a school birthday party.

NOTES
■ The cupcakes can be prepared a day in advance and stored unfrosted in an airtight container. Just wrap tightly in plastic wrap followed by aluminum foil. For the best results, the cupcakes should be frosted just before serving, so the frosting is cold.
■ For those sensitive to wheat, an equal measure of spelt or Lundberg brand brown rice flour can be used to replace the unbleached white flour.
■ For variety, sprinkle 1¼ cups additional chips, coconut, or coarsely chopped nuts on top of the frosting.

Crunchy Amaretti Cookies

Preparation time: 10 minutes to prepare, 20–25 minutes to bake
Yield: 3 dozen cookies

Here's a nutritious version of an Italian favorite. These cookies make a nice accompaniment to a warm cup of chamomile tea.

⅓ cup unblanched whole almonds
2½ cups oat flour

1 teaspoon baking powder
½ teaspoon baking soda
¼ teaspoon sea salt
¼ cup canola oil
½ cup pure maple syrup
2 tablespoons almond butter
1 tablespoon pure almond flavor

1. Preheat the oven to 375°F. Line two 11 x 15-inch cookie sheets with parchment paper and set aside.

2. Using a mini food processor or coffee grinder, process the almonds until they are powder-fine. Transfer to a small bowl and set aside.

3. In a large mixing bowl, whisk together the flour, baking powder, baking soda, and salt until well mixed. Set aside.

4. In a food processor, using the metal blade, combine the oil, maple syrup, almond butter, and almond flavor. Process until creamy, about 1 minute. Pulse the dry ingredients until just incorporated.

5. Using a lightly greased 1¼-inch scoop, scoop the dough out and dip each ball in the almonds, turning gently to coat all over. Place the dough balls 1 inch apart on the prepared cookie sheets (18 cookies per sheet). If a scoop is not available, use the palms of your hands to roll the dough into 1¼-inch balls.

6. Bake on the upper and middle racks of the preheated oven for 20–25 minutes. The sheets should not be touching the sides of the oven. Halfway through the baking period, rotate the sheets from top to bottom and front to back. This ensures proper air circulation and uniformity in baking. The cookies are done when golden in color. Remove the sheets from the oven and let the cookies cool for 5 minutes on the sheets; then, using an angled metal spatula or pancake turner, transfer them to a wire rack until completely cool.

7. Serve with hot herbal tea or a glass of either rice, soy, or nut milk.

NOTE

■ **Oat flour can be purchased in most health food stores or made at home with a food processor by using the metal blade to process 2½ cups rolled oats for 3 minutes, or until powder-fine. For children with gluten sensitivites, an equal measure of Lundberg brand brown rice flour can be used to replace the oat flour.**

Ginger Snap Cookies

■▗■

Preparation time: 10 minutes to prepare, 15–20 minutes to bake

Yield: 3 dozen cookies

We recently spent the New Year holiday in a little Vermont town at the foot of the Green Mountains. After a day of cross-country skiing and making snowmen, it was great to sit in front of a warm fireplace with a hot cup of herbal tea and a plate of these spice-laden treats.

1½ cups unbleached white flour
1 cup whole-wheat pastry flour
2 teaspoons baking soda
2 teaspoons ground ginger
2 teaspoons ground cinnamon
¼ teaspoon ground nutmeg
¼ teaspoon ground cloves
¼ teaspoon sea salt
½ cup canola oil
¼ cup well-mashed banana
½ cup plus ⅓ cup maple sugar
¼ cup molasses
¼ cup pure maple syrup
1 teaspoon pure vanilla flavor

1. Preheat the oven to 375°F. Line two 11 x 15-inch cookie sheets with parchment paper and set aside.

2. In a large mixing bowl, whisk together the flours, baking soda, ginger, cinnamon, nutmeg, cloves, and salt until well mixed. Set aside.

3. In a medium mixing bowl, stir together the oil, banana, ½ cup of the maple sugar, molasses, maple syrup, and vanilla flavor until well combined.

4. With a wooden spoon, gradually add the wet ingredients to the dry, making sure they are well blended before each addition. Scrape off any excess batter from the sides of the bowl.

5. Measure the dough into a 1¼-inch cookie scoop or 1 level tablespoon and roll it between the palms of your hands to shape 1-inch balls. Roll each dough ball, as soon as it is formed, in the remaining ⅓ cup maple sugar until well coated. Place the dough balls 1 inch apart onto the prepared sheets (18 cookies per sheet). Then with the palm of your hand or the bottom of a glass, press down each cookie and flatten to a thickness of ¼ inch.

6. Bake on the upper and middle racks of the preheated oven for 15–20 minutes. For uniformity in baking, rotate the sheets from top to bottom and front to back halfway through the baking period. The cookies are done when firm to the touch. Remove the sheets from the oven and let the cookies cool for 10 minutes on the sheets; then, using an angled metal spatula or pancake turner, transfer them to a wire rack until completely cool.

7. Serve with hot herbal tea or a glass of rice, soy, or nut milk.

NOTES
- For those sensitive to wheat, an equal measure of Lundberg brand brown rice flour or spelt flour can be used to replace the whole-wheat pastry and unbleached white flours.
- For variety, add ½ cup coarsely chopped and toasted hazelnuts, pecans, or macadamia nuts to the cookie dough.

Grandma's Old-Fashioned Apple Cobbler

Preparation time: 15–20 minutes to prepare, 50–55 minutes to bake
Yield: 9 servings

Imagine Grandma's old-fashioned apple pie filled with succulent apples, brown sugar, and sweet, fragrant spices. This crustless foolproof version is apple juice–sweetened with just a hint of honey. The cinnamon brings out the sweetness of the fruit, and the delicate biscuits are a wonderful addition, especially with this special crumb topping.

CRUMB TOPPING
½ cup maple sugar
3 tablespoons whole-wheat pastry flour
⅛ teaspoon ground cinnamon
2 tablespoons Spectrum Spread

APPLE FILLING
1 cup apple juice
¼ cup arrowroot powder
2 tablespoons honey
¼ cup fresh lemon juice
½ teaspoon ground cinnamon
12 medium Golden Delicious apples (about 9 cups sliced)

BISCUIT DOUGH

1½ cups whole-wheat pastry flour

1½ cups plus ⅓–½ cup unbleached white flour

1 tablespoon plus 1½ teaspoons baking powder

¾ teaspoon sea salt

¾ cup canola oil

1 cup plus 1 tablespoon soy milk or rice milk

2 tablespoons honey

1. Preheat the oven to 425°F. Line an 11 x 15-inch cookie sheet with parchment paper and set aside.

2. To prepare the crumb topping, in a small bowl, whisk together the sugar, flour, and cinnamon until well mixed. Add the Spectrum Spread and press with the back of a fork to incorporate and form a crumbly mixture. Set aside.

3. To prepare the filling, in a small saucepan, bring the apple juice to a rolling boil over high heat. Remove from the heat and transfer quickly to a blender. Blend the apple juice on high, and sprinkle in the arrowroot powder until smooth, about 1 minute. Reduce the blender speed to medium. Drizzle in the honey and lemon juice, add the cinnamon, and blend until well combined, about 30 seconds. Transfer this apple juice mixture to a large mixing bowl.

4. Peel, core, and slice the apples; they should be in ½-inch-wide slices at the outside edge. Then toss the apples with the apple juice mixture to prevent discoloration.

5. Pour the apple mixture into an 8 x 8 x 2¼-inch baking pan. Cover with foil and bake on the middle level of the preheated oven for 25 minutes or until the apples are tender. Remove the pan from the oven, and mix the apples to ensure uniformity (apples will still be semifirm). Cover and set aside. Prepare the biscuit dough while the apples are baking.

6. To prepare the biscuits, in a medium mixing bowl, whisk together 1½ cups of both flours, the baking powder, and the salt. Set aside. In a separate bowl, whisk together the oil, 1 cup of the milk, and the honey until well combined.

7. With a rubber spatula, stir the oil mixture into the dry ingredients until a "shaggy" loose dough forms. Turn the dough out onto a lightly floured surface, and lightly sprinkle with the remaining unbleached white flour (about ⅓–½ cup additional flour). Knead gently 5–6 times, or until the dough is no longer sticky. Roll or press dough to a thickness of about 1 inch. Cut the biscuits using a 2½-inch biscuit cutter, dipping it in flour between biscuits. Pat the scraps together and continue to make a total of 9 biscuits.

8. Evenly arrange the biscuits on the prepared sheet so they don't touch each other, then brush the tops lightly with the remaining 1 tablespoon milk, and sprinkle evenly with the crumb topping. Bake on the middle level of the preheated oven for 25–30 minutes or until the bottoms are golden brown. For uniformity in baking, rotate

the sheet from front to back halfway through the baking period. Remove the sheet from the oven, slide the parchment paper onto a wire rack, and let cool for 5 minutes.

9. To assemble the individual desserts, place a scoop of apple filling into a dessert bowl. Top with a biscuit and a dollop of Vanilla Whipped "Cream" (page 225), or nondairy frozen dessert. Proceed this way for the remaining 8 servings.

NOTES

■ **For those sensitive to wheat, the biscuit topping can be prepared using 3 cups of spelt flour or Lundberg brand brown rice flour.**

■ **This cobbler can be prepared all year round. I will often make RASPBERRY PEACH OR CHERRY PEACH COBBLER in the spring and summer months using 8 cups (18–20) peaches (peeled, pitted, and sliced) plus 2 cups raspberries or 2 cups pitted cherries to replace the apples. Note, however, that the peaches and raspberries or cherries need to be prebaked for only 20 minutes, as opposed to 25 minutes for the apples.**

Healthy Pie Crust

Preparation time: 15–20 minutes to prepare, 20–30 minutes to prebake
Yield: two 9-inch crusts

No, it's not an oxymoron—you can *have a healthy pie crust! Consider this one—it's free of all saturated and hydrogenated fats. It's foolproof too, so you gotta love this recipe!*

⅔ cup canola oil plus 1 tablespoon for greasing pans
1½ cups whole-wheat pastry flour
1½ cups unbleached white flour
¾ teaspoon sea salt
⅓ cup ice water

1. Measure ⅔ cup oil into a liquid measuring cup and chill in the freezer for 10 minutes, or until very cold. With additional 1 tablespoon oil, lightly grease and flour two 9-inch pie pans. Set aside.

2. In a large mixing bowl, sift together the flours and salt. Whisk together until well combined. Set aside.

3. Remove the oil from the freezer and drizzle into the flour mixture. Using a fork or dough blender, incorporate until crumbly. Sprinkle in the water, tossing the dough with a fork (work the fork upward from the bottom

of the bowl through the dough) until it is just moist enough to hold together without appearing crumbly. Knead briefly with your hands, only until dough particles are smoothly incorporated, and then shape into 2 equal flat rounds. Wrap 1 round tightly in plastic wrap or a plastic sandwich bag and set aside.

4. Roll the second round out between 2 pieces of waxed paper to a thickness of $1/8$–$1/4$ inch, and 3 inches larger than that of the pie pan (a 12-inch round). To do this, use even strokes and work from the center of the dough cake toward the edges, rolling in different directions to produce an even, round shape.

5. Remove the top layer of waxed paper, place the pie pan upside down on top of the pastry, and slip both hands under the dough to support it as you invert the dough into the prepared pan. Remove the bottom layer of waxed paper, gently fit and lightly press the dough into the bottom and up against the sides of the pan. Using a small knife or scissors, evenly trim off all but 1 inch of the excess dough around the rim of the pan. Reserve the trimmings to patch any thin areas. Fold the overhanging dough into the pan all the way around to form a plump edge. Press evenly and adjust so the dough edge is flush with the top edge of the pan. Finish the edge by fluting: Pinch the outer rim of the dough with the thumb and forefinger of one hand while pushing against the inner rim of the dough with the forefinger of the other hand. Loosely cover the dough-lined pan with plastic wrap and refrigerate or freeze until needed. Repeat the process to prepare the remaining pie crust.

6. To prebake the pie shells, preheat the oven to 375°F. Using a fork, prick the dough on the bottom of each pan at $1/4$-inch intervals, to prevent puffing and shrinkage. Cut 2 disks of parchment paper, 1 inch larger than the diameter of the pans (enough to reach up the sides of the shell), and press into the pans. Fill the paper-covered raw pie shells with either pie weights or dried beans. Bake in the preheated oven on the lower and middle racks for 15–20 minutes, or until the dough has lost its shine. Remove the weights and parchment paper, prick the bottoms again with a fork, and bake an additional 5–10 minutes or until the pie shells are an even golden color (be careful not to scorch the shells since they will bake more rapidly now). For uniformity in baking, rotate the pans from top to bottom and front to back halfway through the baking period. Remove the pans from the oven, transfer to wire racks, and let cool for 15 minutes.

NOTES

■ For a double-crusted pie, roll 1 round, fit it into the 9-inch pie pan, trim the edges, and fill (according to the individual recipe). Roll the second disk of dough into a 12-inch round. Moisten the rim of the bottom crust with water and place the top crust on the pie. Trim the edges of the top crust to an even 1-inch overhang. Fold the exposed edges of the top crust under the bottom crust. Flute the edges of the pie and make 6–8 vent holes in the center of the top crust. Brush the top crust with 1 tablespoon maple syrup mixed with 1 tablespoon water and bake the pie (according to the individual recipe).

■ For a 9-inch tart shell, lightly oil and flour a 9-inch tart pan with a removable bottom. Set aside. Use half the ingredients and follow the directions in steps 1, 2, and 3. Then follow the directions to roll out the dough. Instead of creating a fluted edge, roll the rolling pin across the top of the pan to trim the dough flush with the top. Using a fork, prick the dough on the bottom at $1/4$-inch intervals, to prevent puffing and shrinkage. Cut a disk of parchment paper 1 inch larger than the diameter of the pan (enough to reach up the sides of the shell), press into the pan, and fill the paper-covered raw pie shell with either pie weights or dried beans. Prebake for 15–20 minutes at 350°F or until the dough has lost its shine. Then remove the parchment paper and weights and set the tart shell aside.

■ For children with sensitivities to wheat, 3 cups spelt flour can be used to replace the unbleached white and whole-wheat pastry flours.

Holiday Gingerbread

Preparation time: 10 minutes to prepare, 35–40 minutes to bake
Yield: 6–8 servings

My good friends Kathleen and YongSoo Ha have given parties filled with children and good food for as long as I can remember. Here's a slightly different version of Kathleen's specialty that I make a lot during the holiday season.

1¼ cups whole-wheat pastry flour
¾ cup unbleached white flour
1 tablespoon baking powder
1½ teaspoons ground ginger
1 teaspoon baking soda
1 teaspoon ground cinnamon
½ teaspoon sea salt
½ teaspoon ground mace
¼ teaspoon ground allspice
¾ cup pure maple syrup
½ cup well-mashed ripe banana
⅓ cup canola oil
⅓ cup molasses
2 teaspoons pure vanilla flavor
¼ teaspoon grated orange zest
1 tablespoon maple sugar (optional)

1. Preheat the oven to 350°F. Lightly oil and flour a 10½-inch cast-iron skillet. Set aside.

2. In a large mixing bowl, sift together the flours, baking powder, ginger, baking soda, cinnamon, salt, mace, and allspice. Whisk together until well combined. Set aside.

3. In a 4-cup-capacity liquid measuring pitcher, whisk together the maple syrup, banana, oil, molasses, vanilla, and orange zest until well blended.

4. With a handheld electric mixer on low speed, gradually add the wet ingredients to the dry, making sure they are well blended before each addition. When the ingredients are fully incorporated, increase the mixer speed to high, and beat for 20 seconds to aerate. Scrape off any excess batter from the sides of the bowl. Pour the batter into the prepared skillet and distribute evenly with a spatula. Evenly sprinkle on the maple sugar.

5. Bake on the middle level of the preheated oven for 35–40 minutes. For uniformity in baking, rotate the skillet from front to back halfway through the baking period.

6. The gingerbread is done when the center springs back when touched, or a tester inserted in the center comes out clean. It will be golden brown. Remove gingerbread from the oven and let cool in the pan for 20 minutes. Loosen the edges with a sharp knife and slice into 6–8 equal wedges.

7. Serve the gingerbread on its own or accompanied by a dollop of Vanilla Whipped "Cream" (page 225), or vanilla nondairy frozen dessert, and a slice of candied ginger or candied orange peel.

NOTES
- For Orange Gingerbread, add an additional ¾ teaspoon grated orange zest.
- For those sensitive to wheat, equal measures of spelt or Lundberg brand brown rice flour can be used to replace the whole-wheat pastry and unbleached white flours.
- For special occasions I often make individual gingerbreads using sixteen 3-inch oval molds. Please note: These will require less baking time.

Lemon Marble Pound Cake

Preparation time: 15 minutes to prepare, 100–105 minutes to bake
Yield: 6–9 servings

Golden, buttery, lemon-rich cake with stripes of carob floating throughout—this cake is one of my personal favorites. It is simply delicious on its own, or as a decadent-tasting but light Strawberry Shortcake topped with fresh strawberries swimming in a sweet berry sauce and Vanilla Whipped "Cream" (see Notes).

2½ cups spelt flour
1 tablespoon baking powder
½ teaspoon sea salt
2 tablespoons carob powder
¾ cup orange juice
1 cup pure maple syrup

¾ cup Spectrum Spread
¾ cup well-mashed ripe bananas
2 teaspoons pure lemon flavor
2 teaspoons grated lemon zest

1. Preheat the oven to 350°F. Oil and lightly flour an 8½ x 4¼ x 2¾-inch loaf pan. Set aside.

2. In a large mixing bowl, sift together the flour, baking powder, and salt. Set aside.

3. In a small mixing bowl, sift the carob powder and whisk in 2 tablespoons orange juice until well mixed. Set aside.

4. In a medium mixing bowl, combine the maple syrup, the remaining orange juice, Spectrum Spread, banana, lemon flavor, and lemon zest. With a handheld electric mixer on low speed, blend together until smooth. Gradually add the wet ingredients to the dry (keep the carob mixture set aside), making sure they are well blended before each addition. When the ingredients are fully incorporated, increase the mixer speed to high, and beat for 1 minute to aerate. Scrape off any excess batter from the sides of the bowl.

5. Remove ½ cup of the batter and add to the carob mixture. Reduce the mixer speed to medium, beating for 1 minute or until well combined. Set aside.

6. To alternate colored batters, pour half the yellow batter into the prepared pan and distribute evenly with a spatula. Pour on the carob batter and smooth the surface. Then top with the remaining yellow batter and spread evenly. To marbleize the cake, insert a sharp knife deeply into the batter and make two alternating zigzag formations.

7. Bake on the middle level of the preheated oven for 30 minutes or until the top begins to split. Pull the oven rack out and split the top of the cake: Using a lightly greased sharp knife, make a shallow mark 6 inches long down the middle of the cake. This must be done quickly or the cake may fall. Rotate the cake from front to back, close the oven door, and continue baking for an additional 70–75 minutes.

8. The cake is done when the center springs back when touched, or a tester inserted in the center comes out clean. It will be golden brown. Remove the cake from the oven and let cool in the pan for 15–20 minutes. Loosen the edges with a sharp knife and invert onto a greased wire rack. To prevent the top from splitting, reinvert, and cool completely.

9. Serve the cake on its own, accompanied by a cup of hot herbal tea.

NOTES

■ **For those sensitive to wheat, an equal measure of Lundberg brand brown rice flour can be used to replace the spelt flour.**

■ **To make STRAWBERRY SHORTCAKE, prepare the strawberry sauce: Combine one 10-ounce package frozen** strawberries (thawed) and ¼ cup maple syrup in a food processor fitted with a metal blade. Process for 1 minute or until smooth. Transfer to a medium mixing bowl, stir in 1 quart sliced strawberries until well combined, and set aside. To assemble the individual desserts, place 1 slice of pound cake on a dessert plate. Top with the strawberry mixture and a dollop of Vanilla Whipped "Cream" (page 225). Proceed this way for the remaining 5–8 servings.

Maple Roasted Nuts

Preparation time: 2 minutes to prepare, 10–12 minutes to bake
Yield: 4–6 servings

During the colder months I often roast shelled nuts with a little maple syrup and fragrant spices. The resulting golden treats are great for munching and snacking. I like to put out a large bowl on holidays, but they are perfect any time.

3 cups assorted nuts (almonds, pecans, cashews, peanuts, macadamia nuts, Brazil nuts, walnuts, or hazelnuts)
¼ cup pure maple syrup
¼ cup maple sugar
¼ teaspoon ground mace
½ teaspoon ground cinnamon

1. Preheat the oven to 375°F. Line an 11 x 15-inch cookie sheet with parchment paper and brush lightly with oil.

2. In a medium mixing bowl, toss together the nuts, maple syrup, maple sugar, mace, and cinnamon until well combined.

3. Evenly spread the nuts on the prepared sheet. Bake on the middle rack of the preheated oven for 10–12 minutes or until the nuts are golden and the syrup is caramelized. Remove the sheet from the oven and let the nuts cool for 10 minutes on the sheet; then, slide the parchment paper onto a wire rack until the nuts are completely cool.

4. Serve alone or use these as a topping for cereal, salads, nondairy yogurt, or nondairy frozen dessert.

Mochi S'mores

Preparation time: 5 minutes to prepare, 10 minutes to bake

Yield: 8 s'mores

When we visit the mountains, the children always enjoy the evening campfires accompanied by folk music sing-alongs, and S'mores. Kids love S'mores so much that I decided there must be a healthy substitute for marshmallows. Mochi, made from short-grain sweet rice, puffs up and gets crunchy on the outside and gooey on the inside just as marshmallows do. So this recipe was born, and now kids can have a healthy version of their campfire memories at home.

One 12½-ounce package mochi

One 3–4-ounce dairy-free carob bar, broken into 8 squares

8 graham crackers, broken in halves, or 16 Animal Honey Grahams (page 198)

1. Preheat the oven to 450°F. Line an 11 x 15-inch cookie sheet with parchment paper and set aside.

2. Using a sharp knife, cut the mochi into eight 2-inch-square pieces. Place the mochi pieces on the prepared sheet and bake on the middle rack of the preheated oven for 10 minutes, or until they puff up and turn golden. Remove the sheet from the oven.

3. To assemble the s'mores, place a carob square on a graham cracker half. Top with a mochi piece and then a second graham cracker half, and press together.

4. Serve with a glass of almond milk, rice milk, or soy milk.

NOTE

■ **For those sensitive to wheat, use Animal Honey Grahams prepared with Lundberg brand brown rice flour (page 198).**

Peach Strawberry Jumble Gel

Preparation time: 25 minutes to prepare, 30–45 minutes to chill

Yield: 4–6 servings

This is one of my favorite summer recipes, great as a breakfast, snack, or dessert item. This delicious "gelatin" is loaded with fresh berries and peaches. Plus it's a way to get kids to eat sea vegetables and then come running back for more. (Agar is a sea vegetable derived from the cell walls of certain red algae. It's a good source of B vitamins, in addition to vitamins A, C, D, and K.)

3 cups apple juice
¼ cup plus 2 tablespoons agar flakes
5 medium ripe peaches, peeled, pitted, and sliced
1 pint ripe strawberries, hulled and sliced
2 tablespoons freshly squeezed lemon juice

1. In a medium saucepan, bring the apple juice to a boil over high heat. Reduce the heat to moderate and stir in the agar. Simmer uncovered, stirring occasionally, for 10 minutes or until the agar is completely dissolved.

2. In a large mixing bowl, toss the peaches and strawberries together with the lemon juice until well combined. Transfer to a 7 x 11-inch baking dish and pour in the apple juice mixture. Let cool for 15 minutes; then refrigerate for 30–45 minutes or until jelled.

3. Spoon into small bowls and serve.

NOTE
■ **For JUMBLE GEL FRUIT MEDLEY, use 4 cups of assorted peeled and pitted fresh fruits (grapes, blueberries, plums, and mangoes) as a replacement for the peaches and strawberries.**

Pecan Shortbread Bars

Preparation time: 35 minutes to prepare, 12–14 minutes to roast the nuts, 55–60 minutes to bake
Yield: 20 bars

Okay, imagine this—roasted pecans and rich-buttery shortbread—together! This irresistible combo makes a scrumptious teatime snack, and will devastate even the most hardened sweet-toothed lover of decadent desserts. By the way, it's totally vegetarian and totally healthy—so, show me the shortbread!

1¼ cups pecan halves
1 cup whole-wheat pastry flour
1 cup unbleached white flour
¼ teaspoon sea salt
1 cup Spectrum Spread
½ cup maple sugar

1. Preheat the oven to 325°F. Line two 11 x 15-inch cookie sheets with parchment paper and set aside. To roast the nuts, evenly spread the pecans on one of the prepared sheets and bake in the preheated oven for 12–14 minutes, or until they begin to have a roasted aroma. Remove the sheet from the oven, slide the parchment paper onto a wire rack, and cool the nuts completely. Using a mini food processor or coffee grinder, process the pecans until they are powder-fine, then transfer to a small bowl and set aside. Reduce the oven temperature to 300°F and return the parchment paper to the cookie sheet.

2. In a medium mixing bowl, sift together the flours and salt. Whisk in the finely ground pecans until well mixed. Set aside.

3. In a food processor, using the metal blade, combine the Spectrum Spread and maple sugar. Process until combined, about 30 seconds. Pulse in the dry ingredients until just incorporated.

4. Cut a 10 x 10-inch square of parchment paper. Lay the paper on a cutting board and use it as a template to shape your shortbread. Pat or roll out the dough to a thickness of ⅓ inch. Use a ruler to score the dough into 5 strips lengthwise (each about 2 inches wide) and then crosswise into 4 strips (about 2½ inches wide). With a fork, pierce each piece in three places on a diagonal. Cover the dough with plastic wrap and chill until firm, about 20 minutes.

5. Cut the chilled dough through the second lines. Place the dough bars 1 inch apart on the prepared sheets. Bake on the upper and middle racks of the preheated oven for 55–60 minutes. For uniformity in baking, rotate the sheets from top to bottom and front to back halfway through the baking period. The shortbread is done when the edges are pale golden. Remove the sheets from the oven, slide the parchment paper onto a wire rack, and cool the shortbread completely.

6. Serve with hot tea or rice milk, soy milk, or nut milk.

NOTES
- For those sensitive to wheat, 2 cups of Lundberg brand brown rice flour or an equal measure of spelt flour can be used to replace the whole-wheat pastry and unbleached white flours.
- For traditional SCOTTISH SHORTBREAD: Omit the pecans from the shortbread layer. For LEMON SHORTBREAD: Add 1 teaspoon pure lemon flavor plus 1 tablespoon freshly grated lemon zest to the Scottish Shortbread dough during step 3, then continue as directed through step 5.

Rachael Reid's "Chocolate" Chip Cookies

Preparation time: 10 minutes to prepare, 20–25 minutes to bake

Yield: 16 cookies

A couple years ago, I met a wonderfully gifted chef named Rachael Reid. She graciously welcomed me into her home in Massachusetts. Along with a piping hot cup of herbal tea, she served the most delicious "chocolate" chip cookies I'd ever tasted. After Rachael assured me that these entirely-too-yummy cookies were completely vegan, I asked if she would share the recipe with all of you. She consented with pleasure, which is what you'll be feeling when you try these.

1¼ cups unbleached white flour
½ cup whole-wheat pastry flour
½ teaspoon baking soda
½ teaspoon sea salt
⅓ cup canola oil
¼ cup well-mashed ripe banana
½ cup pure maple syrup
½ cup maple sugar
1 teaspoon pure vanilla flavor
1 cup dairy-free carob chips
⅔ cup walnuts, coarsely chopped

1. Preheat the oven to 375°F. Line two 11 x 15-inch cookie sheets with parchment paper and set aside.

2. To prepare the cookies, in a large mixing bowl, sift together the flours, baking soda, and salt. Whisk together until well mixed. Set aside.

3. In a medium bowl, whisk together the oil, banana, maple syrup, maple sugar, and vanilla until well blended.

4. With a wooden spoon, gradually add the wet ingredients to the dry, making sure they are well blended before each addition. Scrape off any excess batter from the sides of the bowl. Stir in the chips and walnuts until well combined.

5. Using heaping tablespoons or a lightly greased 1½-inch scoop, drop the dough 2 inches apart onto the prepared sheets (8 cookies per sheet).

6. Bake on the upper and middle racks of the preheated oven for 20–25 minutes. For uniformity in baking, rotate the sheets from top to bottom and front to back halfway through the baking period. The cookies are done

when golden in color. Remove the sheets from the oven and let the cookies cool for 10 minutes on the sheets; then, using an angled metal spatula or pancake turner, transfer them to a wire rack until completely cool.

NOTE

■ **For those sensitive to wheat, 1¾ cups of spelt or Lundberg brand brown rice flour can be used to replace the unbleached white and whole-wheat pastry flours.**

Shelly's Banana Cream Pie

Preparation time: 15–20 minutes to prepare, 15–20 minutes to chill
Yield: 8–10 servings

Banana cream pie has always been my favorite dessert. I guess it's fitting that I had to work hardest to make this recipe come out right. After much trying and failing it all turned out yummy.

14 whole-wheat honey graham crackers (½ pound)
¾ cup Spectrum Spread
½ pound silken tofu
2 tablespoons canola oil
1 cup Thai Kitchen Pure Coconut Milk Lite or soy milk
¼ cup honey
¼ cup arrowroot powder
¼ teaspoon sea salt
1 cup pure water
¼ cup agar flakes
2 tablespoons pure vanilla flavor
1½ pounds ripe bananas (see Note)
½ teaspoon carob powder

1. Line the removable bottom of a 10-inch tart pan with parchment paper and set aside.

2. To prepare the graham cracker crust, in a food processor, using the metal blade, process the graham crackers until fine crumbs form. Add the Spectrum Spread and process until well combined. Press the mixture firmly onto the bottom of the pan. Freeze until firm, about 10 minutes.

3. To prepare the filling, in a food processor, using the metal blade, combine the tofu and oil. Process until creamy, about 1 minute. In a small mixing bowl, combine the coconut milk, honey, arrowroot powder, and salt. Whisk together until well blended, and set aside.

4. In a small saucepan, bring the water to a boil over moderate heat. Whisk in the agar and simmer uncovered, stirring occasionally, for 2–3 minutes or until the agar dissolves. Whisk briefly, then pour the coconut mixture into the saucepan. Stirring frequently with an angled-bottom wooden spoon, cook until the mixture begins to thicken, about 2–3 minutes. Remove from the heat, then stir in the vanilla. Restart the food processor, and quickly add the coconut mixture through the feed tube. Run until smooth and creamy, about 1 minute, and set aside.

5. Peel and slice the bananas and arrange them evenly over the bottom of the prepared tart shell. Pour the coconut filling over the bananas and spread evenly. Refrigerate for 15–20 minutes or until well set and firm to the touch.

6. To serve, dust with carob powder, then carefully push up the bottom and slide the tart off the disk and onto a cutting board. Using a sharp knife, slice into 8–10 equal wedges, and serve.

NOTE

■ The quality of the bananas is important for this recipe. They should be firmly ripe, not overripened or bruised. If you want a dynamic presentation you can garnish with extra bananas, Vanilla Whipped "Cream" (page 225), and mint leaves.

Strawberry Rhubarb Tart

Preparation time: 20 minutes to prepare, 65–70 minutes to bake
Yield: 8–10 servings

When was the last time you ate rhubarb? Probably not recently, right? This root has been a traditional part of American fare for generations. In China, it is actually used for its medicinal properties. In this tart, it melts together with succulent strawberries, and is crowned by a maple-flavored lattice crust. What a delicious way to acquaint yourself with an old standard.

1 pound rhubarb (without tops), cut into ½-inch pieces
1 quart strawberries, hulled and sliced
¾ cup plus 1 tablespoon maple sugar
⅓ cup unbleached white flour
2 tablespoons freshly squeezed lemon juice
½ teaspoon pure vanilla flavor
¼ teaspoon sea salt
½ teaspoon lemon zest

1 recipe Healthy Pie Crust dough (page 208), shaped into 2 flat rounds
1 tablespoon soy milk

1. Preheat the oven to 425°F. Lightly oil and flour a 10-inch tart pan with a removable bottom and set aside. Cut a disk of parchment paper to fit the diameter of the pan.

2. To prepare the filling, in a large mixing bowl, toss together the rhubarb, strawberries, ¾ cup maple sugar, flour, lemon juice, vanilla, salt, and lemon zest until well combined. Cover and refrigerate while you roll out the pastry.

3. To roll out the pastry for a 2-crust tart, roll each round of dough between 2 pieces of waxed paper to a thickness of ¼ inch, and 2 inches larger than that of the tart pan (a 12-inch round). To do this, use even strokes and work from the center of the dough cake toward the edges, rolling in different directions to produce an even, round shape.

4. To prepare the bottom crust, remove the top layer of waxed paper from 1 pastry, place the pan upside down on top of the pastry, and slip both hands under the dough to support it as you invert the dough into the prepared pan. Remove the waxed paper, then gently fit and lightly press the dough into the bottom and up against the sides of the pan. Roll the rolling pin across the top of the pan to trim the dough flush with the top. Add the strawberry filling to the pastry-lined pan and refrigerate while you cut the lattice strips.

5. To prepare the pastry as a lattice (woven) tart top, remove the top layer of waxed paper from the remaining pastry. Use a fluted pastry wheel or knife to cut ½-inch-wide strips, and set the 2 smallest strips aside, as extra dough if needed. Remove the filled tart from the refrigerator and arrange the strips on top: First take the smallest strip and place it across one end of the tart. Then take another small strip and lay it perpendicular (at a right angle) on the adjoining side of the tart, overlapping it. Continue in this alternating pattern until you reach the other end of the tart. Carefully roll the rolling pin around the edge of the pan to trim the dough flush with the top. Using a pastry brush, brush the lattice and edges with soy milk, then sprinkle the top of the tart with the remaining tablespoon of maple sugar.

6. Place the tart on top of a cookie sheet and bake in the preheated oven for 65–70 minutes or until the filling bubbles and thickens. Remove from the oven, transfer to a wire rack, and cool completely.

7. To serve, carefully push up the bottom and slide the tart off the disk and onto a cutting board. Using a sharp knife, slice into 8–10 equal wedges and serve alone or accompanied by a dollop of Vanilla Whipped "Cream" (page 225), or vanilla nondairy frozen dessert.

Sunny Day All-Fruit Sundaes

Preparation time: 10–15 minutes

Yield: 4–6 servings

This was our Fertile Earth Farm Sunday dessert send-off. As our guests heard the Champion juicer operating, they suddenly came trickling in from the hot summer sun. First I passed frozen bananas and apple juice through the juicer, transforming them into a deliciously creamy, dairy-free ice cream. The topping was made with fresh fruit and locally grown berries. I hope these sundaes will bring a bit of heaven to your kitchen, as they always do for me.

2 large mangoes, peeled, pitted, and sliced (about 1½ pounds)
2 medium peaches, peeled, pitted, and sliced (about 1 pound)
1 pint strawberries, hulled and sliced
½ pound blueberries
5 medium frozen bananas, cut into 1-inch slices (about 2 pounds) (see Note)
1 cup apple juice

1. In a food processor, using the metal blade, combine the bananas and apple juice. Process until creamy, about 3–4 minutes.

2. In a small mixing bowl, combine the mangoes, peaches, strawberries, and blueberries. Toss together until well mixed and set aside.

3. Spoon the banana "ice cream" into bowls, top with the mango mixture, and serve.

NOTE
■ **Peel the bananas before freezing.**

Super Chip "Ice Cream" Sandwiches

Preparation time: 20 minutes

Yield: 8 sandwiches

These carob-chip-packed cookies, sandwiching vanilla frozen dessert, are a wholesome alternative to commercial ice cream cookie sandwiches and they're so appealing to kids that they can be used as the focal point of a birthday party. Rolling them in chopped nuts adds crunch and flavor.

2 pints vanilla nondairy frozen dessert

1 recipe Rachael Reid's "Chocolate" Chip Cookies (page 217)

2 cups coarsely chopped almonds or nondairy carob chips

1. To assemble each sandwich, allow the frozen dessert to soften slightly. Place 1 scoop frozen dessert on the flat (under) side of 1 cookie. Top with a second cookie, bottom side against the frozen dessert, and press together. Gently pat the almonds into the frozen dessert around the sides of the sandwich. Wrap in plastic and store in the freezer until ready to serve, or up to 1 week.

2. To serve, transfer the ice cream sandwiches to a large serving platter, with the birthday candle sandwich in the center if this is for a birthday party.

NOTES

■ Using a small pointed knife, cut a space in 1 cookie to fit the birthday candle.

■ Kids can assemble these as a party activity and roll them in 2 cups coarsely chopped macadamia nuts, unsweetened flaked coconut, or carob chips to replace the almonds. You can also experiment with the frozen dessert flavors, using banana, strawberry, carob, or almost any mixture to replace the vanilla.

"Sweet Dreams" Ice Cream Cake

Preparation time: 15–20 minutes to prepare, 2–3 hours to freeze

Yield: 10–12 servings

Children love this colorful ice cream wonder-cake because it's eye-catching and delicious. Parents love it because it's easy to prepare and can be made the day before it's served. It consists of alternating layers of carob or chocolate, strawberry, and vanilla nondairy frozen dessert and topped off with your favorite cookies.

10 whole-wheat honey graham crackers (about 5¾ ounces)

½ cup Spectrum Spread

2 pints carob nondairy frozen dessert

2 pints strawberry nondairy frozen dessert

2 pints vanilla nondairy frozen dessert

3 cups coarsely chopped sandwich, carob chip, or shortbread cookies (about 8 ounces)

1. Line the bottom of a 10 x 3-inch springform pan with waxed paper. To prepare the graham cracker crust, in a food processor, using the metal blade, process the graham crackers until fine crumbs form. Add the Spectrum

Spread and process until well combined. Transfer to the prepared pan and distribute evenly. Press the mixture firmly onto the bottom of the pan. Freeze until firm, about 10 minutes.

2. To assemble the cake, place the nondairy frozen desserts in the refrigerator to soften, about 10 minutes. Using a metal spatula, evenly spread on the softened carob or chocolate nondairy frozen dessert. Return the pan to the freezer until the frozen dessert is slightly hardened, about 15 minutes. Spread on the softened strawberry nondairy frozen dessert and return the pan to the freezer until the frozen dessert is slightly hardened, about 15 minutes. Spread on the softened vanilla nondairy frozen dessert. Press on the cookies, cover with plastic wrap, and place in the freezer to harden for at least 2–3 hours.

3. To serve, place the cake in the refrigerator to soften for 10–20 minutes. Run a warm knife around the edge of the cake and release the springform. Using a sturdy pancake turner, transfer the cake from the pan's bottom disk to a chilled serving platter. Slice with a sharp, warm knife.

NOTE
- **May be prepared up to 2 days ahead and frozen, covered.**

Sweet Potato Pie

Preparation time: 15–20 minutes to prepare, 20–22 minutes to bake, 60 minutes to chill
Yield: 10–12 servings

When those fall and winter holidays come, here's your dessert. With a delicious ginger snap cookie crust and a low-fat, caretenoid-packed, colorful filling, your friends and relatives will be lining up for seconds, and maybe even thirds.

1 recipe Ginger Snap Cookies dough (page 205), shaped into a flat round
3 cups peeled, seeded, and cut into 1-inch slices butternut squash (about 12 ounces)
1½ cups peeled and cut into 1-inch slices sweet potatoes or yams (about 8 ounces)
1 cup Thai Kitchen Pure Coconut Milk Lite
¾ cup pure maple syrup
½ cup brown rice syrup
½ teaspoon pure almond flavor
½ teaspoon ground cinnamon
½ teaspoon ground nutmeg
¼ teaspoon sea salt

¼ teaspoon ground ginger

1 cup pure water

¼ cup plus 2 tablespoons agar flakes

1. Preheat the oven to 375°F. Lightly oil and flour a 12-inch tart pan with a removable bottom and set aside. Cut a disk of parchment paper 1 inch larger than the diameter of the pan.

2. To shape the cookie crust, roll the round out between 2 pieces of waxed paper to a thickness of ⅛–¼ inch, and 3 inches larger in diameter than the tart pan (a 15-inch round). To do this, use even strokes and work from the center of the dough cake toward the edges, rolling in different directions to produce an even, round shape. Remove the top layer of waxed paper, place the pan on top, and slip both hands under the dough to support it as you invert the dough into the prepared pan. Remove the waxed paper, and gently fit and lightly press the dough into the bottom and up against the sides of the pan. Roll the rolling pin across the top of the pan to trim the dough flush with the top. Prick the surface with a fork and line it with the prepared parchment paper. Fill the paper-covered raw tart shell with either pie weights or dried beans and bake on the middle rack of the pre-heated oven for 12–14 minutes or until firm to the touch. Remove the weights and parchment paper and bake for 8 more minutes. Remove from the oven, transfer to a wire rack, and cool completely.

3. To prepare the sweet potato filling, place the squash and potato slices on a steamer set into a large pot filled with 1 inch of pure water. Cook covered over high heat until the potato and squash slices are tender when a fork is inserted into their centers, about 10–15 minutes. Remove the steamer and run the squash and potatoes under cool water until they can be handled comfortably. Transfer to a cheesecloth-lined fine sieve and firmly squeeze out and discard as much excess liquid as possible.

4. In a food processor, using a metal blade, combine the squash, potatoes, coconut milk, maple syrup, and rice syrup. Process together until smooth and creamy, about 2 minutes. Add the almond flavoring, cinnamon, nutmeg, salt, and ginger. Process until well combined, about 1 minute. Set aside.

5. In a small saucepan, bring the water to a boil over high heat. Reduce the heat to moderate, stir in the agar flakes, and simmer uncovered for 1–2 minutes or until the agar is completely dissolved. Restart the food processor, pour in the agar mixture through the feed tube, and run until smooth and creamy, about 5 minutes. Pour the filling into the baked tart shell and spread evenly.

6. Refrigerate for 60 minutes or until well set and firm to the touch.

7. To serve, carefully push up the bottom and slide the tart off the disk and onto a cutting board. Using a sharp knife, slice into 10–12 equal wedges and serve alone or accompanied by a dollop of Vanilla Whipped "Cream" (page 225) or vanilla nondairy frozen dessert, and Maple Roasted Nuts (page 213).

Vanilla Whipped "Cream"

Preparation time: 5–8 minutes to prepare, 4–6 minutes to cook, 60 minutes to chill

Yield: 6–8 servings

This is a coconut spin on a dynamite recipe from New York's Angelica's Kitchen. Your favorite desserts will be tops with this topping, which is rich, creamy, and kissed with vanilla.

1 pound silken tofu, well drained
½ cup canola oil
½ cup maple syrup
1 cup Thai Kitchen Pure Coconut Milk Lite
¼ cup pure vanilla flavor
1 tablespoon freshly squeezed lemon juice
1 teaspoon pure lemon flavor
¼ cup arrowroot powder
¼ teaspoon sea salt
1 cup pure water
¼ cup agar flakes

1. In a food processor, using the metal blade, combine the tofu and oil. Process until creamy, about 1 minute. Pour in the maple syrup and process until well blended.

2. In a small mixing bowl, combine the coconut milk, vanilla flavor, lemon juice, lemon flavor, arrowroot powder, and salt. Whisk together until well blended and set aside.

3. In a small saucepan, bring the water to a boil over moderate heat. Whisk in the agar and simmer uncovered, stirring occasionally, for 2–3 minutes or until the agar dissolves. Whisk briefly, then pour the coconut mixture into the saucepan. Stir frequently with an angled-bottom wooden spoon and bring to a simmer until the mixture begins to thicken, about 2–3 minutes. Remove from the heat, restart the food processor, and quickly add the coconut mixture through the feed tube. Run until smooth and creamy, about 1 minute. Pour into a container and refrigerate partially covered for 1 hour or until set.

4. Reprocess for 10 seconds; then serve as an accompaniment to almost any dessert.

NOTES

- An equal measure of soy milk or rice milk can be used to replace the coconut milk.
- This whipped "cream" can be made into Mixed Berry Parfaits layered with ripe seasonal berries (raspberries, blackberries, or blueberries), and strawberry sauce (see Notes, page 212).

Velvety Hot Fudge Brownie Sundaes

Preparation time: 15 minutes

Yield: 8 sundaes

A rich, chocolatey, cake-like brownie topped with creamy vanilla Rice Dream, hot fudge sauce, and roasted peanuts. Simply delicious!

HOT FUDGE TOPPING

1½ cups brown rice syrup

½ cup sifted carob powder

A pinch of salt

½ cup soy milk

1 tablespoon pure vanilla flavor

OTHER COMPONENTS

1 recipe Brownie Blastoff (page 199)

2 pints vanilla Rice Dream or nondairy frozen dessert

1 cup coarsely chopped roasted Valencia peanuts

1. To prepare the hot fudge topping, in a medium saucepan or cast-iron Dutch oven, bring the rice syrup to a rolling boil over moderate to high heat and stir constantly for 30 seconds. Whisk the carob powder and salt into the syrup; make sure all the lumps disappear. Whisk in the soy milk and continue simmering for 2 additional minutes. Stir in the vanilla until well combined, cover, and set aside.

2. To assemble the sundaes, place the brownies into large goblets, dessert bowls, or sundae dishes. Top with scoops of vanilla frozen dessert, drizzle on the hot fudge topping, and sprinkle with roasted peanuts.

NOTES

■ The brownies can be prepared a day in advance. Just wrap together tightly in waxed paper followed by aluminum foil.

■ I often purchase raw Valencia peanuts and roast them myself. To roast the peanuts, place them on a cookie sheet in a preheated 375°F oven for 20–25 minutes. When done they will be slightly golden in color.

Wet 'n' Wild Watermelon Cake

Preparation time: 30–40 minutes

Yield: 8–10 servings

I originally made this on the advice of a friend who told me that his mother used to make a fabulous four-tiered cake from watermelon, using metal molds to press the watermelon into perfectly circular layers. She then decorated it with berries and fresh fruit to create a raw-food cake like no other. Between the bright colors, and children's natural affinity for watermelon, kids will go wild over this one. By the way—I let kids eat this cake as a first course, because it's good for the digestion.

1 large seedless watermelon (at least 9 inches in diameter)

2 large wooden skewers

1 quart strawberries, rinsed, patted dry, and hulled

1 pint blueberries

1 large ripe pineapple, peeled, cored, cut into 1-inch triangles, and tossed in 2 tablespoons freshly squeezed orange juice

1½ pounds seedless green grapes

2 large oranges, peeled and sliced into ¼-inch-thick quarter-moons

3–4 kiwifruit, peeled and sliced into ½-inch-thick cross sections

1 box toothpicks

1. To prepare the watermelon cake layers, use a very sharp long knife to remove 1–2 inches from each end of the watermelon. Slice the watermelon into four 2- to 3-inch-deep cross sections. Using a sharp knife, remove the rind and slice into an 8-inch round layer, a 6-inch round layer, a 4-inch round layer, and a 3-inch round layer. (You should now have 4 watermelon layers, 8, 6, 4, and 3 inches in diameter.)

2. To assemble the cake, use 1 or 2 large spatulas to center the 8-inch watermelon layer on a serving platter. Carefully center the 6-inch layer on top of the 8-inch tier, then center the 4-inch layer on top of the 6-inch tier, and center the 3-inch layer on top of the 4-inch tier. Insert the skewers at even intervals, 1 inch from the center of the 3-inch layer and straight down through the cake until they reach the bottom (trim off any excess skewer from the top).

3. To decorate the cake, skewer the fruits with the toothpicks and press them lightly onto the sides and tops of the watermelon cake, creating a decorative pattern around the surface area. Arrange any leftover fruit on the platter and around the base of the cake.

4. To serve, slice with a sharp knife (removing the skewers and toothpicks as you go) and transfer to dessert plates.

NOTES

- You might want to use miniature cookie cutters to press the pineapple and kiwi slices into decorative shapes before assembling the cake.
- Other fruits can replace any in this recipe (except the watermelon). Consider these fruits, pitted and sliced: nectarines, cherries, peaches, apricots, papayas, and mangoes. Don't use bananas, though; they'll turn brown.

APPENDIX

Party Themes and Menus

There's nothing more fun for children than a party, although parents are known to quake at the prospect of planning one. It doesn't have to be difficult, though, especially when you've got a theme. Following are 6 simple party menus, with themes, designed for 4 children from ages 1 to 8. The healthy foods are for children and adolescents of any age.

To get the ball rolling, create the invitations, color, and mail. All of these lend themselves easily to elaboration with activities, party favors, decorative tablecloths, place cards, party bags, and banners. But remember, you don't have to be fancy to please children. Simple is often best—and easiest. So let's party!

Gone Fishin' Party

Lily Pond Pink Lemonade (page 72)
Ants on Logs (page 104)
Flying Fish Foccacia (Carmela's Authentic Focaccia)
(page 106)
Wet 'n' Wild Watermelon Cake (page 227)

Mexican Fiesta Party

Sunny Sombrero Punch (page 79)
Perfect Party Popcorn Balls (page 123)
Peanutty Neato Burritos (page 122)
Velvety Hot Fudge Brownie Sundaes (page 226)

Mother Nature Party

Kona Coast Coladas (page 71)
Hoppin' Frog Mix (page 117)
Noah's Nuttyjam Jamborees (page 120)
Sunny Day All-Fruit Sundaes (page 221)

PJ in the Day Party

Pillow Party Cherry Cola (page 75)
Nightly Nut Mix (page 120)
Pigs in Blankets (page 124)
"Sweet Dreams" Ice Cream Cake (page 222)

Powwow Party

Soaring Eagle Hot Cider (page 77)
Native Maize Trail Mix (page 119)
Teepee Tacos (page 179)
Chief Cloud's Cupcakes (page 202)

What's Cookin'? Party

Nature's Own Strawberry Punch (page 73)
Bowl o' Crunch (page 104)
Create-Your-Own Pizzas (page 162)
Super Chip "Ice Cream" Sandwiches (page 221)

Optimal Food Combinations and Menu Plans

One way you can avert digestive problems and maximize nutrition is by paying attention to how you combine foods in your diet. There are many theories of proper food combining; here, simply, are some basics to help ensure more efficient digestion and prevent gastrointestinal distress, in both children and adults. We can first look at foods that are light in consistency and then move on to those that are heavier and more concentrated in composition.

To begin with fresh fruits, we have watermelon, a high-water-content fruit that is very rich in minerals and should be ingested alone, on an empty stomach. Other melons can be mixed together, but it is best to exclude other fruits. Grapes can be mixed with other fruits or eaten alone, while tropical and citrus fruits can be mixed together with other fruits such as apples, pears, and berries. However, some people do not always react well to these mixtures, and it's best to take note of any negative symptoms so as to avoid discomfort. Most fruits, such as apples, pears, berries, bananas, peaches, and dates, can usually be combined with grains and flours without any problems.

Greens and starchless vegetables can be eaten with most any food, and when eaten raw they have live enzymes that will aid the digestion process. Of this group, those that can be eaten raw are lettuces, tomatoes, celery, cucumbers, peppers, and most sprouts. With these, you have the makings of a perfect salad with which to begin a meal.

Vegetables that should only be eaten cooked include those of the cruciferous variety, such as broccoli, cauliflower, and cabbage. Dark leafy greens, such as spinach, escarole, collard greens, kale, chard, and dandelions, should be steamed lightly or briefly sautéed. Some vegetables don't appeal to kids when steamed, so serving them with a little olive oil and garlic, or tamari soy sauce, will make them more palatable.

All of these raw and cooked veggies make a perfect accompaniment to protein dishes such as grains, beans, legumes, dairy, fish, poultry, and sea vegetables.

Sea vegetables can be used like any dark green leafy vegetable. They add a delicious element to stir-fries, soups, and stews, or they can be used steamed or in salads. Agar can be used in desserts and combined with fruit and fruit juices, grains, beans, and nut milks.

Starchy and root vegetables, such as potatoes, squash, carrots, parsnips, turnips, peas, and corn, should be cooked enough to allow the starch to be broken down to ensure proper digestion. These vegetables combine well in soups, stir-fries, and casseroles, and make good side dishes to accompany fish and poultry.

Grains are the staple for most of the world's civilizations. Included in this group are rice, millet, wheat, amaranth, quinoa, oats, and buckwheat (kasha); they all mix well with leafy greens and starchless vegetables, and some fruits as mentioned above. When grains are combined with legumes, nuts, or seeds, you get an excellent source of highly absorbable protein. Because animal-source foods are highly concentrated, many people experience indigestion upon consuming them with grains.

Legumes, which include a variety of beans, as well as lentils and split peas, while slightly higher in protein than grains, will combine with most foods in a similar fashion. However, it is best not to combine legumes with fruit.

Nuts and seeds, such as almonds, filberts, pecans, cashews, peanuts, walnuts, sesame seeds, pumpkin seeds, and sunflower seeds, can be mixed together or mixed with dried fruits like raisins, currants, or figs. They can also be added to baked goods, stir-fries, salads, and casseroles. When combined with each other or with grains and beans, they are a highly absorbable, rich source of protein.

Dairy products, including all cheeses, mix best with green and starchless vegetables. Many parents provide their children with grain and dairy combinations such as cheese sandwiches, quiche, and pizza. These combinations, however, can cause digestive discomfort in many, with symptoms that include bloating, gas, constipation, cramping, and diarrhea. So if you notice these problems cropping up after your child eats these foods, a simple solution is to avoid such combinations. Keep in mind that dairy products are some of the most common food allergens in the American diet, and that they're high in fat and sodium as well. In general, they are best totally avoided.

Fish can be eaten with all vegetables, and to a lesser extent, with grains and legumes. However, it's best to avoid combining fish with fruit unless the fruit is used merely as a garnish or condiment. Although cheese and other dairy products are often eaten with fish, digestive consequences often follow.

Eggs are best when combined with vegetables, in baked goods, or by themselves. However, they are gas- and mucus-forming in most people.

THE 14-DAY MENU PLAN

	HEALTHY	VS.	UNHEALTHY
DAY ONE			
BREAKFAST	Alpine Granola (page 83) and oat milk		Sugary corn flakes and cow's milk
SNACK	Carrot sticks		Caramel candy bar
LUNCH	Noah's Nuttyjam Jamborees (page 120)		Cream cheese and grape jelly on white bread
SNACK	Sunflower sprouts		Cheese puffs
DINNER	Denise's Mediterranean Bean Soup (page 129) and Garden's Gift Salad (page 143)		Hamburgers and fries
DAY TWO			
BREAKFAST	Sweet 'Taters and Spice (page 99)		Chocolate toaster pastries
SNACK	Fresh Peaches		Peaches in corn syrup
LUNCH	Carmela's Authentic Focaccia (page 106)		Hot dogs and white bread
SNACK	Bowl o' Crunch (page 104)		Potato chips
DINNER	Rosendale Café Stroganoff (page 173) and Totally Terrific Quinoa Tabbouleh Salad (page 151)		Meat loaf and white rice

THE 14-DAY MENU PLAN (*cont.*)

	HEALTHY	VS.	UNHEALTHY
DAY THREE			
BREAKFAST	Strawberry Millet Cereal (page 98)		Artificial fruit-flavored cold cereal
SNACK	Apple slices and cashew butter		Packaged apple pastries
LUNCH	Pesto Bow-Tie Pasta (page 192)		Boxed macaroni and powdered cheese
SNACK	Green Goddess Smoothies (page 70)		Red licorice sticks
DINNER	Shiitake Butternut Subs (page 155) and Sea Salad Delight (page 149)		Fried steak and boiled potatoes
DAY FOUR			
BREAKFAST	Blueberry Buckwheat Silver-Dollar Pancakes (page 87)		Pancakes and cherry-flavored syrup
SNACK	Raw almonds		Chocolate-covered nuts
LUNCH	Home-Grown Tomato Sandwiches (page 115)		Peanut butter and grape jelly on white bread
SNACK	Red bell pepper slices		Brownies
DINNER	Bite-Size Nori Rolls (page 157), Mellow Miso Soup (page 134), and Quick Cuke Can't-Miss Dish (page 146)		Deep-fried egg rolls and spareribs
DAY FIVE			
BREAKFAST	Scrumptious Scrambled Tofu (page 97), Fakin' Bacon BLT's (page 116), and whole-grain toast		Fried eggs, bacon, and white toast
SNACK	Celery sticks		Chocolate-frosted doughnuts
LUNCH	Buttery White Bean Hummus (page 105)		Fried chicken and instant mashed potatoes
SNACK	Pear slices		Sugar-coated candy "fruit slices"
DINNER	Creamy Curried Potatoes and Peas (page 161) and Turkish Coban Salad (page 152)		Fried pork chops and canned corn

THE 14-DAY MENU PLAN (*cont.*)

	HEALTHY	VS.	UNHEALTHY
DAY SIX			
BREAKFAST	Fantastic Fruit Salad (page 90)		Canned fruit salad in corn syrup
SNACK	Sunflower and pumpkin seeds		Candy corn
LUNCH	Italian Red Lentil Soup (page 132) and mixed green salad		Pastrami on rye bread
SNACK	Rice cakes with sesame butter, honey, and banana slices		Cotton candy
DINNER	Savory Quiche with Mushrooms and Greens (page 174) and Razz-Matazz-Berry Green Salad (page 146)		Pork loin and iceberg lettuce salad
DAY SEVEN			
BREAKFAST	Power Juice (page 76)		Fried eggs and ham on white English muffin
BRUNCH	Pecan Oatmeal Waffles (page 96), The Very Best Chunky Applesauce (page 100), and Rebuilt Waldorf Salad (page 147)		Ham and American cheese on white bread
SNACK	Yellow bell pepper slices		Chocolate ice cream sandwiches
DINNER	Mario's Stuffed Shells (page 189), A Bronx Salad (page 142), and "Gimme-More" Garlic Bread (page 111)		Roast beef, boiled broccoli with melted American cheese, and white bread
DAY EIGHT			
BREAKFAST	Kona Coast Coladas (page 71)		Chocolate milk
SNACK	Monkey Magic Muffins (page 94)		Bagels and cream cheese
LUNCH	Cheese Panini with Salad Greens (page 108)		Crackers and imitation American cheese spread
SNACK	Cucumber slices		Cupcakes
DINNER	Mjadara (page 169) and mixed green salad		Beef fried rice, shrimp toast, and duck sauce

THE 14-DAY MENU PLAN (*cont.*)

	HEALTHY	VS.	UNHEALTHY

DAY NINE		
BREAKFAST	Banana Cream of Buckwheat Cereal (page 85)	Sugar-Sweetened Cereal & Marshmallows
SNACK	Sunflower sprouts	Fried pork rinds
LUNCH	Lunchtime Hummus Sandwiches (page 118)	Salami and butter on white bread
SNACK	Kiwifruit	Rolled pressed fruit with sugar
DINNER	Roasted Autumn Squash Soup (page 136) and mixed green salad	Chicken-fried steak and canned gravy

DAY TEN		
BREAKFAST	Anytime Baked Apples (page 84)	Deep-fried hash browns, fried eggs, sausages, and American cheese on an English muffin
SNACK	Whole-grain rice crackers	Canned salted nuts
LUNCH	Maria's Peanut Noodles (page 190)	Chicken nuggets and fries
SNACK	Clover sprouts	Marshmallow s'mores
DINNER	Glorious Garlicky Greens (page 163), Roasted Sweet Potato Fries (page 173), and Sesame Hijiki (page 176)	Canned beef stew

DAY ELEVEN		
BREAKFAST	Honey Cinnamon Toast (page 92)	White toast and butter
SNACK	Cherries	Cheese-flavored crackers
LUNCH	Eggless Egg Salad (page 110)	Bologna on white bread
SNACK	Perfect Party Popcorn Balls (page 123)	Chocolate bars
DINNER	Children's-Choice Chili (page 159), Golden Pumpkin-Seed Corn Bread (page 112), and Salad Supreme (page 148)	Beef chili

THE 14-DAY MENU PLAN (*cont.*)

	HEALTHY	VS.	UNHEALTHY
DAY TWELVE			
BREAKFAST	Baby Bear Oatmeal (page 85)		Powdered instant oatmeal
SNACK	Plums		Jelly beans
LUNCH	Peanutty Neato Burritos (page 122)		Canned beef ravioli
SNACK	Blueberries		Chocolate ice cream
DINNER	Creamy Spinach and Pine Nut Fusilli (page 186) and mixed green salad		Baked canned ham and pineapple
DAY THIRTEEN			
BREAKFAST	Orange Cream Smoothies (page 74)		Orange drink
SNACK	Raw cashews		Chocolate sandwich cookies
LUNCH	Sweet Corn Chowder (page 140) and crackers		Turkey and mayonnaise on white bread
SNACK	Cantaloupe		Caramel popcorn
DINNER	Spinach Wonton Soup (page 138) and Stir-Fried Sesame Broccoli (page 177)		Boxed elbow macaroni and cheese
DAY FOURTEEN			
BREAKFAST	Rainbow Juice (page 77)		Grape soda
BRUNCH	French Toast of the Town (page 91) and Maple-Glazed Bananas (page 93)		Liverwurst on white bread
SNACK	Cherry tomatoes		Lime-flavored gelatin
DINNER	Mama Palma's Pizza (page 168) and Little Caesar Salad (page 144)		Pepperoni pizza

Nutrient Requirements and Food Values

The tables in this section detail the recommended dietary allowances, per day, of important nutrients, as well as food values for good sources of these nutrients. For the dietary requirements, I drew on the most recent editions (9th and 10th) of *Recommended Dietary Allowances* by the National Research Council's Food and Nutrition Board division of the National Academy of Sciences. Please note that some individuals may require greater or lesser amounts of these nutrients. For advice on your own and your family's intake of these and other important nutrients, consult your health care practitioner.

The food value tables were compiled using the most recent information from the United States Department of Agriculture, the scientific literature, and the food industry itself.

In general, a varied diet of unrefined, minimally processed whole foods, organically grown in nutrient-rich soil, will more than adequately meet the nutritional needs of most children and adults. To get ideas for such a diet, consult the Fourteen-Day Menu Plan in this book.

Note on units of measurement:

IU = *International Units*
mcg = *micrograms*
mg = *milligrams*
RE = *retinol equivalents*
TE = *tocopherol equivalents*

VITAMIN A

GROUP		mcgRE*
Pregnant women		800
Lactating women		1,300
Infants, to	1 yr.	375
Children	1–3	400
	4–6	500
	7–10	700
Adolescent girls	11–18	800
Adolescent boys	11–18	1,000

*1 mcgRE = 1 mcg (3.3 IU) vitamin A or 6 mcg (10 IU) beta-carotene

VITAMIN-A-RICH FOODS

FOOD	SERVING	VITAMIN A (mcgRE)
Sweet potato, cooked	½ cup	2,797
Carrots, cooked	½ cup	1,915
Butternut squash, cooked	½ cup	714
Dandelion greens, cooked	½ cup	608
Kale, cooked	½ cup	481
Mango, raw	½ cup	403
Blue-green algae	1 teaspoon	360
Chicory greens, raw	½ cup	360
Peppers, sweet, raw	½ cup	316
Apricots, raw	3 medium	277
Swiss chard, cooked	½ cup	276
Cantaloupe	½ cup	258
Papaya, raw	½ cup	204
Collard greens, cooked	½ cup	175
Broccoli, cooked	½ cup	108

VITAMIN C

GROUP		MG
Pregnant women		70
Lactating women		95
Infants, to	½ yr.	30
	½–1 yr.	35
Children	1–3	40
	4–10	45
Adolescents, girls and boys	11–14	50
	15–18	60

VITAMIN-C-RICH FOODS

FOOD	SERVING	VITAMIN C (mg)
Kiwifruit	1 medium	75
Papaya, raw	½ cup	63
Orange juice	½ cup	62
Broccoli, cooked	½ cup	58
Guava, raw	½ cup	55
Brussels sprouts, cooked	½ cup	48
Pepper, sweet yellow, raw	½ cup	48
Strawberries	½ cup	43
Grapefruit juice	½ cup	42
Parsley, raw	½ cup	40
Cantaloupe	½ cup	34
Mango, raw	½ cup	29
Sweet potato, cooked	½ cup	28
Kale, cooked	½ cup	27
Cauliflower, raw	½ cup	23

VITAMIN E

GROUP		MGTE*
Pregnant women		10
Lactating women		12
Infants, to	½ yr.	3
	½–1 yr.	4
Children	1–3	6
	4–10	7
Adolescent girls	11–18	8
Adolescent boys	11–18	10

*1mgTE = 1mg or 1 IU

VITAMIN-E-RICH FOODS

FOOD	SERVING	VITAMIN E (mgTE)
Wheat germ oil	2 tablespoons	40.6
Soybean oil	2 tablespoons	25.4
Corn oil	2 tablespoons	23.0
Sunflower oil	2 tablespoons	13.0
Rice bran oil	2 tablespoons	10.6
Safflower oil	2 tablespoons	10.4
Peanuts, roasted	½ cup	9.4
Sesame oil	2 tablespoons	8.0
Peanut oil	2 tablespoons	6.8
Almonds, raw	½ cup	6.6
Pecans, raw	½ cup	3.4
Walnuts, raw	½ cup	3.0
Sweet potato, cooked	½ cup	2.0
Wheat germ, raw	¼ cup	2.0
Sesame seeds	¼ cup	1.2

VITAMIN B$_{12}$ (Cobalamine)

GROUP		MCG
Pregnant women		2.2
Lactating women		2.6
Infants, to	½ yr.	0.3
	½–1 yr.	0.5
Children	1–3	0.7
	4–6	1.0
	7–10	1.4
Adolescents, girls and boys	11–18	2.0

VITAMIN-B$_{12}$-RICH FOODS

FOOD	SERVING	VITAMIN B$_{12}$ (mg)
Blue-green algae	1 teaspoon	12.0
Pollock	3 ounces	3.1
Tuna, light	3 ounces	2.5
Salmon	3 ounces	2.4
Sole	3 ounces	2.1
Muenster cheese	½ cup	1.7
Haddock	3 ounces	1.2
Halibut	3 ounces	1.2
Cheddar cheese	½ cup	0.9
Scrod	3 ounces	0.9
Milk, low fat (2%)	1 cup	0.9
Yogurt, plain, low fat	½ cup	0.9
Mozzarella cheese	½ cup	0.8
Tempeh	½ cup	0.7
Egg	1 medium	0.6

CALCIUM

GROUP		MG
Pregnant women		1,200
Lactating women		1,200
Infants, to	½ yr.	400
	½–1 yr.	600
Children	1–10	800
Adolescents, girls and boys	11–18	1,200

CALCIUM-RICH FOODS

FOOD	SERVING	CALCIUM (mg)
Goat cheese, hard	½ cup	1016
Cheddar cheese, low fat	½ cup	472
Parmesan cheese, grated	3 tablespoons	390
Sesame seeds	¼ cup	351
Milk, low fat (2%)	1 cup	297
Tofu, firm	½ cup	258
Hijiki, dry	½ cup	233
Yogurt, plain, low fat	½ cup	207
Arame, dry	½ cup	195
Almonds, raw	½ cup	189
Blackstrap molasses	1 tablespoon	137
Figs, dried	5 medium	135
Carob powder	¼ cup	90
Sunflower seeds	½ cup	84
Broccoli, cooked	½ cup	36

PHOSPHORUS

GROUP		MG
Pregnant women		1,200
Lactating women		1,200
Infants, to	½ yr.	300
	½–1 yr.	500
Children	1–10	800
Adolescents, girls and boys	11–18	1,200

PHOSPHORUS-RICH FOODS

FOOD	SERVING	PHOSPHORUS (mg)
Pumpkin seeds	½ cup	810
Cheddar cheese, low fat	½ cup	548
Sunflower seeds	½ cup	508
Almonds, raw	½ cup	369
Millet, whole grain	½ cup	355
Rye flour, dark	½ cup	343
Wheat germ, toasted	¼ cup	324
Parmesan cheese, grated	3 tablespoons	254
Tofu, firm	½ cup	239
Milk, low fat (2%)	1 cup	238
Sesame seeds	¼ cup	227
Whole-wheat flour	½ cup	223
Walnuts, raw	½ cup	190
Buckwheat flour	½ cup	170
Rice flour	½ cup	125

MAGNESIUM

GROUP		MG
Pregnant women		300
Lactating women		355
Infants, to	½ yr.	40
	½–1 yr.	60
Children	1–3	80
	4–6	120
	7–10	170
Adolescent girls	11–14	280
Adolescent girls	15–18	300
Adolescent boys	11–14	270
Adolescent boys	15–18	400

MAGNESIUM-RICH FOODS

FOOD	SERVING	MAGNESIUM (mg)
Pumpkin seeds	½ cup	369
Sunflower seeds	½ cup	255
Almonds, raw	½ cup	211
Millet, whole grain	½ cup	185
Soy flour, full fat	½ cup	182
Cashews, dry-roasted	½ cup	178
Filberts (hazelnuts)	½ cup	164
Sesame seeds	¼ cup	127
Tofu, firm	½ cup	118
Wheat germ, toasted	¼ cup	91
Adzuki beans, cooked	½ cup	60
Goat cheese, hard	½ cup	60
Milk, low fat (2%)	1 cup	33
Avocado	½ cup	23
Cheddar cheese	½ cup	16

IRON

GROUP		MG
Pregnant women		30
Lactating women		15
Infants, to	½ yr.	6
	½–1 yr.	10
Children	1–10	10
Adolescent girls	11–18	15
Adolescent boys	11–18	12

IRON-RICH FOODS

FOOD	SERVING	IRON (mg)
Tofu, firm	½ cup	13.9
Pumpkin seeds	½ cup	10.3
Millet, whole grain	½ cup	7.8
Sesame seeds	¼ cup	5.2
Sunflower seeds	½ cup	4.9
Rice bran	½ cup	4.5
Cashews, dry-roasted	½ cup	4.1
Lentils, green, cooked	½ cup	3.3
Blackstrap molasses	1 tablespoon	3.2
Spinach, cooked	½ cup	3.2
Peaches, dried	5 halves	2.7
Wheat germ, toasted	¼ cup	2.6
Raisins	⅔ cup	2.6
Almonds, raw	½ cup	2.6
Pears, dried	5 halves	1.9

ZINC

GROUP		MG
Pregnant women		15
Lactating women		19
Infants, to	1 yr.	5
Children	1–10	10
Adolescent girls	11–18	12
Adolescent boys	11–18	15

ZINC-RICH FOODS

FOOD	SERVING	ZINC (mg)
Pumpkin seeds	½ cup	5.2
Wheat germ, toasted	¼ cup	4.7
Soybean nuts, dry-roasted	½ cup	4.1
Cashews, dry-roasted	½ cup	3.8
Sunflower seeds	½ cup	3.7
Sesame seeds	¼ cup	2.8
Almonds, raw	½ cup	2.1
Adzuki beans, cooked	½ cup	2.0
Tofu, firm	½ cup	2.0
Cheddar cheese	½ cup	1.8
Walnuts, raw	½ cup	1.6
Tempeh	½ cup	1.5
Miso	⅛ cup	1.2
Yogurt, plain, low fat	½ cup	1.0
Milk, low fat (2%)	1 cup	1.0

POTASSIUM*

GROUP		MG
Pregnant women		2,000
Lactating women		2,000
Infants, to	½ yr.	500
	½–1 yr.	700
Children	1 yr.	1,000
	2–5	1,400
	6–9	1,600
Adolescents,		
girls and boys	10–18	2,000

*While no RDA has been established for potassium, the National Research Council's Food and Nutrition Board has made these estimations.

POTASSIUM-RICH FOODS

FOOD	SERVING	POTASSIUM (mg)
Hijiki, dry	½ cup	4,900
Kombu, dry	½ cup	1,933
Arame, dry	½ cup	1,300
Soy flour, full fat	½ cup	1,069
Raisins	⅔ cup	825
Rice bran	½ cup	783
Figs, dried	5 medium	666
Peaches, dried	5 halves	648
Prunes, dried	5 medium	626
Adzuki beans, cooked	½ cup	612
Blackstrap molasses	1 tablespoon	585
Almonds, raw	½ cup	520
Sunflower seeds	½ cup	496
Apricots, raw	3 medium	313
Dates, dried	5 medium	271

Natural Foods Wholesalers

Natural food products can be expensive, especially for families with children. One way to lower your costs is to order your natural foods from wholesalers. This time-saving method enables you to place your orders by phone for home delivery at 35–50 percent off retail prices.

Wholesale companies have virtually everything you would find in a natural foods store, including organically grown produce, grains, beans, nuts, seeds, cereals, flours, packaged foods, beverages, frozen foods, herbs, spices, homeopathic and herbal remedies, environmentally safe cleaning products, health and beauty aids, and vitamins and minerals. These products can be ordered in single units, although it's much more cost-effective to purchase full cases. Case ordering is well worth the effort because it can save you hundreds of dollars in a relatively short period of time.

With a small amount of information, shopping through a wholesaler can be easy. First, you should know that after you call a wholesaler you will receive a catalog of products and an application in the mail. A few companies require $4.00–$5.00 for a catalog, although most will send it free of charge. The scope of the products carried depends upon the size of the wholesaler. In general, the larger distributors will have a broader selection, and be a bit more expensive. An advantage here is more efficient delivery.

Included in the following list of natural foods wholesalers are a number of categories of information that may need explanation.

States: Listed are the states each wholesaler will service. Some wholesalers will deliver only to certain locations in each state on certain days, while others will deliver to all locations. So when calling, ask if and when the wholesaler services your area.

Minimum Order: This is the minimum dollar amount required for home delivery. Some wholesalers will lower your minimum order if you pay a surcharge. For certain individuals or buying clubs this may be cost-effective, and for others it will not be. The minimum order is a monthly one in some cases; in others you may be allowed to order every couple of months. Again, this is information you have to get directly from the company.

Meet Truck on Route: Some wholesalers will permit you to meet the truck at an already scheduled stop at a lowered minimum order. This can be cost-effective if you are unable to meet a large minimum order; however, it may be difficult to predict the exact time a truck will arrive. In addition, some companies apply a surcharge for this service.

Pickup at Warehouse: You may be fortunate enough to live within commuting distance of a wholesaler's warehouse. Some will even allow you to shop on the premises. In this case there may be a minimum purchase required, or a surcharge applied.

UPS: Delivery by United Parcel Service is an option provided by many wholesalers. The range of shippable items will vary, depending on the wholesaler. Some will not ship perishables and glass-packaged items. Also, some will have a minimum purchase required. This method can be convenient if you are in an inaccessible area away from an established trucking route. The UPS option may be especially economical if you order relatively light items, since shipping charges increase with the weight of the package.

Individuals and Buying Clubs: An individual who can meet a minimum order is automatically considered a buying club by most wholesalers. If you're an individual who cannot meet a minimum order, you might consider setting up a buying club, i.e., a group of people—friends, relatives, or neighbors—who pool their time, resources, and buying power to purchase products in large quantities at wholesale prices. As a natural foods buying club you could meet once or twice a month to coordinate ordering, delivery, and division of products. At your meetings you could sample new products, share recipe ideas, and organize support groups. You might even have fun!

For larger buying clubs a nonrefundable surcharge of $10–$15 or an annual membership fee are good ways to pay for phone calls, bags, and other necessary materials.

Foods: This category will let you know if a distributor carries produce in addition to groceries.

FOOD WHOLESALERS

Associated Buyers
P.O. Box 207
Somersworth, NH 03878
(603) 664-5656

States: New Hampshire, Vermont, Massachusetts,
    Maine, Rhode Island, Connecticut
Minimum Order: $300
Meet Truck on Route: No
Pickup at Warehouse: No
UPS: No
Individuals and Buying Clubs
Foods: Produce and Groceries

Bear Foods Wholesale
P.O. Box 2118
125 East Woodin Avenue
Chelan, WA 98816
(509) 682-5535
(800) 842-8049 (in state only)

States: Washington
Minimum Order: $50
Meet Truck on Route: $50

Pickup at Warehouse: No minimum
UPS: No
Individuals and Buying Clubs
Foods: Groceries

Blooming Prairie Warehouse
2340 Heinz Road
Iowa City, IA 52240
(319) 337-6448
(800) 323-2131
or
510 Kasota Avenue SE
Minneapolis, MN 55414
(612) 378-9774
(800) 328-8241 (outside state)
(800) 322-8324 (inside state)

States: Iowa, Minnesota, South Dakota, Montana,
    Nebraska, Illinois, Wisconsin, Michigan,
    Wyoming, Kansas, Indiana
Minimum Order: $500
Meet Truck on Route: No
Pickup at Warehouse: No minimum plus
    $15 surcharge

UPS: No
Individuals and Buying Clubs
Foods: Produce and Groceries

Clear Eye Natural Foods
302 Route 89 South
Savannah, NY 13146
(315) 365-2816
(800) 724-2233
FAX: (315) 365-2819

States: New York, Pennsylvania
Minimum Order: $500
Meet Truck on Route: $250
Pickup at Warehouse: $50 minimum
UPS: $10 minimum
Individuals and Buying Clubs
Foods: Groceries

Country Life Natural Foods
Oak Haven
P.O. Box 489
Pullman, MI 49450
(616) 236-5011
FAX: (616) 236-8357

States: Michigan, Illinois, Wisconsin, Missouri, Indiana
Minimum Order: $200–$250
Meet Truck on Route: No
Pickup at Warehouse: No minimum
UPS: No minimum
Individuals and Buying Clubs
Foods: Groceries

Federation of Ohio River Cooperatives
32 Outerbelt Street, Suite E
Columbus, OH 43213
(614) 861-2446

States: Ohio, Indiana, Michigan, Kentucky, Tennessee, West Virginia, Pennsylvania, North Carolina, Maryland, Virginia, District of Columbia

Minimum Order: $600
Meet Truck on Route: $200
Pickup at Warehouse: $400 minimum
UPS: No
Individuals and Buying Clubs
Foods: Groceries and Produce

Frankferd Farms Foods
318 Love Road, R.D.#1
Valencia, PA 16059
(412) 898-2242
FAX: (412) 898-2968

States: Pennsylvania, District of Columbia, Ohio, Virginia, West Virginia, Maryland, New York
Minimum Order: $300
Meet Truck on Route: No
Pickup at Warehouse: No minimum
UPS: No minimum
Individuals and Buying Clubs
Foods: Produce and Groceries

Genesee Wholesale Natural Foods
R.D. 2, Box 105
Genesee, PA 16923
(814) 228-3205
FAX: (814) 228-3638

States: Pennsylvania, New York, New Jersey, Ohio, Delaware
Minimum Order: $250
Meet Truck on Route: Variable, depending on location
Pickup at Warehouse: No minimum
UPS: No minimum
Individuals and Buying Clubs
Foods: Groceries

Hudson Valley Federation of Food Cooperatives, Inc.
6 Noxon Road
Poughkeepsie, NY 12603

(914) 473-5400
(914) 473-5458

States: New York, New Jersey, Connecticut, Pennsylvania
Minimum Order: $400
Meet Truck on Route: $250
Pickup at Warehouse: $25 minimum
UPS: $25 minimum
Individuals and Buying Clubs
Foods: Produce and Groceries

Mountain People's Warehouse

12745 Earhart Avenue
Auburn, CA 95602
(800) 679-6733
FAX: (916) 889-9544

States: California, Colorado, Hawaii, Idaho, Montana, Nevada, New Mexico, Oregon, Utah, Washington, Wyoming
Minimum Order: $500
Meet Truck on Route: No
Pickup at Warehouse: $200 minimum plus 10 percent surcharge
UPS: No
Individuals and Buying Clubs
Foods: Produce and Groceries

Natural Food Distributing

77 South Main Street
Newtown, CT 06470
(203) 426-2520
FAX: (203) 270-9152
States: Connecticut, New York, Massachusetts, Rhode Island
Minimum Order: $100
Meet Truck on Route: No
Pickup at Warehouse: No minimum
UPS: No minimum
Individuals and Buying Clubs
Foods: Groceries

Neshaminy Valley Natural Foods
5 Louise Drive
Ivyland, PA 18974
(215) 443-5545
FAX: (215) 443-7087

States: Pennsylvania, Maryland, District of Columbia, Virginia, Rhode Island, New York, New Jersey, Delaware
Minimum Order: $250–$350
Meet Truck on Route: No
Pickup at Warehouse: $100 minimum
UPS: $100 minimum
Buying Clubs of at Least Six Persons
Foods: Produce and Groceries

Northeast Cooperatives

P.O. Box 8188, Quinn Road
Brattleboro, VT 05304-8188
(802) 257-5856
(800) 334-9939
FAX: (802) 257-7039

States: New York, New Hampshire, Vermont, Maine, Massachusetts, Connecticut, Rhode Island
Minimum Order: $400
Meet Truck on Route: No
Pickup at Warehouse: $100 minimum for produce, $400 minimum for groceries
UPS: No
Individuals and Buying Clubs
Foods: Produce and Groceries

North Farm Cooperative Warehouse

204 Regas Road
Madison, WI 53714
(608) 241-2667
(800) 236-5880
FAX: (608) 241-0688

States: Minnesota, Wisconsin, Michigan, North Dakota, South Dakota, Montana, Illinois, Iowa, Indiana, Ohio, Wyoming

Minimum Order: $500
Meet Truck on Route: No
Pickup at Warehouse: $100 minimum
UPS: No
Individuals and Buying Clubs
Foods: Groceries

Nutrasource
4005 Sixth Avenue South
P.O. Box 81106
Seattle, WA 98108
(206) 467-7190
(800) 336-8872
FAX: (206) 682-1485

States: Oregon, Idaho, Washington
Minimum Order: $500
Meet Truck on Route: No
Pickup at Warehouse: $250 minimum
UPS: $250 minimum
Individuals and Buying Clubs
Foods: Groceries

Orange Blossom Cooperative Warehouse
1601 Northwest Fifty-fifth Place
P.O. Box 4159
Gainesville, FL 32613
(904) 372-7061
FAX: (904) 372-7988

States: Florida, Alabama, Georgia, North Carolina,
   South Carolina
Minimum Order: $300 or $500 on the Coasts
Meet Truck on Route: $150
Pickup at Warehouse: $25 minimum
UPS: $25 minimum
Individuals and Buying Clubs
Foods: Groceries

Ozark Cooperative Warehouse
P.O. Box 1528
Fayetteville, AR 72702
(501) 521-2667

States: Arkansas, Tennessee, Oklahoma, Missouri,
   Kansas, Texas, Louisiana, Mississippi, Alabama,
   Georgia
Minimum Order: $300–$500
Meet Truck on Route: No
Pickup at Warehouse: $100 minimum
UPS: No minimum
Individuals and Buying Clubs
Foods: Produce and Groceries

Ranchero Produce
726 South Mateo Street
Los Angeles, CA 90023
(213) 627-4131
FAX: (213) 627-3382

States: All
Minimum Order: $200
Pickup at Warehouse: No minimum
All Orders Shipped by Freight
Individuals and Buying Clubs
Foods: Produce

Roots and Fruits Cooperative Produce
1929 East Twenty-fourth Street
Minneapolis, MN 55404
(612) 722-3030
FAX: (612) 722-0882

States: Minnesota, Michigan, Wisconsin, Iowa,
   Montana, North Dakota, South Dakota
Minimum Order: $250
Meet Truck on Route: No
Pickup at Warehouse: $250 minimum
UPS: No
Buying Clubs Only
Foods: Produce

Tucson Cooperative Warehouse
350 South Toole Avenue
Tucson, AZ 85701
(602) 884-9951

States: California, Nevada, Utah, Colorado, Arizona, New Mexico, Texas
Minimum Order: $250
Meet Truck on Route: No

Pickup at Warehouse: No
UPS: $25 minimum
Individuals and Buying Clubs
Foods: Produce and Groceries

Directory of Physicians

Following is a state-by-state listing of physicians who specialize in pediatric allergies, family practice, and environmental medicine. (Inclusion on this list does not constitute an endorsement of any practitioner.) For further information contact:

The American College for Advancement in Medicine (ACAM)
23121 Verdugo Drive, Suite 204
Laguna Hills, CA 92653
(800) 532-3688
(714) 583-7666
FAX (714) 455-9679

The American Academy of Environmental Medicine (AAEM)
4510 West Eighty-ninth Street
Prairie Village, KS 66207
(913) 642-6062

The American Association of Naturopathic Physicians
2366 Lake Avenue East, Suite 322
Seattle, WA 98102
(206) 323-7610

KEY TO ABBREVIATIONS

A	Allergy		
DO	Doctor of Osteopathy	IM	Internal Medicine
DC	Doctor of Chiropractic	MD	Medical Doctor
EM	Environmental Medicine	ND	Naturopathic Doctor
FP	Family Practice	OM	Orthomolecular Medicine
GP	General Practice	Pd	Pediatrics

ALABAMA

Prusch, Gus J., Jr., M.D.	A	(205) 823-6180	759 Valley St.	Birmingham, AL 35226
Brown, Andrew M., M.D.	A/EM	(205) 547-4971	515 South Third St.	Gadsden, AL 35901
Miller, Joseph B., M.D.	A/EM	(205) 342-8540	5901 Airport Blvd.	Mobile, AL 36608

ALASKA

Manual, Russel, I., M.D.	FP	(907) 562-7070	4141 B Street #209	Anchorage, AK 99508
Rowen, Robert, M.D.	FP	(907) 344-7775	615 East 82nd St. #300	Anchorage, AK 99508

ARKANSAS

Warrel, A.M.J., M.D.	A/EM/Pd	(501) 535-8200	3900 Hickory St.	Pine Bluff, AR 71603

ARIZONA

Herro, Ralph F., M.D.	A/EM/FP	(602) 266-2374	5115 North Central Ave.	Phoenix, AZ 85012
Cronin, Michael, M.D.	A/ND	(602) 970-0000	8010 East McDowell Rd.	Scottsdale, AZ 85257

CALIFORNIA

Zinke, Erhardt, M.D.	FP/EM	(714) 249-9449	30111 Niguel Rd. #K	Laguna Niguel, CA 92677
Moss, Charles A., M.D.	FP/EM	(619) 457-1314	8950 Villa La Jolla Dr. #2162	La Jolla, CA 92037
Cathcart, Robert, M.D.	A/EM	(415) 949-2822	127 Second St.	Los Altos, CA 94322
Kim, Duke D., M.D.	Pd	(714) 364-6040	27800 Medical Center Rd. #116	Mission Viejo, CA 92691
Taylor, Lawrence, M.D.	A/FP	(619) 296-2952	2772 4th Ave.	San Diego, CA 92103
Ross, Gary S., M.D.	A/FP	(415) 398-0555	500 Sutter #300	San Francisco, CA 94102
Sinarko, Robert J., M.D.	A/EM	(415) 788-2099	450 Sutter St. #1124	San Francisco, CA 94108
Wempen, Ronald R., M.D.	EM	(714) 546-5325	3620 South Bristol St. #306	Santa Ana, CA 92704
Wakefield, John C., M.D.	EM	(408) 732-3037	500 East Remington Dr. #23	Sunnyvale, CA 94087

COLORADO

Cropley, Charley, M.D.	A/ND	(303) 499-3055	3585 Longwood Ave.	Boulder, CO 80303
Duhon, Crawford, S., M.D.	A/EM	(303) 499-9386	4841 Eldorado Springs Dr.	Boulder, CO 80303
Juetersonke, George, M.D.	FP	(719) 596-9040	3090 North Academy Blvd. #10	Colorado Springs, CO 80917
Denton, Sandra, M.D.	FP	(719) 548-1600	5080 List Dr.	Colorado Springs, CO 80919
Gerdes, Kendall A., M.D.	A/EM	(303) 377-8837	1617 Vine St.	Denver, CO 80206
Stigler, Del, M.D.	A/Pd/EM	(303) 831-7335	2005 Franklin St. #490	Denver, CO 80205

CONNECTICUT

Offgang, Harold, M.D.	A/ND	(203) 798-0533	57 North St.	Danbury, CT 06810
Mandell, Marshall, M.D.	EM/A	(203) 838-4706	3 Brush St.	Norwalk, CT 06850
Cohen, Alan, M.D.	FP/Pd	(203) 799-7733	325 Post Rd.	Orange, CT 06744
Finnu, Jerrold, M.D.	A	(203) 489-8977	333 Kennedy Dr. #204	Torrington, CT 06790
Baker, Sydney, M., M.D.	EM/FP/Pd	(203) 227-8444	40 Hillside Rd.	Weston, CT 06883

DISTRICT OF COLUMBIA

Beals, Paul, M.D.	FP	(202) 332-0370	263 Connecticut Ave. NW #100	Washington, D.C. 20037
Mitchell, George, M.D.	A	(202) 265-4111	2639 Connecticut Ave. NW #C-100	Washington, D.C. 20008

FLORIDA

Cannon, Stanley J., M.D.	A/EM	(305) 279-3020	9085 SW 87th Ave.	Miami, FL 33176
Feldman, Hobart T., M.D.	A/EM	(305) 652-1062	16800 NW Second Ave. #301	North Miami, FL 33169
Chaim, Hana T., D.O.	FP	(904) 672-9000	595 West Granada Blvd.	Ormond Beach, FL 32174
Krischer, K.N., M.D.	A/EM	(305) 584-6655	910 SW 40th Ave.	Plantation, FL 33317

Wunderlich, Ray, M.D.	A	(813) 822-3612	666 6th St. South	St. Petersburg, FL 33701
Parsons, James M., M.D.	A	(407) 628-3399	2699 Lee Rd. #303	Winter Park, FL 32789

GEORGIA

Boyette, Morton D., M.D.	A	(912) 435-7161	425 West 3rd Ave.	Albany, GA 31701
Fried, Milton, M.D.	A	(404) 451-4857	4426 Tilly Mill Rd.	Atlanta, GA 30300
Sin, Young S., M.D.	A/EM	(404) 242-0000	3850 Holcombe Bridge Rd.	Norcross, GA 30092
Schneider, Terril J., M.D.	A/FP	(912) 929-1027	205 Dental Dr. #19	Warner Robins, GA 31088

HAWAII

Frederick, Lam, M.D.	A/FP	(808) 537-3311	1270 Queen Emma Bldg. #501	Honolulu, HI 96813
Clifton, Arrington, M.D.	FP/Pd	(808) 322-9400	P.O. Box 649	Kealakekua, HI 96750

IDAHO

McGee, Charles T., M.D.	A/Pd	(208) 664-1478	1717 Lincolnway #108	Coeur d'Alene, ID 83814
Tyrone, Bellamy G., M.D.	FP	(208) 528-9500	P.O. Box 15	Rigby, ID 83442

ILLINOIS

Aquino, Elizer, M.D.	GP	(708) 719-2191	850 West Irving Park Rd.	Chicago, IL 60613
Rentea, Razvan, M.D.	GP	(312) 583-7793	3525 West Peterson Ave. #611	Chicago, IL 60659
Oberg, Gary, M.D.	Pd/A/EM	(815) 455-1990	31 North Virginia St.	Crystal Lake, IL 60014
Elghammer, Robert, M.D.	Pd	(217) 446-3259	723 North Logan Ave.	Danville, IL 61832
Hrdlicka, Richard, M.D.	A/FP	(708) 232-1900	302 Randall Rd. #206	Geneva, IL 60134
Pfeiffer, Guy, M.D.	A/EM	(217) 234-6441	200 Professional Plaza	Matloon, IL 61938
Benson, Thomas, M.D.	A/EM/Pd	(618) 395-5222	1200 North East St.	Olney, IL 62450
Boxer, Robert, M.D.	A/EM	(708) 677-0260	64 Old Orchard Rd.	Skokie, IL 60077
Marshall, Robert, M.D.	A/EM	(708) 446-1923	700 Oak St.	Winnetka, IL 60093

INDIANA

Anderson, Thomas, M.D.	FP	(219) 686-2202	Church/Main St. P.O. Box 77	Camden, IN 46917
Sparks, Harold, D.O.	A/FP	(812) 479-8228	3001 Washington Ave.	Evansville, IN 47714
Darbro, David, M.D.	A	(317) 787-7221	2124 East Hanna Ave.	Indianapolis, IN 46227
Goodwin, Thomas, M.D.	A/FP/EM	(219) 980-6117	6111 Harrison St. #343	Merrillville, IN 46410
Turfler, David, D.O.	A/FP	(219) 233-3840	336 West Navarre St.	South Bend, IN 46616

IOWA

Nebbeling, David, D.O.	GP	(319) 391-0321	622 East 38th St.	Davenport, IA 52807

KANSAS

Acker, Steven, M.D.	FP	(316) 733-4494	310 West Central #D	Andover, KS 67002
Gamble, John, M.D.	GP/FP	(913) 321-1140	1606 Washington Blvd.	Kansas City, KS 66102
James, Donald, M.D.	EM	(316) 945-5245	1301 North West St.	Wichita, KS 67209

KENTUCKY

Tap, John, M.D.	Pd	(502) 781-1483	414 Old Morgantown Rd.	Bowling Green, KY 42101
Morgan, Kirk, M.D.	FP	(502) 228-0156	9105 U.S. Hwy. 42	Louisville, KY 40059
Kriteck, Stephen, M.D.	FP/Pd	(606) 678-5137	1301 Pumphouse Rd.	Somerset, KY 42501

LOUISIANA

Ardoin, Barbara, M.D.	A	(318) 981-8204	123 Ridgeway Dr.	Lafayette, LA 70505
Dominge, Adonis, M.D.	GP	(318) 365-2196	602 North Lewis #600	New Iberia, LA 70560

MAINE

Haigney, Dayton, M.D.	A	(207) 439-1068	406 Dow Highway	Elliot, ME 03903
Cyr, Joseph, M.D.	GP	(207) 868-5273	62 Main St.	Van Buren, ME 04785
Weisser, Arthur, M.D.	FP	(207) 873-7721	184 Silver St.	Waterville, ME 04901

MARYLAND

Cadoux, Alexander, M.D.	A/FP	(410) 296-3737	2324 West Joppa Rd. #100	Baltimore, MD 21093
Beals, Paul, M.D.	FP	(301) 490-9911	9101 Cherry Lane Park #201	Laurel, MD 20708
Gaby, Alan, M.D.	GP	(410) 486-5656	31 Walker Ave.	Pikesville, MD 21208

MASSACHUSETTS

Asis, Guillermo, M.D.	A	(617) 661-6225	2500 Massachusetts Ave.	Cambridge, MA 02140
Cohen, Richard, M.D.	A	(617) 829-9281	51 Mill St. #1	Hanover, MA 02339
Kaufman, Svetlana, M.D.	A	(508) 453-5181	24 Merrimack St. #323	Lowell, MA 01852
Radwanske, Z.K., M.D.	A/FP	(508) 947-8118	339 Center St.	Middleboro, MA 02346
Englender, Carol, M.D.	A/EM/FP	(617) 965-7770	1126 Beacon St.	Newton, MA 02161
Elson, Barry, M.D.	A	(413) 584-7787	52 Maplewood Shops-Old South St.	Northampton, MA 01060
La Cava, Thomas N., M.D.	Pd	(508) 854-1380	360 West Boylston St. #107	West Boylston, MA 01583

MICHIGAN

Davey, Paula, M.D.	EM	(313) 662-3384	425 East Washington #201	Ann Arbor, MI 48104
Downing, Nedra, D.O.	A	(313) 625-6677	6300 Sashabaw Rd. #C	Clarkson, MI 48346
Born, Grant, D.O.	A/FP	(616) 455-3550	2687 44th St. SE	Grand Rapids, MI 49512
Camp, Herbert Lee, M.D.	A/EM	(517) 631-1254	4011 Orchard Drive #3004	Midland, MI 48641
Walkottin, Ruth, D.O.	A/FP	(616) 733-1989	427 Seminole #111	Muskeyon, MI 49441

MINNESOTA

Dole, Michael, M.D.	FP	(612) 593-9458	10700 Old Country Rd. #350	Minneapolis, MN 55441
Wilder, Walter, M.D.	Pd	(612) 927-5431	6525 Drew Ave. South	Minneapolis, MN 55435

MISSOURI

Schwent, John, D.O.	A/FP	(314) 937-8688	1400 Truman Blvd.	Festus, MO 63028
Sultan, Tipu, M.D.	A/EM/Pd	(314) 921-7100	11585 West Florissant	Florissant, MO 63033
Hill, Doyle, D.O.	A/FP	(417) 926-6643	600 North Bush St.	Mountain Grove, MO 65711

MONTANA

Steele, Charles, M.D.	A	(406) 727-4757	2509 7th Ave. South	Great Falls, MT 59405

NEBRASKA

Millen, Otis, M.D.	FP	(308) 728-3251	408 South 14th St.	Ord, NE 68862

NEVADA

Milne, Robert, M.D.	A/FP	(702) 385-1393	2110 Pinto Lane	Las Vegas, NV 89106
Fuller, Rayal, M.D.	A/EM	(702) 732-1400	3720 Howard Hughes Pkwy.	Las Vegas, NV 89109
Broodie, Douglas, M.D.	FP	(702) 324-7070	309 Kirman Ave. #2	Reno, NV 89502

NEW HAMPSHIRE

Moore, Michele, M.D.	FP/EM	(603) 357-2180	115 Key Rd.	Keene, NH 03431
Nicoletti, Andrew, M.D.	A/DC	(603) 898-5500	289 Lawrence Rd.	Salem, NH 03079

NEW JERSEY

Magaziner, Allan, D.O.	EM/FP	(609) 424-8222	1907 Greentree Rd.	Cherry Hill, NJ 08003
Ali, Majid, M.D.	A	(201) 586-4111	95 East Main St.	Denville, NJ 07834
Leder, Robin, M.D.	A	(201) 525-1155	235 Prospect Ave.	Hackensack, NJ 07601
Harris, Charles, M.D.	A/FP	(908) 506-9200	1520 Rt. 37 East	Toms River, NJ 08753

NEW MEXICO

Luciani, Ralph, D.O.	FP	(505) 888-5995	3917 West Rd. #2	Albuquerque, NM 87110
Krohn, Jaqueline, M.D.	P/EM	(505) 662-9620	Los Alamos Med.Ctr. #136	Los Alamos, NM 87544
Shrader, W.A., M.D.	A/EM	(505) 983-8890	141 Paseo de Panalta, #A	Santa Fe, NM 87501

NEW YORK

Izquierdo, Richard, M.D.	A/FP/Pd	(212) 589-4541	1070 Southern Blvd. Lower Level	Bronx, NY 10459
Wojcik, Joseph, M.D.	A/EM	(914) 793-6161	525 Bronxville Rd. #1G	Bronxville, NY 10108
Yutsis, Pavel, M.D.	A/FP/Pd	(718) 259-2122	1309 West 7th St.	Brooklyn, NY 11204
Patel, Kalpana, M.D.	A/Pd/EM	(716) 883-2611	191 North St.	Buffalo, NY 14201
Rapp, Doris, M.D.	Pd/A/EM	(716) 875-5578	2757 Elmwood Ave.	Buffalo, NY 14217
Bergman, William, M.D.	A/FP/ND	(212) 684-2290	Hahnemann Health Associates 50 Park Ave.	New York, NY 10016
Levin, Warren, M.D.	A/EM	(212) 696-1900	World Health Medical Group 444 Park Ave. South 12th Fl.	New York, NY 10016
Teich, Morton, M.D.	A/EM/Pd	(212) 988-1821	930 Park Ave.	New York, NY 10028

Block, Nell, M.D.	A/FP	(914) 359-3300	14 Prel Plaza	Orangeburg, NY 10962
Rogers, Sherry, M.D.	A/EM/FP	(315) 488-2856	P.O. Box 2716	Syracuse, NY 13220
Boris, Marvin, M.D.	Pd	(516) 921-9000	75 Froelich Farm Blvd.	Woodbury, NY 11797

NORTH CAROLINA

| Laird, John, M.D. | A/FP | (828) 683-3101 | Rt. 1 Box 7 | Leicester, NC 28748 |
| Wilson, John, M.D. | A/EM | (704) 876-1617 | P.O. Box 6981 | Statesville, NC 28687 |

NORTH DAKOTA

| Leigh, Richard, M.D. | A/EM | (828) 775-5527 | 2314 Library Circle | Grand Forks, ND 58201 |
| Briggs, Brian, M.D. | FP | (701) 838-6011 | 718 SW 6th St. | Minot, ND 58101 |

OHIO

| Cole, Ted, M.D. | A/FP/Pd | (513) 779-0300 | 9678 Cincinnati-Columbus Rd. | Cincinnati, OH 45241 |
| Ressenger, Charles, M.D. | DO | (419) 668-9615 | 853 S. Norwalk Rd. P.O. Box 374 | Norwalk, OH 44857 |

OKLAHOMA

Philpott, William, M.D.	OM	(405) 390-3009	17171 S.E. 29th St.	Choctaw, OK 73020
Hagglund, Howard, M.D.	A/FP/EM	(405) 329-4458	2227 West Lindsey #1401	Norman, OK 73069
Farr, Charles, M.D.	A	(405) 691-1112	10101 South Western Ave.	Oklahoma City, OK 73139

OREGON

Peters, Ronald, M.D.	A/FP	(503) 482-7007	1607 Siskiyou Blvd.	Ashland, OR 97520
Morgan, Joseph, M.D.	Pd/A/EM	(503) 269-0333	1750 Thompson Rd.	Coos Bay, OR 97420
Gambee, John, M.D.	A	(503) 686-2536	66 Club Rd. #140	Eugene, OR 97401
Peterson, Noel, M.D.	A/ND	(503) 636-2734	560 First St. #204	Lake Oswego, OR 97034
Tyler, Jeffrey, M.D.	Pd	(503) 255-4256	163 NE 192nd Ave.	Portland, OR 97527

PENNSYLVANIA

Chung, Chin, M.D.	Pd	(814) 455-4429	210 East 2nd St.	Erie, PA 16507
Kerry, Roy, M.D.	A	(412) 588-2600	17 Sixth Ave.	Greenville, PA 16125
Maulfair, Conrad, D.O.	A	(215) 682-2104	P.O. Box 71	Mertztown, PA 19539
Galperin, Mura, M.D.	FP	(215) 677-2337	824 Hendrix St.	Philadelphia, PA 19110
Buttram, Harold, M.D.	A/FP/EM	(215) 536-1890	5724 Clymer Rd.	Quakertown, PA 18951

SOUTH CAROLINA

| Rozeman, Theodore, M.D. | FP | (803) 796-1702 | 2228 Airport Rd. | Columbia, SC 29169 |
| Lieberman, Allan, M.D. | EM | (843) 372-1600 | 7510 Northforest Dr. | N. Charleston, SC 29420 |

SOUTH DAKOTA

| Argabrite, John W., M.D. | EM | (605) 886-3144 | P.O. Box 1596 | Watertown, SD 57201 |

TENNESSEE

Crook, William, M.D.	Pd/EM	(901) 423-5400	681 Skyline Dr.	Jackson, TN 38301
Wanderman, Richard, M.D.	Pd/FP	(901) 683-2777	5575 Poplar Ave. #112	Memphis, TN 38119

TEXAS

Hamel, Charles, M.D.	A/EM	(817) 468-7755	4412 Matlock Rd. #300	Arlington, TX 76107
Johnson, Alfred, M.D.	A/EM	(214) 368-4132	8345 Walnut Hill Lane #205	Dallas, TX 75231
Marsh, George, M.D.	A/EM/FP	(903) 962-4247	P.O. Drawer H	Grand Saline, TX 75140
Battle, Robert, M.D.	A/FP	(713) 932-0552	9910 Long Point Rd.	Houston, TX 77055
Stewart, Everett, M.D.	A/FP	(806) 793-8963	3812 24th St.	Lubbock, TX 79410
Izen, Joseph, M.D.	A/EM	(713) 941-2444	3301 Plainview St. #8	Pasadena, TX 77504

UTAH

Harper, Dennis, D.O.	A/FP	(801) 288-8881	5263 S. 300 W. #203	Murray, UT 84107
Remington, Dennis, M.D.	A/FP/EM	(801) 373-8500	1675 North Freedom Blvd. #11E	Provo, UT 84604

VERMONT

Anderson, Charles, M.D.	A/FP	(802) 879-6544	175 Pearl St.	Essex Junction, VT 05452

VIRGINIA

Patel, Sohinj, M.D.	A	(703) 941-3600	7023 Little River Tpk. #207	Annandale, VA 22003
Huffman, Harold, M.D.	FP	(703) 861-5242	P.O. Box 197	Clinton, VA 22831
Cranton, Elmer, M.D.	A/FP	(540) 677-3631	Ripshin Road—Box #44	Troutdale, VA 24378

WASHINGTON

Block, Murray, D.O.	A/FP	(509) 966-1780	609 South 48th Ave.	Yakima, WA 98908
Wilkinson, Randall, M.D.	FP	(509) 453-5506	302 South 12th Ave.	Yakima, WA 98902
Cranton, Elmer, M.D.	A/FP	(206) 458-1061	P.O. Box 7510	Yelm, WA 98547-7510

WEST VIRGINIA

Corro, Prudencio, M.D.	A	(304) 252-0775	251 Stanaford Rd.	Beckley, WV 25801
Kostenko, Michael, D.O.	A/FP	(304) 253-0591	114 East Main St.	Beckley, WV 25801

WISCONSIN

Kadile, Eleazar, M.D.	A	(414) 468-9442	1538 Bellevue St.	Green Bay, WI 54311
Kroker, George, M.D.	A	(608) 782-2027	P.O. Box 2408	La Crosse, WI 54602
Robertson, Allan J., M.D.	FP	(414) 259-1350	10520 West Bluemound Rd. #202	Milwaukee, WI 53226

WYOMING

Smith, Gerald, M.D.	EM	(307) 632-5589	5320 Education Dr.	Cheyenne, WY 82009

Index

addictive food allergies, 58
additives
　in food, and hyperactivity, 60
　in water supply, 27
aflatoxins, 20, 44
after-dinner eating, 6
agar, 42, 43, 62, 235
alachlor, 26
alfalfa sprouts, 43
alginic acid, 42
allergen-free cooking, 61–63
allergies, 6, 58–63
　to cow's milk, 14
　to eggs, 15
　testing for, 60–61
　and unborn babies, 59
almond milk, 80–81
aluminum cookware, 56
amaranth, 35
amaranth flour, 62, 63
amaretti cookies, 203–4
amasake, 51
amino acid profile, 10
animal products, nutritional purity
　of, and factory farming, 14–18
animals, inhumane treatment of,
　15–18
antioxidant nutrients, 18
apple cider vinegar, 53
apples
　baked, 84
　carrot apple juice, 68
　cobbler, 206–8
applesauce, 100–101
aquifers, 24
arame, 43
arrowroot, 55, 62, 63
asthma, 14
avocadoes, guacamole, 113–14

bakeware, 56
baking powder, 55
　corn-free, 63
balsamic vinegar, 53

bananas
　banana cream pie, 218–19
　and cream of buckwheat cereal,
　　85–86
　maple glazed, 93–94
barley, 35
　and mushroom soup, 135
barley flour, 62
barley malt, 50–51
basil, crostini, with tomato, 127
basmati rice, pilaf, 156–57
beans, 37, 44, 236
　soup, Mediterranean, 129
　white bean hummus, 105
beef, 17–18
benzene, 20, 26
beverages, 67–81
　during eating, and digestion, 6
blackstrap molasses, 51
bleached flour, 34
blueberries, in buckwheat pan-
　cakes, 87–88
blue-green algae, 19, 52
bottled water, 31–32
bovine spongiform encephalopathy
　(mad cow disease), 17–18
bow-tie pasta, and pesto, 192–93
bran, 33
bread
　French toast, 91
　garlic, 111–12
　honey cinnamon toast, 92
　pumpkin-seed corn bread, 112–13
breadsticks, herbed, 114–15
breakfast foods, 82–102
breast milk, 14
Brewer's yeast, 19
broccoli, stir-fried, with sesame,
　177–78
Brostoff, Dr. Jonathan, 59
brownies, 199–200
　in hot fudge sundaes, 226
brown rice flour, 62
brown rice pasta, 62

brown rice syrup, 50–51
brown rice vinegar, 53
buckwheat
　and blueberry pancakes, 87–88
　cream of, and banana cereal,
　　85–86
buckwheat flour, 62
bulgur, 36
burritos, 158–59
　peanutty, 122–23
butternut squash, and shiitake subs,
　155–56
butters, 45, 62

Caesar salad, 144
cakes
　carrot cake muffins, 88–90
　"ice cream," 222–23
　pound, lemon marble, 211–13
　watermelon, 227–28
calcium
　foods rich in, 246
　RDA, 246
　and vegetarianism, 19
canning, 5
canola oil, 48, 62
carbohydrates, complex, 33
carbon filters, 29
carbonyl compounds, 20
carcinogenic pesticides, 10
carob ("chocolate"), 52–53
　chip "ice cream" sandwiches,
　　221–22
　"chocolate" chip cookies, 217–18
　hot "chocolate," 73
　hot fudge brownie sundaes, 226
　milk shake, 68–69
carrots
　apple carrot juice, 68
　carrot cake muffins, 88–90
　lemony carrot pear juice, 71–72
casein, 14, 62
cast iron cookware, 56
celery, snack, with nut butter, 104

cellulose triacetate membrane (CTA), for water purification, 30
cereal grain juices, 52
cereals
  banana cream of buckwheat, 85–86
  granola, 83
  hot rye muesli, 92–93
  oatmeal, 85
  strawberry millet, 98–99
  walnutty apple granola, 101–2
certification, of organic farming, 12
cheese
  and macaroni, 188–89
  nachos, 118–19
  panini, with salad greens, 108
  soy, 41, 62
chemical adulteration, of fruits and vegetables, 9–11
chemical contaminants
  in fish, 16
  in water supply, 26
chemical fertilizers, 9, 10
chemical pesticides, 9–10
cherries, party cola, 75–76
children
  cooking with, 3–4
  exposure to junk food, out of the home, 7
  and knives, 3
  portion sizes for, 4
  variety in meals of, 4–5
  vulnerability to chemical farming, 10, 11
chili, 159–60
chili dogs (veggie), 182
chips
  nachos, 118–19
  snack mix, 104–5
chlorella, 52
chlorination, of water supply, 25
chlorine, 27
chlorophyll, 18, 43, 44, 52

"chocolate" (carob), 52–53
  chip "ice cream" sandwiches, 221–22
  "chocolate" chip cookies, 217–18
  hot "chocolate," 73
  hot fudge brownie sundaes, 226
  milk shake, 68–69
chowder, corn, 140
cider, hot, 77–78
cinnamon
  croutons, 108–9
  and honey toast, 92
citizen outrage, about toxic chemicals in foods, 11
citrus fruits, 235
cobalt, 19
coban salad (Turkish), 152
cobbler, apple, 206–8
cocoa, 52–53
coconut milk, 46
coconut oil, 47
coladas, Hawaiian, Kona Coast, 71
colas, cherry, 75–76
colic, 59
community-sponsored agriculture (CSA), 13
companion crops, 12
complex carbohydrates, 33
compost, 11–12
condiments, 55
cookies
  amaretti, 203–4
  "chocolate" (carob) chip, 217–18
  ginger snap, 205–6
  oatmeal chip, 200–201
cooking
  allergen-free, 61–63
  with children, 3–4
  with teenagers, 8
cookware, 56
copper cookware, 56
corn, 35
  pumpkin-seed corn bread, 112–13
  sweet corn chowder, 140
corn flour, 62

corn-free cooking, 63
corn oil, 63
cornstarch, 55, 63
corn syrup, 63
cottonseed oil, 47
coulis, with gnocchi, sweet peppers and tomato, 187–88
couscous, 36
cow's milk, 14
"cream," whipped, vanilla, 225
crop rotation, 12
crostini, tomato and basil, 127
croutons
  cinnamon, 108–9
  deluxe, 109–10
cruciferous vegetables, 235
cucumbers, salad dish, 146
cupcakes, 202–3
cyclic food allergy (type II allergy), 58, 59

dairy-free cooking, 62
dairy products, 14, 236
dark leafy greens, 235
date sugar, 49
desserts, 196–228
digestion
  and food combining, 235
  tips for easy, 6
directory, of physicians, 258–64
distilled water, 30
  bottled, 31
dried fruit, 49, 236
drinking water, bottled, 31
drinks, 67–81
dulse, 43
durum wheat (semolina), 34
dyes, on vegetables and fruits, 10–11

eating
  pace of, 6
  seasonal, 5
ecosystems, damage to, from modern factory farming, 10
egg-free cooking, 62